# MIGRATION, REPRODUCTION
# AND SOCIETY

# Studies in Critical Social Sciences Book Series

Haymarket Books is proud to be working with Brill Academic Publishers (www.brill.nl) to republish the *Studies in Critical Social Sciences* book series in paperback editions. This peer-reviewed book series offers insights into our current reality by exploring the content and consequences of power relationships under capitalism, and by considering the spaces of opposition and resistance to these changes that have been defining our new age. Our full catalog of *SCSS* volumes can be viewed at https://www.haymarketbooks.org/series_collections/4-studies-in-critical-social-sciences.

*Series Editor*
**David Fasenfest** (SOAS University of London)

*Editorial Board*
**Eduardo Bonilla-Silva** (Duke University)
**Chris Chase-Dunn** (University of California–Riverside)
**William Carroll** (University of Victoria)
**Raewyn Connell** (University of Sydney)
**Kimberlé W. Crenshaw** (University of California–LA and Columbia University)
**Heidi Gottfried** (Wayne State University)
**Karin Gottschall** (University of Bremen)
**Alfredo Saad Filho** (King's College London)
**Chizuko Ueno** (University of Tokyo)
**Sylvia Walby** (Lancaster University)
**Raju Das** (York University)

# MIGRATION, REPRODUCTION AND SOCIETY

Economic and Demographic Dilemmas in Global Capitalism

ALEJANDRO I. CANALES

Haymarket Books
Chicago, IL

First published in 2019 by Brill Academic Publishers, The Netherlands.
© 2019 Koninklijke Brill NV, Leiden, The Netherlands

Published in paperback in 2020 by
Haymarket Books
P.O. Box 180165
Chicago, IL 60618
773-583-7884
www.haymarketbooks.org

ISBN: 978-1-64259-354-9

Distributed to the trade in the US through Consortium Book Sales and Distribution (www.cbsd.com) and internationally through Ingram Publisher Services International (www.ingramcontent.com).

This book was published with the generous support of Lannan Foundation and Wallace Action Fund.

Special discounts are available for bulk purchases by organizations and institutions. Please call 773-583-7884 or email info@haymarketbooks.org for more information.

Cover design by Jamie Kerry and Ragina Johnson.

Printed in United States.

10 9 8 7 6 5 4 3 2 1

Library of Congress Cataloging-in-Publication Data is available.

# Contents

List of Figures   VIII
List of Tables   IX

Introduction   1

1 **Migration and Reproduction: Basic Premises**   14
 1 Three Glances at the Reproduction Approach   16
  1.1 *Demography and Population Reproduction*   17
  1.2 *Reproduction in the Thought of Pierre Bourdieu*   20
  1.3 *Gunnar Myrdal and the Principle of Circular and Cumulative Causation*   24
  1.4 *Migration and Reproduction: A Preliminary Synthesis*   27
 2 From the Social Reproduction of Migration to Migration as Reproduction of Society   28
 3 Conclusion: Migration and Reproduction   32

2 **International Migration in Neoclassical Economics: a Critical Perspective**   34
 1 Approaches of Neoclassical Economic Theory and of the New Home Economics   35
 2 Limitations of Neo-classical Theory: Imperfections of the Market   39
 3 Rational Choice: Theoretical or Axiomatic Principle?   43
 4 Neoclassical Economics: an Ahistorical Theory   46

3 **Migration and Development: Three Theses and a Corollary**   54
 1 Migration and Development: the Pitfalls of a Misleading Discourse   57
  1.1 *The Immigration Issue in Host Countries*   57
  1.2 *Is Migration a New Development Paradigm for Origin Countries?*   60
 2 Migration and Development: a Critical Perspective   65
 3 Conclusion: Three Theses and a Corollary on International Migration   70
  3.1 *Corollary: Towards a Global Model of Understanding Migration*   75

## 4 Migration and Reproduction: Beyond the Critique of Methodological Nationalism  77
  1. Globalization as a Critique of Methodological Nationalism  80
  2. Transnational Communities and Transnationalism  85
  3. Migration, Social Networks and Transnationalism  91
  4. Migration and Reproduction  94

## 5 The Role of Migration in the Global System of Demographic Reproduction  102
  1. Thesis  102
  2. From Demographic Transition to a Global System of Reproduction  102
  3. International Migration and Demographic Change in Sending and Receiving Societies  108
     - 3.1 *Ageing Population and the End of Demographic Transition*  108
     - 3.2 *The Second Demographic Transition*  113
     - 3.3 *The Demographic Dividend: Dynamics of Population in Origin Countries*  116
  4. Demographic Change and Migration: Towards a Global Model of Population Reproduction  119
  5. Migration and Demographic Change: the Contradictions of the Model  124
  6. Conclusion: Dilemmas and Contradictions of a Model  130

## 6 Migration and the Reproduction of Capital  135
  1. Thesis  135
  2. From the Circular Flow of Income to the Reproduction of Capital  136
  3. Labor Migration and the Reproduction of Capital  141
     - 3.1 *Deindustrialization and Tertiarization in the New Labor Matrix*  142
     - 3.2 *Immigration and Labor Deficit*  147
  4. Transnationalism, Social Networks and Remittances: the Reproduction of the Labor Force  154
  5. Conclusion  163

## 7 Migration and Social Reproduction  168
  1. Thesis  168
  2. Social Networks and Social Reproduction  169
  3. Migration and Social Reproduction in Host Societies  173
     - 3.1 *Globalization and Employment Polarization*  175

3.2　*Racializing Social Inequality and Class Structure in the United States*　180
　　　3.3　*Migration, Work and Social Reproduction in Advanced Societies*　185
　4　Migration and Social Reproduction: Towards a Global and Comprehensive Vision　188

8　**The Central Place of Migration in the Reproduction of Advanced Societies**　196
　1　Thesis　196
　2　International Migrations: the Theoretical-methodological Debate Revisited　196
　3　Migration and the Reproduction Approach　201
　4　The Central Place of Migrations in Advanced Societies　204
　5　The Contradictions of the Model: Demographic Replacement　207

9　**Latinos in the USA: the New American Dilemma**　210
　1　Thesis　210
　2　Demographic Change and Ethnic Replacement　212
　3　The Racialization of Inequality and the New American Dilemma　220
　　　3.1　*Occupational Segregation and the Racializing of Social Inequality*　223
　　　3.2　*Productivity, Wages and Economic Discrimination*　226
　4　Final Reflections: Latinos and the New American Dilemma　233

**References**　237
**Index**　257

# Figures

1  Asset/vulnerability approach applied in international migration   62
2  The migration-society-reproduction relationship from three levels of analysis   76
3  The three components of the Reproduction Model   99
4  Population pyramid, selected receiving countries   111
5  Ageing Index in selected receiving countries   112
6  Total Fertility Rate. Selected receiving countries   115
7  Latin America, 1950–2100. Demographic Dependency Ratio and Demographic Dividend   118
8  Latin America, 2000–2010. Export of Demographic Bonus by country of origin migration rate of working age population (%)   122
9  International migration and global regime of demographic reproduction   124
10  Latin America, 1950–2100. Working age population growth (thousands)   125
11  USA, 1970–2060. Population by ethnic origin (millions of people)   127
12  USA, 2012 and 2060. Population pyramid, whites and Latino population   128
13  Arizona, California, Florida, Nevada, New Mexico and Texas. Population by ethnic groups, and population pyramid   131
14  Labor migration and reproduction of capital   140
15  USA, 2016. Third World immigrants by major industry groups   147
16  Spain and United States. Labor force deficit   149
17  Global flow of remittances (billion US dollars)   157
18  Remittances by receiving country (%)   158
19  USA and Europe (15 countries). Employment growth and occupational polarization   177
20  United States of America. Ethnic composition of occupational strata   181
21  California, Texas, Florida, Arizona, Nevada and New Mexico, 2016. Ethnic composition of occupational strata   183
22  United States of America and selected states. Ethnic composition of population by income strata, 2016   184
23  United States of America, 2016. Employment of Latinos (migrants and natives) in selected personal services (%)   187
24  International migration and social reproduction in global society   192
25  The centrality of international migration in advanced societies   205
26  California, 1900–2015. Population by major ethnic group   216
27  USA, 1980–2060. Population pyramid, white non-Latino and Latinos   219
28  USA. 2002–2015. Labor force deficit (millions of people)   221
29  USA, 2000–2015. Growth of GDP by ethnic origin of labor force   222

# Tables

1. United States and European Union (15 countries). Employment by major industry groups (thousands of people)   145
2. United States, 2000–2015. Labor force growth by ethnic and migratory origin and age groups   151
3. United States of America. Gross domestic product by ethnic origin of labor force   152
4. United States of America. GDP and economic growth by ethnic origin of labor force   153
5. USA, 2008. Characteristics of immigrant households sending remittances   159
6. USA. 1780–2060. Population by main ethnic groups   215
7. USA 1970–2050. Births by ethnic origin of mother   217
8. USA. 2016. Population occupied and total population by major ethnic groups and occupational and income strata   224
9. California. 2016. Population occupied and total population by major ethnic groups and occupational and income strata   225
10. USA. 2003–2015. Annual net transferences of earnings between major ethnic groups of workers (dollars 2009)   229

# Introduction

*Never deny wherever you come from*
*Whatever you have, come from wherever you come*
*Come from Denmark, or from Chiloé*
*The world is a great ark of Noah*[1]
    The Rose of the Winds
    MAKIZA / ANITA TIJOUX

∴

If anything characterizes social sciences, it is the aptitude to account for the dynamics and depth of society's problems of which it is part. It is a simple reflexivity process: through social sciences, society knows itself better. For this reason, the research problems, agendas and academic programs, are and always will be, social problems each time and place. The problems that social scientists research only acquire meaning when confronted with their society. There is no social discipline, or area of social sciences which does not have as its ultimate aim, the study of society.[2]

No doubt that international migration constitutes one of the central issues of contemporary society. Both at the level of countries and societies of origin and at the host country level, along with the most diverse supranational organisms and international cooperation, migration is part of the prevailing social and political agenda. At the current juncture, unlike in the past, international migration has not only intensified, but also *extensified,* becoming more diversified in its origins, destinations, migratory forms and profiles of the subjects involved, as a result of the accumulation of processes all of which we call globalization.

A walk along certain areas of any large western city, like the *Raval* in Barcelona, *East LA* in Los Angeles or *Brixton* in London, would undoubtedly cause a peculiar sensation to the uninitiated visitor. Most of the people they encounter, belong to an ethnic and demographic group from other parts of the world who

---

1 Original in Spanish: "Nunca niegues donde tu provengas. Tengas lo que tengas, venga de donde vengas. Vengas de Dinamarca, o de Chiloé. El mundo es un gran Arca de Noé".
2 As Moore indicates, "an axiom of the social sciences is that the social research reflects the concerns of its time" (Moore, 2008:57).

speak unintelligible languages and even sometimes dressed in a quite natural picturesque way, because in fact that is "their place" and it is the visitor who seems out of context. Such a sensation is not only produced by the manners and aspects of the residents, but also by the whole morphology of the place, ranging from the shops external appearance and the products they sell to the smells and colors that are perceived which do not correspond to what is usually considered as native. This situation has also been extended to some of the large cities of Latin America, as are the cases of the *Charrúa district* in Buenos Aires, where a growing colony of Bolivian immigrants settle (Sassone and Mere, 2007), or *Little Lima*, in the center of Santiago, which currently accommodates a recent and growing community of Peruvian immigrants (Stefoni, 2009).

The most relevant in this case is that these neighborhoods are not a curiosity for tourists eager to find exotic images for their photos (though they may be) or a kind of theme park that shows a living testimony of the daily life in other parts of the globe. Although the visitor may have the feeling that they have been inadvertently transported to another continent, in fact what he observes is a typical West globalized district, as native and unrepeatable as any other, outside the First World.

As a matter of fact such experience does not suppose a unique character of the current world. The numerous *Chinatowns* and *Little Italies* scattered all over the planet, many of which are among the longest established and most traditional neighborhoods of the cities concerned, show that international migrations are not a phenomenon of recent years. While it is often conveniently forgotten, its history is as ancient as human existence on the Earth itself. To be more precise, it goes back to the appearance of the first international borders. In fact, with the only exception of the so called countries of settlement (The United States, Canada, Argentina, Australia and New Zealand), all Western countries and Japan expelled considerable population contingents until well into the twentieth century, accounting until that time for the main international emigration. Even countries as developed at present as Italy, Spain or Ireland kept on being the focus of important emigrations until approximately thirty years ago, which is also frequently forgotten.

Migratory dynamics, in turn, reinforce make the interdependence among countries, so characteristic of globalization, irreversible, in such a way that each one of the migratory routes that link in a regular manner a country of origin with another of destination is consolidated progressively. According to the mechanism that Massey (1990) has named as *cumulative causality*,[3] every

---

3 As we shall see later, this is a term originally developed by Myrdal (1957), based on the idea in which the social and economic inequalities do not tend to be mitigated by the economic development, but to be reproduced and supported in time. Massey recaptures this concept, for the analysis of migration, proposing the thesis that the same social and familiar networks

migratory movement establishes the conditions for new migrations of people to which this migrant is related. It is for this reason that when a route has been established, the increments are no longer linear and acquire an exponential character, creating close ties between both countries in a process that is fed back without interruption. A brief review of the migratory movement figures since the seventies of the last century up to the present day[4] confirms the existence of this type of population flow between the Caribbean Basin (Mexico, Central America and the West Indies) and the United States, between the Maghreb and some European Mediterranean countries (France, Italy and Spain), between Hindustan and the United Kingdom, between Southeast Asia and Australia or between the rest of China and the Guangdong province (though not precisely an international flow), to cite just some of the best-known examples showing to what extent this phenomenon has spread across the globe.

Experience shows that in all these cases, the first population movements are the trigger for a growth in contacts of all kinds between both countries. Immigrants return to their countries of origin for vacations and are visited by friends and relatives, they send home goods purchased in the host country but also consume goods produced in the country of origin which have to be imported, they transfer remittances to their relatives and send news of employment opportunities for new migrants, receiving in exchange information about events affecting their families and making decisions about them. We could of course go on citing examples of a web of contacts of ever increasing density.

To meet the increase of exchanges a whole communication and transport infrastructure is developed (establishing and expanding the regular flights, improving telecommunications systems, institutionalizing money-transfer mechanisms) that, in turn, facilitates new migratory movements, leading to the appearance of what might be called *migratory circuits* between both countries. Consequently, one of the characteristics of migration nowadays is that it is no longer limited to a flow of people, but increasingly drives a no less important flow of material and symbolic goods, information, capital and cultural values among the territories and communities linked by these migratory circuits. An important consequence of this is that this network can reach such

---

on which any migratory process rest, set up a material and symbolic support that enables its reproduction as a social process, even beyond the persistence or not of the structural factors that triggered it in a beginning.

4 Although any choice of dates at the time of separating the stages of a historical process must have an important arbitrary component, experts agree in pointing out that the current phase of migration as historical phenomenon would have begun with the energy crisis of 1973 and the consequent restructuring of the productive model that led to the conversion of the western countries in postindustrial societies. In this regard, see Castles and Miller, 1993; Pioré, 1979; Portes and Rumbaudt, 1996.

an extension and depth that the countries of origin and destination become a migratory binomial that in practice works as an integrated system. In fact, in many cases, immigration acquires an increasing influence on the evolution of key elements of host countries structures as are its demographic pyramid or the characteristics of the supply in the labor market (Canales, 2013).

Considering these dynamics of contemporary migration, as well as its social and political significance, we must also admit that in spite of all our attempts to systematize the social reality, it will always go several steps ahead of our research work and reflection. The dynamics of international migration in the current times, clearly reflect this loss-making situation. The growing integration among countries caused by globalization has rendered many of the theories and concepts from which the phenomenon of migration had been addressed obsolete. This phenomenon in addition, adopts innovative ways that are reluctant to be tightly corseted in the classic molds.

This level of uncertainty does nothing but feed a profound and profuse political, social and academic debate on migration issues such as its causes and consequences in this globalized world. Thus, from diverse political and ideological trenches, we frequently listen to the most varied speeches and proposals regarding how to understand migration, and the most important, what to do with it in these times. From those who advocate the entire closing of borders, massive deportations, criminalization of undocumented status, construction of retaining walls that far outweigh any king or feudal lord of the Middle Ages, to those in opposite and antagonistic positions, who promote the entire abolition of national borders and the free transit of people and workers, and even the possibility of establishing a formula of global or supra-national citizenship.

Despite this wide range of positions, the academic and political debate has been heavily dominated by conservative visions that usually question the role of migration in the transformation of society.[5] It is a matter of positions and approaches that not only reproduce outdated theories and conceptualizations of the current reality, but also, fall prey to methodological frameworks that keep them from seeing and analyzing the new facets that not only migration adopts, but also society itself. These traditional approaches are victims of at least two

---

5 A clear example of this is the minimum and slightly significant progress that has happened in different Global Forums on Migration and Development (Delgado, Márquez and Puentes, 2010). In these, the vision of the developed countries usually predominates, the main areas of destination of contemporary migration, which not only impose their interests, but also, limit the possibilities of a global consensus on the matter, and have been reluctant to sign and/or ratification diverse international agreements on human, social, labor and political rights of immigrants.

methodological weaknesses of great importance which leads them to visions and proposals that are politically biased. On the one hand, they reproduce the so-called *methodological nationalism* which is an epistemological inheritance of the world view of Modernity, upon which the whole modern thought and social theory would have sustained its principle of correspondence between Nation, State and Territory (Beck, 2000a; Wimmer and Glick Shiller, 2002).

On the other hand, they are equally imprisoned by a methodological dualism, which leads them to separate and analyze in isolation from each other, the causes and consequences of migration in societies of origin with regard to the causes and consequences in receiving societies. This led to the formulation of a framework of analysis and understanding, different and opposed to international migration, depending on whether it implies an analysis of migration in the places of origin or in those of destination, separating arbitrarily the two areas and spatial dimensions which in any migratory process are always inextricably linked. For some (receiving countries), migration is problematized according to social, economic and cultural problems, its volume and slow or the lack of assimilation abilities of immigrants. In sending societies, on the contrary, the debate on migration centers on the hypothetical opportunities and apparent benefits that migration and remittances could represent as engines of economic and social development. For some the fear, for others hope.

From our perspective, we believe that these approaches are mistaken not only in the vision on migration, but also in their inability to understand the new dynamics and changes in contemporary society. In those discourses, the problem is that they keep on analyzing migration and society based on conceptual categories and methodological frameworks that belong to a society which is ceasing to exist, and they haven't been able to comprehend a society which is being built, in whose process, international migration configures a component of paramount importance.

Thus, beyond its technical and methodological preciousness (that is to say, the use of sophisticated statistical and econometrics models, extensive studies involving many cases and countries, etc.), what is certain is that in all these studies, the observation and description of migrations and migrants together with their own specific problems, is from the point of view of a society that no longer exists and that neither gives an account nor reflects the problems of migration and migrants in today's society. Consequently, these approaches contribute little or nothing to understand the dynamics of current societies, nor its daily reproduction, transformation, diversity, social and spatial heterogeneity, and even less, to understand the international migration role in all these processes.

In these times of globalization, every society is influenced by a local-global system of networks and relationships, which are deriving in the deterritorialization of social life (Appadurai, 1990). All the spaces of a local society (national), become deterritorialized, remaining traversed by this local-global relations system. In this context, the social sciences, and the studies on migrations in particular, face the challenge of building frameworks of analysis that involve thinking about the world and the social phenomena as components of globalized societies.

The study of migration is part of these theoretical-methodological challenges. In fact migration is in itself, a phenomenon from which an entire system of local-global relationships is recreated. Therefore, the analysis of migration nowadays involves accepting these challenges and thinking of migration as a component that contributes to the globalization of contemporary society. On this matter, we believe that the main theoretical-methodological weakness of the debate concerning current migrations, lies not so much in the answers as in how argumentations are thrown in favor or against, but, fundamentally, in the way in which the question has been constructed concerning migration in the light of current times, meaning, in social fields from where its function, causes, and consequences are problematized in different aspects of social life.

In this sense, it seems especially relevant, to recapture the transnationalism and transnational communities approach, since its formulation arises precisely from the indication and questioning of this epistemological and theoretical weakness in current migratory studies. Transnationalism is not only an emergent social phenomenon, but also stands as a paradigm that allows us to interpret the peculiarities of international migration in an age of globalization. That is why the development of this new paradigm is one of the primary needs of social sciences in addressing the phenomenon of international migration.

On one hand, the configuration of transnational communities shows us that increasingly, migrants are not such people who leave the society of origin and no longer belong to it. On the contrary, through migration and migrants, the origin societies, communities and families, simply expand towards other territories, reconfiguring and expanding their spatiality by incorporating other places where they reproduce.

For receiving societies, on the other hand, the immigrants have also stopped being people who come from the outside, from external territorial contexts (foreigners, we used to call them). In fact, the category of analysis "society of destination" is no longer relevant in the context of the globalization of societies. Indeed, in the globalization process, the so-called "society of destination" only blurs its territorial borders, becoming a globalized space, where there is neither an interior nor an exterior, but the same society turning into a globalized space. In the global society, its spatiality is only territorially restricted and bounded by the contours of its *mundialization*.[6]

In this regard, the current migration places of destination, are not "national societies", in the classic sense, but places of a common globalized society. To the extent that the global society has been globalizing, the traditional categories of "origin" and "destination", referring to local places that are articulated and integrated by means of migration and transnational communities that are configured from it. Thus, migration becomes, a local-local interconnected field that contributes to the configuration of the spatiality of a global society.

This is the dilemma of current migration to which the models of transnationalism and globalization offer us possible frames for its understanding. We cannot comprehend the contemporary migratory process without adopting a global vision, that is, from the globalization of societies, and in particular, without considering the role that migration has to play in this process.

Now, it is precisely this vision of migration, as component of the structuring of a global society, that allows us to restate its construction as an object of study and problematization. What is relevant then, is to analyze and discuss its role in the dynamics and movements of society, that is, its contribution to the reproduction and transformation of the global society.

This is the thesis we want to develop in this book. To propose not only a pure and simple model of analysis, but rather, a framework from which to understand and think of contemporary migration, that is, a model of analysis to be understood and conceived as a component of the structuring of society in an age of globalization. In this regard, it is a question of not losing sight of transformations taking place in current society, as well as the particular social age we live in, of which migration is an important part. That is why we propose to analyze migration from the perspective of society's *reproduction*.

From this Reproduction approach, while the studied object is international migration, we must take into account that this is just a *mediation* to enable a greater understanding of the dynamics of society as a whole. For the time being, the question is not so much about migration in society itself, but about its role in the reproduction of contemporary society. In this sense, we propose three fields in which migration assumes an important role.

– First of all, in a class society like ours, reproduction means necessarily that a class structure is reproduced, that is, inequalities that differentiate and oppose them one against the other. In this context, we wonder how migration contributes and is part of class structure and social inequality reproduction

---

6  And nothing is more global nowadays, than first world societies and cities. For more details, see Sassen, 2007 and 1991.

in the global society. In this regard, Sassen (2007) raises the point of how current migration contributes to the reproduction of a new global class of disadvantaged. We add that through their engagement in domestic services for wealthier groups, immigrants also contribute to the reproduction of these middle and high social classes in host countries.
- Secondly, at the economic level, it also raises concern about the role and function of migration in the simple and extended system of economy and capital reproduction (accumulation). In this sense, we can say that it is essentially a labor migration. What is important then is how its role as labor force, contributes to economic growth, and by these means, to the capital globalization and relations of production together with capital accumulation. Or in other words, how migration allows to articulate capital reproduction with the labor force reproduction.
- In the third place, at demographic level, the question is about the role of migration in the configuration of a global regime of demographic reproduction that signifies a system that articulates the patterns of demographic reproduction (births-deaths, migration) which are configured locally. This is particularly interesting in the case of developed country demography which is the main destination for contemporary migrations. The second demographic transition along with ageing of population, constitute a demographic context that does not seem to ensure the reproduction of population.

In view of that, immigration, especially the one linked to Third World countries, contributes in a triple process.
- On the one hand, it provides the necessary demographic contingents to ensure the reproduction of population.
- On the other hand, it provides the necessary active population (labor force) contingents to fill in the gaps left by the insufficiency of the local demographic reproduction pattern, and thereby contribute to sustain and to maintain the reproduction of the capital.
- Finally, it does not only contribute to the reproduction of the population in general, but also to the demographic base of social class differentiation. Immigrants are not only a labor force for the capital, but also, a growing fraction of them, are the labor force used in the most diverse personal services necessary for the daily reproduction of medium and high strata population belonging to the native population.

Now, it is equally relevant and of the utmost importance, to take note that, given the demographic volumes that international migration implies at present, it must be said that it does not only contribute or is part of reproduction in the places of destination (population, capital and class inequalities reproduction), but also, and through the same mechanisms of reproduction, it contributes to the transformation of these societies. In this regard, our thesis raises that the way in which these three mechanisms operate and interact in the reproduction of society (population, capital, social classes), is in itself the engine, the origin of transformation of society.

In the case of the United States, for example, since the 1980s has undergone a transition process that takes it from the traditional demographic structure based on an undisputed predominance of the white majority to a peer structure where whites will cease to be an absolute majority and will share their primacy position with the Latino population (Canales, 2015). It is a process of *demographic replacement* that is based on two major trends: (i) the decline of the white population as a result of ageing and low birth rates; and (ii) the rise and growth of Latinos as a result of immigration and their highest birth rates.

We are not the first to speak in terms of a process of demographic replacement to refer to the consequences of immigration in contexts of very low birth and ageing populations. In a 2001 report, the United Nations used the concept of replacement migration, which defined it as

> the international migration that would be needed to offset declines in the size of population and declines in the population of working age, as well as to offset the overall ageing of a population.
> United Nations, 2001:7

Coleman (2006) conceptualizes this same phenomenon as the *Third Demographic Transition*, and documents it for the case of the more developed European countries. This author points out that if current migratory and demographic trends continue, by 2050 immigrants would account for 36% of the population in England and Wales, 29% in Holland and Italy, and 24% in Germany.

In both cases, they focus on the eventual *demographic replacement* of the native population by immigrants in contexts where low fertility and high levels of ageing do not make it possible to ensure the demographic reproduction of the native populations and thus provide the necessary labor force to sustain their economies. In both cases, the focus is not so much on the dynamics and characteristics of immigration, as in the context of demographic decline that characterizes the developed countries, the main destinations of contemporary international migration.

In the USA case, it is estimated that the population of Latin origin (so-called *Latinos* or *Hispanics*), went from being a mere 14.6 million in 1980, to more than 50 million people in 2010, a figure that represents, more than 17 % of the resident population in that country. Also, according to estimates made by the

Census Bureau of that country, it is projected that the coming forties decade of this century (this is, in only 30 years more), non-Latino white population will no longer be an absolute majority to represent 49% of the entire population of this country. Also, it is estimated that the Latin population will exceed 120 million, representing more than 30% of the country's population.

This data illustrates the magnitude of the demographic change which is already underway in the United States and that will be manifested in an unprecedented transformation of its ethnic and migratory composition. The conjunction of these processes, white population decline and Latino population growth, give rise to changes in the ethnic composition currently experienced by the population of the United States. According to estimates from the Census Bureau, these dynamics would imply an eventual process of *ethnic and demographic replacement*, making the United States transition from having historically been a *white country* to being a *society of demographic minorities*.

This demographic change raises a stage of transformation of the current ethnic and demographic composition of American society, which involves among other things, a questioning of the current concentration of the social and political privileges in the hands of whites. This is the *New American Dilemma* around which the class struggle of the 21st century in the United States will be structured.

Diverse voices arise today from the conservative sectors of this country, announcing an endless number of calamities and perverse effects of these changes. The best example of it is Jared Taylor in an interview of late 2016 with Jorge Ramos. Here we only extract some sentences that illustrate what we have been raising here.[7]

J. Ramos:
*So you would like to live in a white only country?*

J. Taylor:
*Well, not necessarily white only, but in a country that is clearly based on a European model, which whites will basically remain overflowing majority in perpetuity ... And what happen with my people ... You are promoting a process that will turn my people into a minority ... You want more power for*

---

7 Samuel Jared Taylor is a white nationalist. He is founder and editor of the American Renaissance magazine, and president of the New Century Foundation, a group described as a white supremacist. Taylor supported Donald Trump's presidential campaign and described his rise to government as "a sign of growing white consciousness". An extract from this interview can be found in https://youtu.be/qkwD5CC2up4.

> *Latinos, at the expense of the power of my people ... And you want more and more and more.*

These excerpts from the interview clearly reflect the fear that has begun to seize the white supremacists. Their problem is not only because of the presence of "others", purely and simply, but because of the fact that these others tend to be many, and threaten to be more than "us".

For Jared Taylor and white supremacists, the fear of Latinos is not only because of the cultural diversity it implies but because of its population growth that puts at risk the ethno-demographic primacy of the white population. His current fear comes from something more simple, practical and direct. It is the fear of losing their demographic majority status, it is the fear that causes them to have to share their privileges and their power with those minorities that they despise. It is the fear that the United States will no longer be a *country of whites and for whites*, a society where ethnic diversity was tolerable to the extent that it was a matter of minorities subordinated to the primacy of whites.

Unlike the traditional racist discourse, for the first time it is a position that is on the defensive. Their fear is to become a demographic minority which would imply the loss of power they have exercised for centuries. For them, the issue of ethnic and cultural diversity would be totally tolerable as long as this does not compromise their demographic primacy and their position of power vis-à-vis other ethnic groups. Everything is tolerable insofar as it does not violate its model of society: European and white supremacy.

Taylor and the current white supremacists were not the first to pose this situation of *risk of white hegemony* in the face of Latino population growth and immigration. Twenty years ago, Samuel Huntington pointed to the threat Mexico might pose to the United States, placing the risk not only in cultural and identity terms, but especially in terms of its different demographics, with particular emphasis on the risk that, by the end of The 1990s represented the rise of Mexican and Latin American immigration against the ageing of the white population (Huntington, 2004).

Philip Martin and Martin Ruhs posed the same problem almost a decade ago in the form of a virtual *Trade off Numbers vs. Rights* (Ruhs and Martin, 2008). According to these authors the problem with current immigration is that it is *too numerous*, which does not allow ensuring the distribution of *privileges and rights* for all immigrants. In other words, the cake of Human Rights is very limited and cannot be distributed among all immigrants, which requires their reduction to socially and politically controllable volumes. What these authors do not explain, however, is based on what criteria the distribution of human rights is established, so that it would reach the entire native population but not for all immigrants. It is clear that behind this dilemma there is a discriminatory bias: because of their status as migrants, they do not have the same right to access their human rights. That is, a circumstantial condition – to be migrant – is superimposed on an essential condition: human being.

The truth, nevertheless, is that they are only reacting to a demographic change that will substantially readjust the political balances and the distribution of the political and economic power among the different ethnic and demographic groups in this country.[8]

It is necessary to point out, however, that these immigration volumes, are a reflection of the magnitude of the demographic deficit or shortfall that the current regime of population reproduction in these countries is generating. That is to say, the magnitude of demographic impact that immigration generates is not due to immigration in itself, but to the demographic insufficiency that is generating the increased ageing population in these countries as well as the decline in fertility levels, sometimes even below those of demographic reproduction in the long term in other words, the ageing and demographic decline causes that, at present, both the economic dynamics and the social population reproduction in the developed country, depends straight on the contributions that immigration makes, especially the ones coming from the Third World countries, where they still live in the last stages of the first demographic transition. Nevertheless, the ageing and demographic decline as such, cause that immigration leads to a deep transformation of the receiving countries ethnic composition (Coleman, 2006).[9]

Within this framework, we can understand the depth and historical significance of the dilemma that developed countries face at present, namely:
– An alternative is to insure the demographic and economic process of reproduction based on the adoption of a policy of openness and tolerance to immigration, which brings, nevertheless, an ethnic and cultural transformation of its population;

---

8  A manifestation of the political impacts of this shift on the ethnic and demographic composition of North American population, took place at the presidential elections of 2008 and 2012, where the so-called *Latino* vote allowed the reelection of President Barak Obama, becoming a key factor in the election results in this country.

9  The current case of California, Texas, Florida, Arizona, New Mexico and Nevada are a clear indication of what we are affirming. In all of these states the traditional demographic supremacy of non-Hispanic white people practically has been diluted by the influence of Mexican and Latin-American immigration. In the particular case of California, non-Latino whites are an ethnic minority, and are already outnumbered by the Latino population, who are currently the main ethnic group (Canales, 2017).

- Or a radical control and halt of mass immigration policy is adopted, but at the risk of entering into a process of demographic unsustainability that threatens not only the population, but also the economic and social stability in this country.

It is a question of a dilemma of demographic nature but that has direct economic, social and political implications. The importance of this lies in the impact that an eventual reduction of the active population would have on the development of the productive and economic forces of the country. In other words, if immigration is not maintained, the economy and demography of advanced societies would turn out to be seriously compromised. However, maintaining immigration entails the risk of structural changes in the population resulting in an eventual demographic and ethnic replacement of the native population by immigrants and their descendants.

To assure its current and future reproduction, these societies must be open to the possibility not only to become multicultural, but also to a society where the current composition of social and ethnic majorities and minorities could be radically disrupted. The problem is that, as Obama pointed out in his last speech, these transformations would take place in a context where racism and migration remain a powerful force dividing our societies (*The New York Times*, 2017, January 10th).

Considering the above, in this book we propose a model of analysis that allows positioning the context of this dilemma, as well as its possible causes and consequences.

CHAPTER 1

# Migration and Reproduction: Basic Premises

> *I'm a globetrotter, with no course fixed*
> *I founded the place where I Tumble*
> *¡This is my world!*[1]
>> The Rose of the Winds
>> MAKIZA / ANITA TIJOUX

∴

International migration constitutes one of the priority issues in any social agenda and contemporary politics. One can hear speeches and proposals of diverse nature and from diverse political and ideological trenches. From those who propose an entire control, the closing of borders, migrant criminalization etc., up to whom advocate the free transit of people and workers, multiculturalism as a sign of times and many others. Nevertheless, in this melting pot of positions, the debate has been dominated by an epistemic vision of the Migration-Development relationship which is based on the methodological nationalism. This is a methodological inheritance of Modernity which consists on supporting the thought and the social theory by the principle of correspondence between State, Nation and Territory in modern society, (Beck, 2000a). Based on this meta-theoretical principle, the modern social thought and Sociology, in particular, made of national societies an object of study in itself, independent of each other (Goic, 2007).

In contemporary society, and observing the scope of globalization process, a theoretical and methodological rupture arise in relation to the way of observing and analyzing the social processes. With globalization, each society is cut across by a local-global system of networks and relations, which are deriving in the social life deterritorialization (Appadurai, 1990). All the spaces of a local society (national), are deterritorialized, being traversed by a local-globalized system of relationships. In this context, the challenge for the social sciences is

---

1 "Soy una trotamundo, sin fijo rumbo me fundo. Al lugar donde yo tumbo ¡Así es mi mundo!". Original in Spanish.

to think of the world and the social phenomena as components of globalized societies.

Thus, the analysis of international migration, constitutes a case of particular relevance in this theoretical and methodological challenge because it configures in itself one of these relations that support the local-globalized interconnected system. In this sense, our interest is precisely, to propose a turning point in the debate of migration so as to take on the challenge implied in the thinking about societies and social processes from their globalization processes.

A first point to take into account, is that this challenge leads us to no longer think about new answers to the classic question about the relationship between migration and development, but rather, to the need of changing the perspective from which we ask the question. In other words, the theoretical-methodological weakness of the debate is not only put on the answers and arguments that are given in favor of or against, but also and fundamentally, on the manner in which the issue of migration and development has been built.

In a globalized world, international migration, its causes and consequences, must be thought of and analyzed in global terms. This thesis allows us to restate the very concept of international migration. From the traditional vision, imbued with methodological nationalism, migration by definition was thought as a flow coming from abroad, and therefore as an external factor to the society and to the Nation State, and this, regardless of the possibility of generating positive externalities, and promoting diverse positive dynamics in the host society, or be able to act in the opposite direction.

In the context of a globalized society, on the other hand, migration stops being an external phenomenon, to constitute a process within society. It's not just that migration, as a social process, is internalized as an intrinsic and proper dynamic of these societies. Rather, because of globalization, it is society itself the one that has expanded its social and territorial limits. Thus, as society gets globalized, we can no longer conceive migration as a problem that comes to us from abroad, but rather as a social phenomenon generated by the same factors that are shaping the global society.

Taking up Giddens (1986), we can affirm that in a global society, migration constitutes a component and a factor that contributes to the *structuration* of society, and therefore, to its dynamics and movement in a process that upholds its reproduction and transformation. It is precisely this vision of migration as a component of the global society structuring, which allows us to rethink its construction as an object of study and problematization.

If migration is a component in the constitution of society, what turns out to be relevant then, is to analyze and to debate its role in the dynamics and movement of society, meaning, its contribution to the reproduction and transformation of global society. This is precisely, the object of analysis and reflection that we want to exhibit in this book. In methodological terms, this proposal raises a double challenge, namely:

- On the one hand, we must never lose sight of the fact that through the study of migration, what we basically are looking for, is to understand some of the problems of contemporary society. Although the matter under observation is international migration, we must bear in mind that it is only a medium for coming to an understanding of society as a whole. Meanwhile, the question is not about migration itself, but its role in the Reproduction of Society.
- On the other hand, this perspective of society and migration analysis, requires categories and concepts that account for these different processes, as well as its corresponding levels of analysis. It is a question of categories and concepts which along with giving an account of the vicissitudes of the international migration, allow us to make the leap to the understanding of the vicissitudes of contemporary society.

## 1   Three Glances at the Reproduction Approach

Undoubtedly, the concepts of social capital and familiar networks, turn out to be basic and fundamental to understand the support and, in particular, the reproduction of migration as a social process (Durand and Massey, 2003). Through this social fabric built upon migration, migrants reproduction is also taking place, along with their families and communities, and in the case of contemporary international migration, it takes on a transnational and translocated form. Also, the concept of cumulative causation turns out not only to be an illustrator of this situation, but it synthesizes all its meaning and social significance (Massey, 1990).

In the same sense, de Haas (2007) takes up the concept of survival strategy, to give an account of this very situation. Familiar networks are becoming social resources (social capital), on the basis upon which migrants, their families and communities can develop diverse strategies to deal with their own survival. The success of these survival strategies is based on the strength of these family and community networks that contribute to the survival, support and reproduction of migrant family and community.

Beyond what we could reflect on and debate concerning the validity and internal consistency of this approach concerning social networks (either as survival strategies, social capital or cumulative causation mechanisms), our interest is that from this we may move towards a new field of problematizing and understanding migration as a social process.

It is a question of giving an additional turning to this reflection, reconsidering the vision and sense that the original authors (Myrdal, Bourdieu, among others) imprinted on these terms and concepts (circular cumulative causation, social capital, social networks, strategies of reproduction) as categories of analysis for the study and understanding of not only individual's social reproduction (migrants, their communities, in this case), but above this, the vicissitudes and dynamics of the society reproduction in itself, especially in relation to the reproduction of its social inequalities, class structures, structural heterogeneities and regional asymmetries.

In this regard, the *Reproduction* approach provides us with the necessary tools to face these theoretical and methodological challenges. In this sense, we would like to present a reflection concerning this Reproduction concept, based on three different but complementary developments. We initiate taking up what Demography indicates on this matter, to continue with Bourdieu's contributions and the debate in Latin America on reproductive strategies, finishing with Myrdal's concept on circular and cumulative causation.

### 1.1  *Demography and Population Reproduction*

Migration constitutes first and foremost, a fundamental component of the demographic dynamics of populations. In this regard, it turns out to be pertinent and relevant, to take up what Demography notes on migration as a component of demographic population reproduction. Likewise, it turns out, that Demography offers us a suitable methodological input to understand what we are proposing.

In Demography, against the commonly accepted view, the object of study is not the population in itself, that is to say, pure and simple volumes and trends. More than two centuries have passed since Demography has already transcended from being mere statistical information about populations, to go deep into the study and analysis of the dynamics of population reproduction. As Livi Bacci points out (1993) population is not just a stock of persons, but a "set of stable groups of individuals formed, linked by bonds of *reproduction* ... population, then, will be defined as such if it has continuity in time and if this continuity is ensured by links of reproduction that connect parents and children and guarantee the succession of generations" (p. 9 and ss. our emphasis).

In this context, the specificity of demographic analysis which sets it apart from mere population statistics, is precisely to regard its subject of study, population as a reproductive system sustained over time (Pérez, 2013).

In other words, the field of Demography study transcends population itself understood as mere stocks conventionally defined, as well as the mere description of its profiles, components and structures; to become more involved with all those issues and aspects that affect and determine its core of knowledge:

*population reproduction*. Volumes, trends, profiles, components, among others, are topics only of interest to demography as it determines reproduction in time and space concerning population.

To Julio Pérez's definition, we can add an additional turn. Demography's concern about population reproduction is not considered in abstract, but in its historical and social dimension. In this sense, we reconsider Leguina's definition for whom under capitalism, "the population reproduction process is part of a wider process: the labor power process of reproduction" (Leguina, 1981:3).

Thus the ultimate goal, which gives historical and social significance to Demography, is that through studying population reproduction, the reproduction process (and transformation) of societies to which these populations belong are aimed to be understood. In other words, as a social science, and not as mere social statistics of populations, the Demography field of study transcends even populations to penetrate into the social world and societies. Through the study of the demographic reproduction of population, the objective is to contribute to the analysis and comprehension of society reproduction. In essence, the Demography object of study, as any social science, is Society itself, which is studied and analyzed through one of its components: Population, and in particular, the conditions for its reproduction.

From this reflection on the field of study of Demography, we can extract three lessons of particular interest to us.

- On the one hand, the concept of REPRODUCTION, as the essence of society and populations study. It is a question of understanding the continuous movement of society, through the movement of its population.
- On the other hand, the concept reproduction does not mean pure and simple repetition, but also involves social transformations along time. Precisely, the idea of society movement tells us about its permanent change, in which nothing remains, but everything moves, and in this movement, everything changes and transforms.
- Finally, this vision of populations as reproductive systems, indicates that although in the past it was possible to "isolate" some of these "demographic systems of reproduction", and to analyze them independently (such would be the case of the demographic studies of "national" populations, for example), at present, on the other hand, and opposite to the advance of globalization that is leading to a progressive planetary integration, this territorial division loses sense, and it will only be possible to speak of a single demographic system reproduction: global population (Pérez, 2013).

In the most basic and widely accepted formulation in the field of Demography, it is indicated that population reproduction is sustained by two components of demographic dynamics. On the one hand the natural component of growth which corresponds to the phenomena of birth and mortality. On the other hand, the social component of population growth, that refers to the phenomenon of migration. It is a question of components that have their own dynamics which don't always coincide with every historical period, and that have a differentiated impact on demographic structures and reproduction.

In this model of analysis, migrations are a central factor for understanding the demographic process of population reproduction, at least from two perspectives:
– On the one hand, directly contributing to the increase in population, by adding to (or subtracting from, as it may apply) the total volume of people that make up the population of a country, region or entity.
– On the other hand, contributing indirectly, by modifying the population structure by age and gender, from both source and destination of migratory flows. By this means, it also has an impact on the dynamics of birth and death of the populations involved.

Curiously, nevertheless, the modern theories of population have focused on analyzing and shaping the reproduction of population by focusing exclusively on the components of its natural growth, disregarding migration (internal and international). Paraphrasing the economic terminology, it would seem that it is a question of "closed demography" models, that is to say, population under study and analysis, does not develop demographic interactions with its environment, and therefore, there are no human displacements or flows of people abroad. It is not just a question of null migratory balances (emigration compensates immigration), but that such flows of people do not exist, neither departure nor arrival. Such is the case, for example, of the Demographic Transition approach, which is not but a historical summary of the trend in birth and mortality rates in the European countries between the eighteenth and nineteenth centuries, but that inexplicably makes a total abstraction of this dual role of migration in population reproduction.

These approaches face a double methodological weakness we are interested to recapture in the following chapters. On the one hand, it is obvious that these are partial and biased, to the extent that they disregard a central component of the demographic reproduction. But on the other hand, they perhaps fall into a more serious bias, characteristic of methodological nationalism that lies behind them. On having been sustained in "closed demography", they are also unable to grasp the complexity of the processes of demographic interaction among different regions, countries and nations. This even prevents them from asking questions regarding a comprehensive system of demographic reproduction, since such a concept, is simply beyond its vision and field of problematization. A demographic system of this type, should be based on models of "open demography", where the demographic relationship between populations (migrations principally) would constitute one of its fundamental support.

## 1.2 Reproduction in the Thought of Pierre Bourdieu

As well as for Demography, the *reproduction* concept turns out to be basic and central, the same is true in the case of Pierre Bourdieu's Sociology. According to this author, one of the basic and fundamental issues that need to be solved by Sociology, is that of "knowing why and how the social world lasts and perseveres in its manner, how the social order is perpetuated, that is to say, the whole relationship of order constituting it" (Bourdieu, 2011:31).

To answer this basic question of social science, Bourdieu moves away from both the structuralism, according to which are structures that carrying the principle of perpetuation, are reproduced with the collaboration of agents subjected to its own conditions and constraints; and from the interactionism and the methodological individualism (marginalism) according to which the social world is a product of acts of constructions that agents are performing every moment, in a sort of continuous creation.

Given the contrast individual–structure and facing the emphasis and reductionism that political economy has made as regards to the role of the economic-productive structures, Bourdieu's proposal is that of opening the analysis of society's reproduction to other fields of analysis and understanding this society's reproduction movement (Bourdieu and Passeron, 1977). It deals with a set of mediations which are manifested as systems of cultural, symbolic, political and demographic reproduction, among others, that consequently, allow a more complete and comprehensive understanding of the historical vicissitudes concerning this opposition between reproduction and social transformation.

Economy, although undoubtedly necessary, is not enough by itself to understand the reproduction of class structure in modern society. Therefore, there arises the need to incorporate other dimensions of social life that also contribute to reproduction. We refer to the fields of culture, politics, social, demography, education, and so many others (Bourdieu, 1980). In these other dimensions we can find that social class structures, differentiation and inequality are also reproduced. In these social fields non-economical capitals are constructed, (social, cultural, symbolic, political, etc.) which also take part and contribute to the social class structures reproduction (Bourdieu, 2011).

Society is not only economy (even though it may be). Likewise, *class* is not only an economic category, that is to say, only determined and produced by economical processes, but it is also a cultural, symbolic, political, social and demographic category. Class not only means production relationships (even though it may be), but also of kinship, marriages, fecundities, familiar structures, education, systems of succession, symbolic and cultural structures, etc.

This vision of reproduction and society, is what allows us to draw attention to the need of analyzing and conceptualizing the function of migration in society reproduction. In this sense, we understand that migration social process configures a social field, where, at the same time that concrete social subjects are being reproduced (migrants, their families and communities), there is a contribution to other social fields, subjects and structures reproduction.

In this regard, we can return to the reference that Bourdieu makes in relation to the role of the educational system in social reproduction, and in particular, the reproduction of social and political differentiation structures. In words of Bourdieu and Passeron, "the classical theories tend to sever cultural reproduction from its function of social reproduction, that is, to ignore the specific effect of symbolic relations in the reproduction of power relations" (Bourdieu and Passeron, 1977:10).

In terms of migration analysis, we can point out that in general, the traditional approaches often dissociate migration reproduction as a social process in itself from its role in the society reproduction, particularly, in the reproduction of class relationships and structure of social inequality, of which migration and migrants are a part.

Within this framework, in Bourdieu's proposal the concept of social reproduction strategy is fundamental for the integrated analysis of the diverse ways in which social life is reproduced, and in particular, how the different mechanisms of domination and dependence are reproduced, i.e., the dynamics and social class reproduction (Gutiérrez, 2011).

The concept of social reproduction strategies has its origin in Bourdieu's investigation related to matrimonial strategies and inheritance practices in Kabila and Bearn (Bourdieu, 1980 and 1976). With this concept, Bourdieu faces structuralism, much in the news during those years, and proposes what Gutiérrez pointed out as a *relational understanding of the social world*. According to this author, "the different reproductive strategies are explained only relationally, in a dual sense: within the context of the system (in a family or in a group of families belonging to a class or fraction of class) and within the global social space, where the practices within this system are related to the constitutive practices of the others, articulating social and differential ways of reproduction" (Gutiérrez, 2011: 23–24).

According to Bourdieu (2011), the use of the category *strategy of reproduction*, must be sustained in the articulation and integration of both the structural conditions that weigh upon the agents (moving away from the proposal of the methodological individualism) as to the possibilities of active responses to the same coercion (also moving away from the mechanistic and structuralism visions much in vogue during those years).

Bourdieu's approach turns out to be central for our proposal of analyzing and understanding migration as a strategy of social reproduction, which not only contributes to the reproduction of migrants themselves and their families, but above all, it is part of the reproduction mechanisms of social structure in contemporary society. In this sense, we are interested in returning to the same meaning that Bourdieu gave to his concept of *strategies of reproduction*, as a category of analysis and mediation, which at the same time allows us to understand both the agent and subject action as well as the reproduction of the social system as a whole, that is to say, the social structures and society.

In its study on marriage and inheritance practices in Kabila and Bearn, Bourdieu points out how the matrimonial strategies that individuals and families develop, not only allow the lineage reproduction, privilege positions, and/or family economic capital, but also, through those same matrimonial strategies, the structures of differentiation and social inequalities are reproduced upon which lineages, privileges and economic capitals are sustained. In this sense, the matrimonial strategies are not only strategies of family reproduction or survival, but above all, are mechanisms of reproduction of both community and its social inequalities upon which differentiation and social stratification are structured.

In the same perspective, in Latin America during those years, the discussions were focused on the scopes of the *survival strategies* notion and their uses in the study of family and communities reproduction in conditions of poverty, marginality and social vulnerability. In Latin America, the analysis of social reproduction forms of families under marginality and poverty conditions, already have a long record even prior to the initial studies of Bourdieu. The anthropological works of Oscar Lewis (1961) and of Larissa Lomnitz (1977), are pioneers in illustrating how the familiar structures and the relationships of kinship, *compadrazgo* and friendship (social networks we call them now) are the basis for survival in situations of poverty and social exclusion in Mexico City in those times. In both cases, it turns out to be clear that the structures and familiar relations are mechanisms (later to be called strategies) that allow the reproduction in conditions of poverty and marginality.

Based on those works, a field of particularly fertile investigation is opened in Latin America, which gave rise to a large number of investigations as well as comparative studies and theories on survival strategies of poor families in the most diverse contexts.² Also, in the seventies the concept extends towards the study of migratory processes, job search and labor insertion, development of family businesses, informal and rural economies, the setting up of unions and marriages, among many other fields of study.

Equally, at the end of the seventies, a self-reflective process occurs through which a critical review and proposal around this concept is made, both in its methodological aspect as in the conceptual and theoretical one. Thus, from a functionalist vision, Mora y Araujo (1982) launched a devastating critique to the historical-structural approaches of the epoch, demonstrating its methodological flaws and functionalist biases (paradoxically) that underlie them. Also, from different views, Zemelman (1982) and Przeworsky (1982) recapture and deepen this critique, at the same time proposing different ways of solving it. The first one, by appealing to a theoretical-methodological approach of *mediations*. It is a matter of rebuilding the category of survival strategy as a field of mediations between the macro-structural determinants and the micro-social behaviors, in the old subject–structure opposition. Likewise, Przeworsky, in the same direction of establishing these *meso* levels, raises the issue that the term "survival strategy" turns out to be misleading and inaccurate. What in fact families and individuals face are *option structures*, and social, class, ethnic and genre differences, among many others, are manifested as structures of different options. These option structures not only refer to structural and material factors or determinants, but also to the profiles of individuals, family situations, cultural and symbolic structures, systems of power, among many others.

In spite of their differences, it should be noted that both Zemelman and Przeworsky, refer a reconceptualization of the term "survival strategy". Both cases, *mediations* as well as *option structures*, are theoretical-methodological proposals oriented to delimit fields of thought and reflection, in which it is possible to recapture the movement of society, through its reproduction. These reflections and self-critiques allowed Latin-American thinking to take an adequate distance and throw off the narrow margins that structuralism imposed on them to open up the debate of contemporary sociology. The idea of establishing mediation areas between the micro and macro levels, is bound up with the thought of Bourdieu, Coleman, Alexander and others, and resulted in both

---

2   An example of this are the research and investigations to be carried out by the Working Group on the Process of Population Reproduction from CLACSO Commission on Population and Development which were published in 5 volumes of the series *Population, Reproduction and Development* between the years 1974 and 1985.

creative and fertile developments for the analysis and comprehension of the most diverse social problems (Salles, 2003; Salles and Tuiran, 2003).

## 1.3 Gunnar Myrdal and the Principle of Circular and Cumulative Causation

A third concept we are interested in recapturing, corresponds to that of *Circular and Cumulative Causation*, originally proposed by Gunnar Myrdal in 1957. In the first place, it is necessary to remember the moment and the historical context in which Myrdal proposes this concept. His interest was to understand how the economic and social inequality takes place and reproduces, both at a global scale and within each country. In other words, why some regions of the world succeed in developing while others are kept in the underdevelopment, and why conditions of ethnic and social inequality are perpetuated within societies, for example in the case of the African American population in the United States.

As regards the uneven economic development, Myrdal raises that neither the theory of international trade nor the neoclassic economic theory provide "an explanation in causal terms, of how the facts of international economic inequalities have come into existence, and why there is a tendency for the inequalities to grow" (Myrdal, 1957:21). The concept of stable balance, basic principle of orthodoxy in economic theory, turns out to be not only insufficient, but also completely divorced from the processes of differentiated economic development observed in the global economic system.

According to the neoclassical theory, the differences in the regional or national growth rates, would tend to balance with the free trade and free mobility of the production factors. In contrast to these ideas, Myrdal raises the opposite thesis, according to which once a region or country obtains a growth advantage, it will tend to sustain it through the mechanisms of circular and cumulative causation that its own economic growth induces. More specially, "by themselves, migration, capital moves and trade are rather the media through which cumulative process evolves – upwards in the lucky regions and downwards in the unlucky ones. In general, if they have positive results for the former, their effects on the latter are negative" (Myrdal, 1957:27).

Like other economists at the time (Robinson, 1956), Myrdal thinks that society and economy are dynamic and changeable, never statics, and furthermore, never stable. The balances do not exist, but continuous imbalances, movements and transformations that reproduce these imbalances and inequality.[3]

---

[3] In this sense, the scientist concern is to build frameworks of analysis and understanding of this continuous society movement, reproduction and transformation.

In this frame, he raises the principle of *circular and cumulative causation*. In opposition to the economic balance approaches, he points out that, "the essence of a social problem is that it concerns a complex of interlocking, circular and cumulative changes" (Myrdal, 1957:26).

It is particularly interesting the way in which Myrdal gives meaning to this process. It is not a question of any interaction process, but of a phenomenon of cumulative causation, based on a principle of circular interdependence. Both terms, *cumulative* and *circular*, give sense to this principle of causation. The economic and social inequality both worldwide and at regional levels, is explained by this principle:
– On the one hand, there exists a reciprocal causation between development and underdevelopment, this circular causation makes one factor (development) the cause of the other (underdevelopment), and *vice versa*.
– On the other hand, it is accumulative, since development generates and accumulates development, simultaneously underdevelopment reproduces and accumulates underdevelopment. This unequal accumulation is, in turn, caused by (explained by) this circular development–underdevelopment.

According to Myrdal, the underdevelopment not only reproduces itself, but in the same process, it causes the reproduction (*accumulation*) of development, and inversely, development not only reproduces itself, but in the same process, it causes the reproduction (*accumulation*) of underdevelopment. This is what we might name as the principle of cumulative circularity on which reproduction of economic inequality at the international and regional levels are sustained.

It is clear that Myrdal's concern is not just the situation of underdevelopment in some regions, or inequality on a global and regional scale, but how these situations are reproduced and sustained over time. Why some of them grow and accumulate development, while others remain at a standstill and accumulate underdevelopment. Likewise, the answer the author gives, turns out to be even more pertinent and relevant through his proposal of the circular and cumulative causation. In effect, this concept is based on a perspective of analysis that seeks to articulate and integrate in a same model of understanding, the conditions of some (developed), with the conditions of others (underdeveloped), and more precisely, seeks to explain how the development reproduction of some is not in abstract, but influenced and determined by this relationship of inequality that oppose the situation of underdevelopment of others. Therefore, the context (the relation of inequality) becomes a structuring factor, conditioning the reproduction of some or others, and by this means, a factor of self-reproduction, as a context of inequality between developed and underdeveloped regions.

Myrdal had previously developed this same principle of circular and cumulative causation in its analysis on the social situation of the African-American population in the United States (Myrdal, 1944). On this matter, a simplified version of Myrdal model (but not less enlightening), can be synthesized in the action and reciprocal interaction of two factors. On the one hand, the A-factor, that would be *white people's prejudice*, which sustains the discrimination against the black people in its different forms, and on the other hand, the B-factor that would be *black people's low standard of living*, that is to say, their condition of poverty, patterns of behavior and ways of life associated to a social situation concerning ethnic discrimination. According to Myrdal,

> these two factors are mutually interrelated: the Negroes' low level of living is kept down by discrimination from whites, while, on the other side, the Negroes' poverty, ignorance, superstition, slum dwellings, health deficiencies, dirty appearance, bad odor, disorderly conduct, unstable family relations and criminality, stimulate and feed the antipathy of the whites for Negroes.
> MYRDAL, 1957:28

This example allows to illustrate the operation of these circular and cumulative causation principles.

- In the first case, we see on one side the A-factor (prejudice of white individuals) is caused by the B-factor (poverty, patterns of behavior and ways of life of black individuals). But in turn, the A-factor (prejudices) is a social condition that generates and causes the B-factor (ways of life). Thus, both factors are reciprocally determined in a system of *ad infinitum circular causation*. It is "a cumulative process of mutual interaction in which the change in one factor would continuously be supported by the reaction of the other factor, and so on in a circular way" (Myrdal, 1957:29).
- Equally, this process is *cumulative* since this situation of inequality generated by the ethnic discrimination condition, strengthens itself in a double sense. On a first level, the initial positions reproduce themselves: the poverty of black people makes them reproduce as poor, at the same time as prejudices made by white reproduce discrimination towards the blacks. On a second level, the reproduction of these initial positions is mutual: black people *accumulate* poverty, behaviors and life styles, all of which oppose them to white people. This very fact, in turn, makes the latter accumulate prejudices and behaviors that reproduce the ethnic discrimination condition. Conversely, prejudices and discrimination accumulated by the white

individuals, makes its counterpart, the black individuals, reproduce and accumulate poverty, life styles, etc.

### 1.4 Migration and Reproduction: A Preliminary Synthesis

These approaches outline the premises on which we sustain our proposal to analyze the contemporary international migration. If we could sum it up in a phrase, we would say that it is a question of passing from the analysis and understanding of the migration reproduction as a social process, to understand and analyze migration as a factor, among others, of Society Reproduction. In this sense, these approaches help us in this heuristic and cognitive exercise where the Reproduction concept is central in the whole proposal.

- On the one hand, from the perspective of Demography the population reproduction constitutes the vector on which its object of study and problematizing is constructed. From this we recapture the already exposed idea that through population reproduction (and the role of migration in this case) what is essentially the focus of interest is to understand and analyze the dynamics of society reproduction. It is a question of not losing sight of the fact, that through migration and population, we are observing the society itself, its dynamics, and its continuous movement in the reproduction-transformation dialectics. It is a matter of looking at society through social processes that reproduce and transform it.
- Thus, in the words of Bourdieu, from this glance referred to society reproduction, it raises the methodological need of working with analytical perspectives, that's to say, categories and models of analyses that articulate the perception of the micro and macro, the subject's actions and its structural determinants. In this sense, it is necessary to recapture Zemelman's proposal (1982) with regard to the role of mediations as a logical reasoning and to the importance of a thought concerning society and social affairs to be built based on a system of mediations through which it is possible to reconstruct the articulation between the different fields, levels and dimensions of the social issue.
- Finally, Myrdal circular and cumulative causation perspective, goes in the same direction. The concept of circular causation is of particular relevance. Through it, we can restore and apprehend the processes of reproduction of one part (underdeveloped world, poor, migrants, etc.) and the other (developed world, rich, white people, native, etc.) in its circular and cumulative movement, which is nothing but the reproduction of a society that contains both of them. The reproduction of one side can be seen as the opposite to

the other's reproduction. Equally, the reproduction of both can't be seen any other way but as a mere reproduction of the structures of inequality that oppose one against the other, and that separate and categorize individuals in relation to others.

Meanwhile, this is the general analytical framework on which we sustain our proposal to understand international migration as a component of world reproduction as a system. This vision, although it seems to imply a certain distance with some of the currently most accepted approaches concerning analysis of migration (we refer to the approach of social and familiar networks, which focus its study on analysis of migration as a social process), in fact, it corresponds to a theoretical and methodological exercise that is sustained in those same approaches, in order to move forward in the analysis of society itself. In particular, on the basis of these approaches we want to ask ourselves how this social self-reproduction of migration, accounts for a significant part of the processes of reproduction of societies as a whole.

In fact, our proposal takes as a starting point, precisely, this principle of the cumulative causation, which allows to talk about migration as a social process, and not just as a demographic phenomenon and less still, circumscribed only to its economic and structural determinants. For this reason, it is not our interest to establish a debate on this approach, but on the contrary, to support it, in moving towards other fields of problematizing migration from which we could arrive at new meanings and scopes of the social process of migration.

Meanwhile, without these principles of cumulative causation and social reproduction of migration (based on the system of social capitals and familiar networks) we could not make the step to a proposal of a model which enables us to understand the role of migration in the society reproduction processes. Undoubtedly, this exercise of incorporating new problematizing fields, involves a review and re-elaboration of the categories of analysis that are commonly used in studies on migration, especially in terms of adjusting and adapting them to the targets and scopes of our particular proposal and model of understanding migration.

## 2  From the Social Reproduction of Migration to Migration as Reproduction of Society

It is widely accepted that in the origin of any migratory flow, there are usually structural triggers no matter if it is a question of economic, social or political factors, or even natural disasters. Nevertheless, this migration causal determination not always turns out to be enough to make a migratory process initiate.

In effect, migration as a social process, never takes place in the abstract, or only motivated by equally abstract structural causations. For its launching it must be sustained, like many other social processes, by a system of networks and social relations through which individuals interact with one another.

In this sense, although the structural factors serve as migration drivers and triggers, once it happens, the social and familiar networks are those that allow its support and reproduction. Through migration, these networks and systems of social and familiar relations are activated and expanded beyond the territorial limits of the home community. In the case of international migration, this expansion is also international, in that it has been categorized as the formation of transnational communities. What is outstanding in this, is that through this system of familiar networks and social relationships (social capital), migration becomes a mechanism for migrant social reproduction, along with their families and community.

One of the most accepted approaches in the academic world, is precisely that which is studying the social process of migration and the analysis of social and familiar networks that are activated by migration itself. One of the basic concepts that has been proposed by this approach, is precisely that of *cumulative causation*, which allows to explain how, once the social process of migration has broken out, a series of mechanisms has been activated (social and familiar networks, relations of solidarity, reciprocity, institutions like the *compadrazgo*, among others) that allow its maintenance and reproduction in itself and by itself, even regardless of the factors that at the beginning could have triggered it (Massey, 1990; Durand and Massey, 2003).

Nevertheless, beyond the relevance, importance and contributions that have emerged from this vision, we think that it is a question of a partial and incomplete recovery of Myrdal *circular and cumulative causation* concept and approach, which we have already reviewed, and hence, it does not account for the depth, complexity and radicalism of this theoretical proposal. On this matter, we can indicate two areas in Myrdal's proposal that in our opinion, have not been properly retaken. The first one refers to the role of migration trigger factors (and of the cumulative causation processes), and the second one to the absence of the circular character of cumulative causation processes.

i) According to our interpretation of Myrdal, we think that the structural factors and migration triggers are always necessary for migration reproduction as a social process, to the extent that they are always part of the mechanisms that account for the principle of *circular and cumulative causation*. There is no doubt that the social capital and familiar networks are a series of mechanisms that are activated by migration and favor its self-reproduction and, in a way, they are very particular because at the moment they are activated and empowered by the beginning of the migration process; internal mechanisms are activated that configure ways and forms in which migration reproduces itself and perpetuates as a social process.

Nevertheless, the principle of circular and cumulative causation is not restricted to the role and importance of internal factors that is to say to those that are intrinsic and configure the process in itself. Therefore, to think about the migration social process only in terms of its *cumulative causation*, refers more to a migratory *inertia* than to Myrdal's concept of circular and cumulative causation. In effect, the physical inertia concept, tells us that once an object is put into motion, it will remain in such a state indefinitely, until an external force acts on him either to stop it or to apply some acceleration force that alters its movement and/or its direction. In this sense, the migratory inertia refers to the fact that once structural factors trigger and activate a migratory process, this generates the necessary mechanisms (social networks) to remain and reproduce until an external force (political, social, economic factors) acts, either to stop it, re-direct it or, re-launch it.

On the contrary, the circular and cumulative causation indicates precisely, the necessary coordination and integration among the diverse factors which, from diverse levels and fields of action, determine the development of a population group, the development of a region, or in general, the dynamics and reproduction of the social process that is being analyzed. As Myrdal indicates, the principle of circular and cumulative causation raises that "the main scientific task is, however, to analyze the causal interrelations within the system itself, as it moves under the influence of external forces as well as by the power of its own internal processes" (Myrdal, 1957:30).

In other words, the principle of the circular and cumulative causation raises a methodological requirement, in the terms that the analysis cannot be reduced neither to the description and characterization of the inner impulses of each social process, nor to the mere observation of the presence of external or structural factors that trigger this social process. On the contrary, the demand is in terms of thinking that both factors (external and internal) make up a system of interrelations between circular and cumulative causation, which must be analyzed and described as a whole.[4]

ii) The cumulative causation principle helps to understand the mechanisms that keep and reproduce the social phenomenon (migration, in this case)

---

4   Keeping a distance from the analysis and its dimensions, this idea is similar to that proposed by Zemelman (1982), Salles (2003) and other authors, when referring to the need for mediations in social analysis. This is, the need for fields of mediation between the micro and macro levels, between the subjects and the structures.

regardless of the structural causes that would have triggered them. Nevertheless, it does not facilitate the understanding of the second level of analysis that Myrdal prints to his approach which refers to the circular causation. It is not an unimportant question, as the circularity of the processes is what allows us a better understanding of economic inequality reproduction, and in particular, of the duality development-underdevelopment.

In our concrete case, we can say that focusing on the cumulative causation in itself, only helps to understand the reproduction of migration, but it does not allow to understand the mechanisms of the social inequality reproduction from which migration sets up one of its components. Not only that, but the cumulative causation in absence of circular causation, is a way of making abstraction of this social inequality condition which explains so much migration in itself, as its reproduction as a social process.

Myrdal makes an analysis regarding the duality Development-Underdevelopment. On the one hand, he points out that there are evident internal mechanisms that make underdevelopment reproduce itself. It is equivalent to the so called poverty trap, where the poor cannot get out of this situation, just because they are poor: their low level of education keep them from finding good quality and better paid jobs all of which limits their income options and reproduce their poverty situation. The same can be said with regard to education, health, living conditions, housing segregation, among many other aspects.

This is the aspect of cumulative causation of poverty self-reproduction which we could extend to migration analysis as a social process. In general, any social process activates these self-reproduction mechanisms. Nevertheless, Myrdal also talks about a circular causation, which in case of the duality development-underdevelopment remains clearly illustrated. Here the object of analysis is no longer the situation of development or underdevelopment of a region in itself, in abstract or in the absence of one another; the object of analysis is the situation of inequality, the economic and political asymmetries that characterize the relationships of some developed regions compared to the underdeveloped ones. When the underdevelopment of a region is reproduced, (by causation to circulate cumulative mechanisms) it is also reproduces its position and the situation of inequality and asymmetry in relation to the developed ones.

Here the relevant aspect is the scope of the analyzed problem. Myrdal is not only interested in the underdeveloped regions, but in the reproduction of the inequality and economic asymmetries that are established between the developed regions and the underdeveloped ones. To the extent that development and underdevelopment are part of the same economic system, it turns out to be practically impossible to reduce the analysis and explanation of the underdevelopment situation only to the mechanisms of cumulative causation. On the contrary, both in theoretical and methodological terms, the principle of circular and cumulative causation raises the demand of incorporating in the same analysis model, the factors and mechanisms that involve its reciprocal and *circular* causation.

In this regard, it is not ventured to affirm that the radical nature of Myrdal's approach, lies precisely in this view through which he wonders the ways in which the reproduction of some people (developed on one side and white people on the other) is articulated with the reproduction of others (underdeveloped on one side, black people on the other). Its radicalism lies in the fact that his concern is not restricted to reproduction conditions of some *or* others but to the forms and reproduction conditions of some *and* others, and particularly, to the reproduction of inequality between some *and* others.

His answer is equally radical: it is the reproduction of some that generate and cause the reproduction of others, and therefore, the reproduction of inequality between both. Or what is the same, the cumulative causation of some, cannot be understood without the cumulative causation of others, in a scheme according to which it is the circularity of these cumulative causations that are the center of the whole analysis, the base of the whole process, it is what reproduces to some *and* the others. Therefore, the cumulative causation does not achieve by itself the explanatory and understanding power of social phenomena if it is not integrated into the processes of circular causation that articulates and projects them towards the whole reproduction of which they are an integral part.

## 3   Conclusion: Migration and Reproduction

In this book we want to propose an analysis model of international migrations as a reproduction process component of contemporary society. To do this, we depart from the premise that international migration activates mechanisms that articulate and integrate in the same process the social reproduction of migrants and their communities of origin, with the social reproduction of the native population into destination societies (especially the middle and upper classes).

Also, from the Reproduction perspective, we can not only integrate in the same model both phenomena but, in addition, state that they are not but two faces of the same global process: the reproduction at a global level of a social structure in which we can identify different strata, groups and social classes which are different and distant but articulated and integrated into their social reproduction. Through migration intersection fields of local processes related to social reproduction are configured, some of them located both in the origin communities and others in destination areas of migration. These are processes that although different and distant, through migration they turn into what we may call a global process of social reproduction.

This process of local-global articulation given through international migration, is not solely composed of analytical categories purely and simply (work, migration, transnational communities, individuation, labor market, reproduction, globalization, among others), but also, and fundamentally, it is the articulation and opposition of social subjects, this is, of classes, strata and social groups, as well as of their unequal positions in a social structure.

In this sense, our thesis is that in this era of globalization, international migration constitutes a component of the world system reproduction. In particular, through migration a structure of *social inequality* takes place and reproduces, which, in this case, also adopts a *transnational* form. But we must not delude ourselves. In this perspective, the transnational is not only migration in itself, but the whole reproduction system of social inequality of which migration is part.

CHAPTER 2

# International Migration in Neoclassical Economics: a Critical Perspective

*I know how to make the way when I walk, a walker*
*That's why I do not have a representative flag*
*it's not my name that matters, what matters is what I make*
*To value man for the quality of his work*[1]
            The Rose of the Winds
    MAKIZA / ANITA TIJOUX

∴

International migration is, without a doubt, one of the main concerns of contemporary society. Whether in the countries of origin or those of arrival, migration is on the social and political agendas of nations. Discussions and proposals of various kinds can be heard coming from different political and ideological stations. From those proposing total control, closing borders, criminalizing migrants and many policies of the same ilk, to those recommending freedom of movement for people and labor, and multiculturalism as a sign of the times, on an equally long list. In the academic world, the study of migration has also been approached from a variety of theoretical points of view.[2]

In spite of there being a vast array of positions, academic and political discussion of the subject has been strongly dominated by conservative views of

---

1 "Sé hacer camino al andar caminante; por eso no tengo bandera representante; da lo mismo mi nombre, lo importante es lo que hago; valorar el hombre por la calidad de su trabajo". Original in Spanish.
2 For a comprehensive view of the range of these theoretical approaches, see, to start with, the work of Massey et al. (1993), which provides an ample revision of the most relevant theories, and includes an interesting and adequate proposal for classifying them on the basis of the scope of their proposals, the areas and scales they focus on, and the most abstract theoretical currents they form a part of. Also, although the range is smaller, it is worth consulting the equally rigorous work of Herrera (2006), who reviews the theories and includes in her publication those that have been applied to the study and analysis of internal and international migrations.

society that tend to question the role of migration in society and its transformations. The most notable approaches here are those of neoclassical economics and the methodological individualism, which in their various formulations, seek to provide theoretical and conceptual support for such discussions of a conservative nature of the causes and consequences of migrations in contemporary society.

Taking the above into account, in this text we present a critical revision of neoclassical theory, both in its original formulation and in its re-elaboration as the so-called new home economics.

## 1 Approaches of Neoclassical Economic Theory and of the New Home Economics

In neoclassical economic theory, we can find three approaches used to analyze and conceptualize the phenomenon of migrations. It should be noted, that these approaches are not only for international migration, but also cover displacements within each nation, with a major emphasis on rural to urban movements. However, in all cases, the analytical framework used is based on the principles of rational choice, and of methodological individualism.

Ever since the first formulations of neoclassical theory were made, in the second half of the nineteenth century, it has been much influenced by Newtonian models of the world, in which economic actors, whether individuals, households or companies, are regarded as atoms, subject to laws of universal validity, economic rationality and perfect competition (de la Garza, 1998). Seen in this way, migration and the spatial mobility of people, can only be considered a field in which these basic premises of neoclassical theory, with all the varieties of it that may be derived on the way, apply.

In effect, analysis is centered on studying the conditions and determining factors of the decision taken by each actor with regard to whether or not to start a process of migration, and when and how to do it and where to go. This makes the unit of analysis *par excellence* the individual subject, who acts in isolation and independently of the action of other individuals. Further, although the unit of analysis in some approaches may be the household, or the family, the basic principle is the same, in so far as the unit of analysis acts and decides in a way that is independent of the action and decisions of other family units.

Also, whether it is the individual, in one case, or the family and household, in another, the decision is still always taken according to principles of rational choice, meaning the optimization at all times of the allocation of resources. Optimization is achieved on the basis of a traditional classical analysis of costs and benefits, where what varies between one option and another is not the principle involved in taking the decision but the elements included as costs and as benefits.

From a macroeconomic point of view, the central argument of neoclassical theory is that movements of the population have their basic origin in a situation of wage level inequality (in real, not nominal terms) between the migrants' countries of origin and those of their arrival (Todaro, 1976; Stark, 1991). On the basis of rational choice, it may be said that to the extent that the difference in wages is great enough to compensate for the economic and subjective costs of migration, there is an economic (cost-benefit) motive for people to migrate (Sjaastad, 1962).

Although the growth model of two sectors and an unlimited supply of labor, developed by A. Lewis (1954), was quickly replaced by other more sophisticated models including more variables, and less restrictions, the basic premise was kept. Migration is the effect of inequalities in wages, which express the different rates of productivity in each region. In this sense for workers and for the economy as a whole, migration from sectors (or regions) with a low rate of productivity (generally, rural zones, undeveloped countries), to sectors (or regions) with a higher rate of productivity (urban industrial zones, developed countries), is beneficial. Migrants are motivated by the better wages associated with the higher rates of productivity in the places they migrate to, while in macroeconomic terms there would be a net gain, because what is gained in productivity in the regions migrated to, is more than what is lost in the regions of origin.

Other authors have broadened this theory, and point out that in the case of better qualified workers, the variable that carries the most weight is no longer the difference in wages, but differences in rates of return, which makes it possible to include in an analysis of the decision to migrate, the contribution made by other factors, such as differences in the economic situation, in other words opportunities for the individual (or the family) to make progress, working conditions, quality of life, and other indicators.

In microeconomic terms, a certain amount of complexity is added to the original idea by the argument that the cost-benefit differences of migration should be weighted on the basis of the probabilities that the migration will be successful, that is, that the country of arrival will be reached and employment obtained that provides a large enough difference in pay from that which would have been obtained in the country of origin. This analysis, then, includes in its models differences in the unemployment rate as a proxy variable for the probability of finding a job, as well as the different economic costs of moving from one country to another (Borjas, 1990; Stark, 1984; Todaro, 1969).

At any rate, what matters is that the decision is taken by individuals as a function of optimizing the allocation of resources, seeking to maximize income and profits, in the face of the restrictions imposed by the labor market (unemployment rate, for example) and the costs of the move itself, on the basis of the widely accepted assumptions of perfect competition, which would imply basically unrestricted knowledge of job opportunities and working conditions (wages, etc.), the free movement of production factors, and the principle of rational choice, along with the existence of a large number of economic agents (companies and workers, in this case) none of whom has the power to intervene in the determination of the other variables of the labor market (Ritchey, 1976).

The first reworking, or rather adjustment and alignment of neoclassical theory, came from the idea that the actors do not always have all the information, that is, information on the markets is not free nor available to everyone. Considering that the decision to migrate necessarily implies a relatively long time horizon, the original proposal included the thesis that the actors (migrants, in this case) would behave in accordance not only with information they possessed at the time, but also on the basis of what future situations were expected to be like, both in terms of possible benefits and of the costs and risks of migration. This however presupposed that the actors not only had complete information for the present but also for the future behavior of the markets and their basic variables (wages, unemployment rates, and others).

Thus the supposition of free and perfect mobility and knowledge of the facts about the costs and benefits of migration, and of the dynamics and behavior of the basic variables, was called into question. This led to the formulation of the hypothesis of adaptive expectations (Cagan, 1956) and of another, that of rational expectations (Muth, 1961; Lucas, 1972). In the first case, the vision and expectations of the future are said to be a function of the behavior that the variables and certain economic events have shown in the past, and in the second case, that of the hypothesis of rational expectations, there is an additional assumption that people learn from their mistakes and successes, especially if these start to be systematic, which makes it possible to make corrections and improve predictions of the future. So in the second case, even though it also holds to the principle of uncertainty regarding the future behavior of variables and economic phenomena, it adds a factor of adjustment that allows errors to be not systematic but accidental.

In this way, though still uncertain, future expectations allow decisions to be taken in the present about migrating, returning, or not migrating, and these decisions are then adapted to how the values of the variables evolve and are modified in the course of time. Expectations of the future, and the decision to migrate, are thus adapted to circumstances, where the only certainty is that of an uncertain world, with partial, incomplete and biased information.

With regard to the *new economics of labor migration*, this is an application of the so-called *New Home Economics* to international migration. The new home economics itself is really an extension of the basic principles of rational choice of the neoclassical school, to a series of phenomena in which the unit of analysis and observation is not the individual but the household or the family. An example is the analysis of the decision on how many children to have, which led to the economic theory of fertility (Becker, 1960).[3] Another example refers to expenditure on the health and education of children, which rather than being seen as a type of consumption, is conceived of as a process of investment in the formation of human capital. In general, the new home economics is interested in analyzing, from the perspective of rational choice, various aspects of social life that had hitherto remained outside the scope of neo-classical economic theory (Becker, 1966).

This new approach of economic theory notes in particular that the economic analysis of the behavior of individuals should consider not only the rationality of the subject, but also include the household (and the family) as an intermediate space where a second level of economic rationality operates, and this can on certain occasions override the benefit of the individual in favor of that of the domestic unit (De Haas, 2007). As a consequence of this point of view, what becomes relevant now is not the analysis of cost-benefit (rational choice) at an individual level, but at a collective level within the household. So what is relevant is not the strategies and decisions of individuals but strategies and decisions adopted collectively in the household.[4]

---

3   The original proposal was somewhat provocative, as it claimed children were an *inferior* good, because empirical data showed that fertility and the number of offspring tended to reduce as income increased. In response to this curious paradox, the economic theory of fertility noted that what really happened was that as the level of income of couples or families rose, although the number of children did decrease, at the same time expenditure on each of them increased (more and better education, health, toys, pattern of consumption and lifestyle, etc.). In which case the application of basic principles of neo-classical economic theory would allow the claim that children were a *superior* good, in terms of the fact that as the level of income increased, though the quantity might be less, the *quality* improved (Becker, 1981).

4   Although these might seem to be more or less recent theoretical claims, in fact they were first formulated by the Russian scholar Alexander Chayanov (1986) who lived from 1888 to 1937 and is probably the first economist to have extended the analysis based on rational choice of the neo-classical school to the study of the economy of households in Russia at the end of the tsarist period, that is in the late nineteenth and early twentieth centuries. On the basis of principles of the marginalism in price theory (theory of marginal utility, marginal cost, marginal productivity) from Austrian School Economics (Böhm-Bawerk, 1959), he analyzed decisions of consumption-investment made by peasant families in the Russia of the time.

Following the principles of rational choice, this new approach of neoclassical theory proposes that, as distinct from the decisions of individuals, in the case of households and domestic units, the function to be optimized is not maximizing expected income but minimizing risk for the household. In this sense, the decision is taken as a function of the general levels of wellbeing of the household, and not of each individual separately. This implies that the strategy of resource allocation of the household follows a principle of resource diversification into several different uses, a strategy that reduces the risk that would have been incurred by assigning all resources to a single activity[5] (Massey, et al., 1993).

In spite of the differences between them, all of these approaches follow the same basic principles of neoclassical theory, where rational choice is the fundamental and most crucial premise. It is on the basis of this principle, that the action of *homo economicus* (or *domus economicus*, we might add for the new household economics) is defined, and what changes in each case is rather more a question of the variables to be included as a function of optimization than the principle of optimization as such.

## 2    Limitations of Neo-classical Theory: Imperfections of the Market

Now rather than discuss the validity and internal consistency of the neoclassical approach to migration, whether in its original formulation or in its derived form as the new home economics, what we wish to point out here is its weaknesses for the understanding of migration in its actual historical context. We shall concentrate our reflections on two levels, one on the criticism that markets do not necessarily work under the assumptions of perfect competition proclaimed by the neoclassical school, and the other on the ahistoricism which neoclassical economic theory generally shows.

As a number of authors have pointed out before, capitalism does not work on the basis of principles of perfect competition but on the contrary, most

---

In fact, it is not by chance that this author should have been taken up in the nineteen seventies by anthropologists, demographers and sociologists to study the conditions of social reproduction of impoverished families whether in urban or rural zones of Latin America, and that his ideas led to the formulation of concepts like that of survival strategies (Cortés, 1980, Rodríguez, 1981), which even today, thirty years later is referred to by English speaking and European writers and others (de Haas, 2007).

5   A new version, with a certain degree of formal and discursive sophistication added, of the timeless old principle of not putting all your eggs in one basket. Still a big step forward for neoclassical economic theory, no doubt.

commonly and generally markets work on the basis of oligopolistic or duopolistic competition, when they are not directly dominated by monopolistic situations (Robinson, 1969). These are market conditions substantially removed from what neoclassical theory maintains, under which therefore the operation of the markets does not guarantee the optimal allocation of resources.

On the level of the labor market, the formation of dual and segmented markets should also be considered, as they imply another type of restriction on the entry of workers. They make the basic variables of the labor market, crucial for individuals taking the decision of whether to migrate or not, to be seriously distorted by restrictions on labor mobility from one type of activity and occupation to others better remunerated, with better perks and better levels of security, etc.

As commonly noted in critical literature, the labor market does not work like the potato market (Meller, 1982), which means there are substantial differences in the way prices (wages) and quantities (employment and unemployment) are determined in the labor market. Contrary to the neoclassical view, the problem of unemployment (and wages) is not a microeconomic phenomenon, that applies only to the corresponding market (buying and selling the power of labor), but is essentially a macroeconomic problem. In fact classical macroeconomic theory states that the determination of wages and unemployment depends directly on what happens in the markets of goods and finance at a macroeconomic level. Wages and unemployment are therefore essentially macroeconomic variables, not only because of their social and political implications but also because of the economic factors that determine their levels, tendencies and magnitudes, as well as the consequences their values and determinations have in other markets and for macroeconomic dynamics.

Further, modern macroeconomic theory also emphasizes the macroeconomic determinants of the labor market. Meller (1982) points out that according to economic theory:

> (any) existing imbalance in the market of goods, produces an imbalance in the labor market (and as a result, unemployment); at the same time, this imbalance in the labor market feeds back and increases the original imbalance in the market of goods.[6]
> 
> MELLER, 1982:77

---

6 "(Cualquier) desequilibrio existente en el mercado de bienes, produce el desequilibrio del mercado de trabajo (y en consecuencia, desocupación); por otra parte, este desequilibrio del mercado del trabajo retroalimenta e incrementa el desequilibrio inicial del mercado de bienes". Original in Spanish.

The situation becomes even more complicated as the labor market is particularly sensitive to the political, economic and social conditions prevailing in other parts of society. Wages, for example, are not only an indicator for the price of merchandise being traded in a market, but spill over socially and politically into the rest of society, as an indicator of the value of labor power, making them a fundamental component of the distribution of income and social inequality, among other aspects (Noriega, 1994).

In the same sense, several authors argue that the price of work force (i.e. wages) does not depend only and exclusively on the productivity rates of the workers, but also and fundamentally on the prevailing political and social conditions at any juncture, and especially on the capacity of the workers to negotiate with other actors (business people, investors, politicians, and so on). Therefore wages are not purely and simply an economic variable but a variable whose rate is determined socially and politically.

From the point of view of institutionalist theory, for example, economic markets, especially those of strategic importance, like the labor market, do not operate merely as interactions between rational economic agents, but form a complex system of interactions and relations between various social, political and economic institutions (Chang, 2011; Hodgson, 1998). Of vital importance in the case of the labor market, is the action of the unions, of the State, of business associations and of political parties. The way they interact is not governed just by criteria of rational choice but is also based on the correlation of forces prevailing at any one time, and on the structural contexts of the moment.

This is particularly true of the insertion of migrants into the labor and employment market, where the very condition of being a migrant, is a factor of social vulnerability and a lack of political protection that explains the situation of asymmetrical power relations affecting them directly, and stops them from insisting on their rights in determining the level of their pay and in general the working conditions they are employed in (Bustamante, 2002).

These asymmetrical power relations expose migrants to different forms of labor discrimination. The condition of being a migrant (and commonly also of not having papers) creates a situation of social and political vulnerability, which translates into discrimination in wages, employment, labor insecurity, and into other disadvantages that directly affect the working conditions and pay of migrant workers. In this case we can see how, independently of the rules of the economic operation of the labor market, other social and political rules are at work and end up dominating the former, becoming the principle determinants not only of the value, rates and tendencies of the basic variables of the labor market (wages, employment, labor conditions), but also of the marked differences between different groups of workers (migrants, and residents, in this case).

Here one should add a reference to comments on neoclassical theory made by studies focusing on social networks. These point out that it is not sufficient for there to be differences in wages or of an economic nature, and in living conditions in general, as it is just as important for the individual (or the household) to have access to jobs and labor markets that would make it possible for them to enjoy improved living conditions (Massey, et al.; 1993). In this sense, amongst other points questioned is the neoclassical assumption of rational choice, whereas on the contrary it is affirmed that the labor market (as well as other economic and social institutions) does not work solely and exclusively on the basis of rational choice mechanisms, but of equal importance to it are the presence and mediation established by a series of social institutions that work with a great variety of rationalities, not necessarily reduceable to the logic of costs and benefits (Requena, 1991).

Such is the case of social and family networks, that turn out to be necessary both for supporting the process of migration itself and for making it possible to have access to the labor market, accommodation, a household, etc. in the arrival community. In other words, day to day life is not only sustained by institutions and principles of rational choice, but also and fundamentally by much more complex and diverse social and cultural phenomena that are certain to escape the precepts of neoclassical economic theory (whether in its traditional formulation or in that of the new home economics).

In this sense, important contributions have been made by economic sociology and institutional economics that directly contradict the neoclassical principles for explaining how the labor market works, and in particular, with regard to the insertion of migrants into the labor market. We refer in the first place to the approaches concerned with dual or segmented markets (Pioré, 1979), and then to approaches concerned with social capital as a mechanism for migrants to have access to the labor market. In the first case, the question is one of structural factors that explain the formation of differentiated labor markets, for residents and migrants, in which the conditions of employment, wages, benefits, etc. are markedly different. Of relevance is the fact that in many cases this segmentation of the market is not an abstraction but is found in the same company and economic sector, with workers having different conditions of employment and labor protection coexisting in the same productive plant.

In the second case, we refer to microsocial factors, that is, to the social and relational capital of migrants, which works as a mechanism of protection and provides the migrant worker with mechanisms and tools from other areas of life (family, society, community) with which to face the situation of vulnerability and labor discrimination that predominates in the labor markets he can have access to (Sassen, 1995; Portes, 1998). Here the most relevant point is that this social and relational capital is one of the principle mechanisms through which the labor market operates and through which migrants gain an entry into it, and this point helps to move the workings of the labor market even farther away from neoclassical economic theory's dictates as to how it should work. Working migrants, far from being actors who make decisions on the basis of a principle of rational choice, of optimization, act on the basis of extra-economic principles, that is, on the basis of logics and premises rooted in areas of life completely separate from and quite incompatible with economics and its rationality of *homo economicus* (Bourdieu, 2005).

## 3   Rational Choice: Theoretical or Axiomatic Principle?

These criticisms concentrate on questioning the validity of the basic assumptions of the neoclassical model, especially in relation to the imperfections of the markets. They go on to propose alternative models with which to establish new focal points of analysis of economic processes, and in the present case, of migration in particular. This applies for example to theories of imperfect competition, theories on the segmentation of labor markets, and theories of economic sociology, many of which have their own derivations and analytical models for the study of international migration (Pioré, 1979; Portes, 1995).

There is a second level of criticism which is more interested in noting some of the methodological differences of the neoclassical approach, which derive from the principles upon which it was built. I would mention first the principle of rational choice as a factor for explaining decisions to migrate or not, and then the ahistorical character of this economic theory. With regard to the decision on whether or not to migrate, the principle of rational choice refers more to *how* a decision is taken, that is, to the principles and logical criteria taken into account, than it does to *what* decision is taken and *why* this and not another was preferred, something it is incapable of addressing and explaining. The decisions taken (in this case on whether to migrate or not) are dictated more by factors in the household and contextual and historical factors. We can see this in a simple example, which refers precisely to the decision to migrate.

We take the case of two households, in the same community. One of them has members of the household living at home and others who have migrated, while the other has members of the household living at home and other members of the family working in local economic activities. In other words, we have two domestic units, and the social capital of one of them is sustained by migration networks and that of the other is sustained by local networks of employment.

It is most likely that the first domestic unit will choose to strengthen its migration strategy, while the second domestic unit will choose to strengthen its presence in the local economy. In fact, for this second domestic unit, with no migration networks, it would be highly irrational to decide to migrate, as starting a migration process would be a decision significantly increasing risk and thus introducing an element of uncertainty into levels of family wellbeing.

Equally, for the family that does have migration networks, taking the opposite decision, of not migrating but integrating members of the family into local labor markets, is just as much a high risk option, as the household does not possess the information, the connections or the necessary experience to guarantee employment that would not put the stability and wellbeing of the family at risk. On the contrary, staying with the migration strategy would be the most rational choice, as it implies making better use of the household's resources, of its accumulated experience of migration, of the information at its disposal and in general of its social and family capital.

So both these households, following the same principle of rational choice, of minimizing risks, nevertheless are led to take different decisions. For one household, optimization is achieved through more migration and for the other, with no migration. Evidently rational choice does not explain the decision to migrate, which is taken on the basis of the different social capital of each of the domestic units.

If the principle of rational choice is the basis of all the decisions of the household (and there is no reason to suppose that some households are less rational than others, or that some decisions are less rational than others), then it is not a principle that makes it possible to differentiate between the decision of one household and that of another. Therefore it is not a principle allowing the migration of some households and the non-migration of others to be explained. The differentiation in the decision making of the two households derives rather from the structural conditions of each household and its contextual and historical conditions, in which the households are unlike each other.

However, neither family structure nor historical context are included as variables or explicative factors of migration in the neoclassical model, whether in its macroeconomic formulation, or in traditional microeconomic theory, or in the so-called new home economics.

This is the logical problem underlying the principle of rational choice. If all the behavior of individuals (let us say, all actions and options of an economic kind or of relevance to the study) is decided on the basis of rational choice, then this principle does not help us to differentiate one decision from another, one action from another, one individual from another. They are all equally rational. However, in fact, the decisions and actions of individuals are not all the same, but clearly different. Really, it is this difference, the distinctive features of actions and decisions, which needs to be explained and theorized about.

The corollary of all this is obvious. Beyond questions of whether the principle of rational choice is valid, the way it is actually formulated does not allow us to use it to explain the behavior of persons, at the level of the individual or at the level of the household. And anyway the principle itself defines a tautological situation, which automatically disqualifies it from being a theory. If every decision is taken rationally (on the basis of costs and benefits) then you reach the paradox that in a single household, if the decision to migrate is taken, that is the most rational choice, but if the opposite decision is taken, so is that. There are no elements in the decision itself that make it possible to determine whether it was taken on the basis of rational (cost-benefit) criteria or not. On the contrary, neoclassical economic theory itself is based on the assumption that actors always take decisions following a principle of rational choice (cost-benefit). What varies in each case, that is, in each formulation of the theory, is whether the process is one of maximizing income or one of minimizing risk, but in both cases the criterion is one of optimizing the allocation of resources, in the first case those of the individual and in the second case, those of the household.

In other words, the principle of rational choice works more as a general axiom, that cannot be demonstrated, or questioned, and is valid by itself, than as a theoretical principle on the basis of which attempts to explain the behavior and decisions of people and their households are made. So as a general axiom, it makes no sense to discuss whether it is valid or not, but neither is it sensible to base an explanation of the migratory behavior of individuals and/ or their households, on a principle as general as this.[7]

As a general axiom, it may serve to build theories to explain the behavior and decisions of persons, but as an axiom it can never replace the theory or be used as a theoretical axiom to explain directly for each concrete and historically definable case, the behavior and decisions of these individuals. The problem of the neoclassical approach (in any of its formulations) is that it remains at this level of general abstraction, at the level of general axioms, without leading to a theory of migration as such. As pointed out by de la Garza (1998), in this respect neoclassical theory is more like the formal sciences, for example mathematics which starts from indemonstrable axioms from which theorems

---

7 After all, it goes against every principle of scientific rationality to want to base a theory on an unprovable axiom.

and corollaries are deduced, which in turn may be tried against reality but not in Popper's sense of verification/refutation of the theory.

The validity of the theory in these cases is not given by submitting it to reality, which would imply a form of exposure to methods of refutation, as explained by Popper (1968). What makes it valid is its internal coherence, the logic with which the theorems and corollaries have been extrapolated, as in mathematics, where the methods for validating theorems are equally abstract and based purely on logical analysis, not on processes of empirical testing, which would imply exposing the theory to the risk of being verified or refuted.

This is evidently a distinctly positivist criticism, following Popper's postulates of verification and validation of a theoretical framework (Popper, 1965). From this Popperian positivist perspective, neoclassical theory is only a worn out story, with great internal logical coherence, based on irresistible logical reasoning, but because it derives from unverifiable axioms, like that of rational choice, it has turned into an irrefutable theory, in other words a metaphysical tale and not a body of scientific knowledge.

## 4   Neoclassical Economics: an Ahistorical Theory

This leads us to the second focal point of criticism against the methodological pillars sustaining the neoclassical approach. In concrete terms, our interest is in discussing the intrinsic difficulty for neoclassical theory to incorporate into its formulations and analytical models, the historical dimension of the processes it is theorizing about. For the neoclassical school, empirical analysis is based on a hypothetical-deductive model, that is to say, on starting from abstract models to deduce hypotheses of general validity that will be the methodological guide for studying concrete historical cases (de la Garza, 1998b). In no case does it imply steadily incorporating new dimensions of the real, that is, of its historical dimension. The real, that is to say the concrete object of study being analyzed, thus maintains the same level of abstraction and ahistoricism as the theoretical models used for its analysis and comprehension.

In the case we are concerned with, what is interesting is that, using neoclassical theory, not only the terms considered, of migration and development, but the relation between them and their mutual structuring (causes and consequences of one upon the other) tend to be studied on the basis of general models, without considering the historical contexts in which both these processes are framed. To put it more simply, in neoclassical approaches there appears to be no attempt to recover the historical genesis of these processes, or of the relations between them, and even less to revise and reflect on the concepts and categories used to take account of them. In this way, using the neoclassical school, the theories of and approaches to migration and development that it leads to do not cease to be theories of a general character, valid indeed for any and every situation of migration and development but insufficient for analyzing and explaining historical and concrete processes of migration and development.

This does not mean we believe it is necessary to always aim for the concrete to a point of absurdity, that is, to differentiate each and every migratory movement theoretically, rather that it is necessary to establish the historical and geographical limits of each theory, which in our case refers to all approaches to the relation between migration and development. A general theory of migration and development that uses the same arguments, the same categories of analysis, the same models and the same causal relations to explain rural-urban migration in the early days of capitalism in Europe, and international migration at the end of the 19th century and the beginning of the 20th century, or to explain international migration in the global society of today, may be a good starting point for an introductory course on population mobility, but is certainly not enough for understanding the range and limitations of the relation between migration and development at each of these stages of capitalist development.

So, for example, to say that migration is always explained by factors of attraction and repulsion, may be a good start for an undergraduate student, but in no case is it a model that allows the conditions of migration at every historical juncture to be understood and explained. Precisely what differentiates one model of migration from another, for example rural-urban migration in Latin America in the 20th century from contemporary international migration in the same region, is the fact that in either case the factors of expulsion and attraction are quite different. In this sense what is required of a theory is that it should tell us in concrete terms what these factors are and how they work at each historical juncture.

With general theories at this level of abstraction it is impossible methodologically to analyze, evaluate and understand the vicissitudes of the relation between migration and development in our times. The only thing achieved with general theories of this type is precisely the making of statements that are so general as to be unquestionable but are not useful for designing programs, proposals and models to analyze and comprehend the relation between migration and development in contemporary society. This charge of ahistoricism may at first seem to be a rather reckless and exaggerated claim. However, to understand the sense of our methodological criticism of these approaches, we can make an analogy with an everyday universal climate phenomenon, which is rain.

On the basis of simple principles of the atmosphere it is possible to elaborate a general theory (which has indeed been elaborated) that both allows us to define what rain is and also to explain how it is generated. Using the principle of gravity and going on to atmospheric factors that explain the processes of condensation of water, among many other aspects, a general model has been created that explains the phenomenon of rain very well.[8]

However, in spite of the obvious theoretical validity an explanation of rain as general as this may have, it is quite inadequate for explaining two very simple phenomena related to rain. First, how can the same phenomenon of torrential rain be catastrophic in certain geographical and historical contexts, and in others, a blessing? A general theory based on simple atmospheric principles may well explain the rain, but is unable to explain the climate phenomena of *El Niño* or *La Niña*, let alone their very distinct consequences in different social and geographical contexts.

It is obvious that the description and explanation of these concrete historical situations cannot be derived from what the general theory of rain has to say, but, on the contrary, their explanation must be sought in what the general theory does not say, that is, in what was hidden and cast aside in the process of abstraction leading to the generalization: namely the historical and geographical context that all the rain occurs in.[9]

The phenomenon of *El Niño* clearly illustrates this inadequacy of the general theory, and provides us with a mirror in which to see the inadequacies of general theories of migration. As is well known, the phenomenon of *El Niño* is dictated by a series of climate, historical and social circumstances that have led to so-called global warming. Of relevance here is, first, that this is a climate phenomenon that is historically determined. We therefore require a history of rain and climate that explains not climate and rain in general, but their dynamics and characteristics in the current historical context of global warming. Secondly, it is a phenomenon that needs to link, in the same model of analysis, situations deriving from processes as dissimilar as they are complementary, such as global climate, ecology, capitalist industrialization, demographic growth, and consumer society, amongst others. Finally and of no less relevance is the fact that the study of the impact or consequences of *El Niño* should also be conducted in terms of the particular historical, social and geographical

---

8  In fact, in the *Enciclopedia Hispánica*, rain is defined as atmospheric water precipitation, produced by the effect of the condensation of vapour contained in the clouds, which falls to the ground through the effect of terrestrial gravity. The condensation is explained by the joint action of three factors: atmospheric pressure, atmospheric humidity, and temperature.
9  Change the word "rain" to "migration" and all will be made clear.

conditions in which this phenomenon is manifested.[10] That is, it is not enough to have a theory that links these different dimensions, as it is necessary for the theory to recover the historicity of the phenomenon, both with regard to its causes and in respect of its consequences.

Something similar occurs with the case of migration. It is not enough to have a general theory of migration like the traditional formulations of neoclassical economic theory, not even one that includes other dimensions of the migration process in its analysis, such as the new home economics. Whatever the theory, it must be founded on the historicity of the phenomenon of migration, that is, on the history of its structural causes, and of its consequences in the course of its development on its different scales and levels (economic, social, demographic, cultural and political, among others).

In ontological terms, space and time are conditions of existence. As ontological conditions of being, they are always present in every phenomenon, whether of the physical or of the social world. So the analysis, understanding and comprehension of any social phenomenon should necessarily include them, or risk falling into generalities that are as obvious and empty as they are true. In our case this means trying to recover the historical (time) and geographical (space) conditions of the migration phenomenon, and its relation to processes of economic development, ontological conditions that as we have seen are not in the analytical models for analyzing and understanding migration that derive from neoclassical economic theory. This is a methodological inadequacy that is found both in the macroeconomic approach and in its extension into what is called the new home economics.

In the case of neoclassical macroeconomic theory, for example, we may point out that due to the degree of abstraction and generality it possesses, the principle of wage inequality can be applied equally to explaining international migration today (in a global postmodern society) and to explaining international migration 100 years ago. However this is clearly a case of two completely distinct phenomena, that is, waves of migration in different directions, of a different character and having a different economic significance, all of them aspects that cannot be recovered and specified by this theory.

Further, even accepting that wage inequalities (or differences in the quality of life, of working conditions, etc.) might explain labor force mobility, it is clear that this theory of migration can never explain the origin of the

---

10  In a single city the rain falls on everyone but it does not fall equally. Not everyone is equally susceptible to the effects of a storm. There are sectors that are more exposed to the risk of flooding than others, and this is due to factors of an urban, social, economic, political and geographical type, amongst others. For some it literally never rains but it pours.

inequalities, that is, the historical and structural bases of regional differences in wages and pay. Also, although such a theory can state that migration will act as a mechanism of adjustment or balance for such inequalities, whether or not this is true,[11] what is important is that to the extent that a phenomenon (wage inequality) is not explained by the theory, it would be inconsistent with the methodology adopted to use the theory to explain transformation of the phenomenon. In other words, it is impossible to say that migration may act as a balancing factor in wage inequalities when the theory applied has not explained the determining factors of the inequality.

We can propose something similar for the case of the so-called new home economics and its derivative the new labor force economics. Certainly migration can be understood as a resource which households facing situations of impoverishment, vulnerability or other social or economic risks, can have recourse to. However there is no way these strategies of survival for the family can be useful for understanding and explaining why the situation of vulnerability and impoverishment has occurred. Or to put it another way, on the basis of this theory it can be understood that migration may be a strategy for dealing with the social situation of the household, but it can never explain the overcoming of a social situation whose determining factors have not been previously conceptualized and explained by the same theory.

This theory also shows a degree of generality that is like that of the traditional neoclassical approach (both at a macro and at a micro level), in so far as the same theory serves to understand migration in postindustrial society and rural-urban migration in 19th century capitalist society. In both cases, migration can be understood as one of the family's strategies, as a resource households can accede to deal with a situation of precariousness or economic insufficiency. However, because it is so general, it has the same methodological deficiencies that we laid out for the case of the traditional neoclassical approach.

Now to synthesize the arguments that are critical of these neoclassical approaches, and are commonly used in the study of migration, we can ask: how then is it possible for a single theory to serve for explaining phenomena as distinct as current migration in a postindustrial society, and migration in the capitalist economy of the 19th century, when the differences between the one and the other wave of migration are so evident? In fact the differences are not only to do with the structural and historical contexts which are unlike each

---

11  There are economic theories that speak of a tendency to diverge as opposed to tendencies to converge. See Myrdal, 1957 and Stiglitz, 2012, not to mention Neo-Ricardian or Structuralism authors such as Prebisch, 1950 or Robinson, 1979 and 1969, among others.

other, but also with kinds of migratory flow that are dissimilar in their modalities, spatial patterns of origin and destination, and their social and economic character and significance. In the framework of neoclassical theory, one should therefore ask how the relation of migration to development is to be understood, when the migration process and the process of development are evidently social and economic phenomena that are historically determined.

We can return to the example of a general theory of rain to help us understand this critical position better. As with general theories of migration (such as those laid out in this section), we can ask how it is possible for a single theory of rain to explain the torrential rains that fall in South-East Mexico and also the sporadic rains that fall in the North of Chile? Also, following the same line of reasoning, we should also ask how it can be possible to explain on the basis of this one general theory of rain such radically different effects and consequences of the two types of the rainfall, which in the first case produce recurrent catastrophes (in South-East Mexico) and in the other case, produce the wonders of a flowering desert (in the North of Chile)?

The answer is quite simple: by abstracting from the historical, geographical and climate contexts of each case and keeping only what both have in common: purely and simply, rain. A general theory of rain can only explain what all examples of rainfall have in common. The specifics of each place, such as the consequences or effects of the rain on the geography and climate of the environment, for example, are phenomena that lie outside the scope of explanation provided by such a theory. Or, which amounts to the same thing, they are phenomena that require other theoretical frameworks for them to be explained or understood. The corollary is obvious. A general theory of rain does not serve to explain the forms and concrete causes of rain in one region or another, nor to evaluate the differentiated impacts of rains in one region or another, nor to design programs and proposals for action to help the most vulnerable groups to face the risks of flooding, storms and other dangerous situations originating in the particular type of rainfall of each region.

Thus, returning to the case of the relation between migration and development, we can now say that just as the particular effects of rain in one case and another (the occasional short-lived flowering in the North of Chile, and the periodical flooding in South-East Mexico) cannot be explained by a general theory of rain, so neither can the particular effects of international migration in each historical context (contemporary global society or national society at the end of the 19th century) be explained by a general theory of migration, at least none like those expounded in this section. This is evidently no mean conclusion to reach. How can we use these theories of migration to study and understand its relation (causes and effects) to the process of development, when development itself as well as its relation to migration, is something outside the range of competence for these theories to explain?

Just as we need to drop the general theory of rain to explain the effect of rain in North Chile or the effect of rains in South-Eastern Mexico, and explore more concrete and specific theories of the climate in each place, so, to be able to understand the dynamics of migration and of how it is linked to processes of development, we must also drop these general theories of migration and explore theories tackling the processes of development at any one time (History) and any one place (Geography, Regions).

The case of the neoclassical approach to labor migration, based on a principle of wage inequalities, allows us to illustrate the point. In effect, on the basis of this approach, focused on wage inequalities, we are supposed to be able to understand equally well the wave of international migration a hundred years ago from some European countries to the Americas and Australia, and the labor migration today from countries of the South to regions of the developed North. However, any historian of migrations can tell us that these are completely different social phenomena, not just because of the direction of the migration flows but also because of their social, demographic and economic significance.

To explain the different aspects of international migration in one historical period and another, we must go beyond the principle of wage inequality, so as to be able to include other lines of reasoning and other scales and levels of analysis. Thus, for example, consideration may be given to the demographic situation in Europe a century ago, when in the midst of its Demographic Transition, the continent generated an excess population that was expelled to unpopulated regions undergoing capitalist expansion, such as the United States of America, Canada, Australia, Argentina, and others.

However, by bringing into the analytical model of migration the theory of demographical dynamics and its differentiated forms in places of origin and places of arrival, we are really directly challenging the validity of the neoclassical principle of wage inequalities as an explanation for international migration. In effect, we could well ask whether wage inequalities are the cause of migration, or migration is not rather explained by a factor of demographic imbalances, or indeed, to the contrary, whether it is explained by a factor of capitalist expansion which, amongst others things, makes this demographic imbalance apparent while at the same time creating wage inequalities.

Whatever the position assumed, what matters in either case is that by accepting more complexity into the line of argument we are really throwing the neoclassical theory of migration based on wage inequalities into the garbage. As a theoretical principle, wage inequality cannot be the basis for explaining both migratory phenomena at once, or for explaining either one of them on its own.

In this sense, taking the concrete case of international migration in the current global postmodern society, to explain its causes and consequences in relation to processes of development we need to start from theories and conceptual frameworks that will explain the social and economic processes of contemporary society, on the basis of which we can develop a framework for understanding migration and its role in contemporary, global and postmodern society.

CHAPTER 3

# Migration and Development: Three Theses and a Corollary

*But my place is both here and wherever*
*Four cardinal points, four heads*
*You will see that nationality is not the big deal*
*but rather to turn with the winds like La Rosa*[1]
   The Rose of the Winds
   MAKIZA / ANITA TIJOUX

∴

In the last years we have witnessed a renewed interest on international migration, occupying a privileged place in the national governments political agendas as well as in the most diverse international agencies and supranational institutions (FOMIN, 2004; World Bank, 2006; OIM, 2003). This is not only an academic interest in an emerging phenomenon, but it is also a political and social interest, considering the quantitative dimensions that migration has acquired in the last decades, as well as its social, cultural and economic potential impact. In this sense, since the mid-nineties diverse programs and government policies have been prompted, and numerous publications have proliferated as well as forums, conferences and meetings of experts of high level have taken place, where we can find discussions and agreements on diverse strategies and recommendations to enhance the impact of migrations in the development processes of origin countries.[2]

---

1  "Pero mi lugar es tanto aquí como donde sea. Cuatro puntos cardinales, cuatro cabezas. Verás que la nacionalidad no es la gran cosa. Si no más bien gira con los vientos como La Rosa". Original in Spanish.
2  As examples, we can mention the *Global Forum on Migration and Development*, which since 2007 is celebrated each year; the *High level dialogue on international migration and development*, organized by the United Nations in 2006, as well as the *Ibero-American Meeting on migration and development* organized by the Ibero-American Secretariat (SEGIB) and held in Madrid in July of 2006.

Although it is outlined that the Migration-Development relationship is a complex multifaceted phenomenon, at the end of the day the debate has been under the hegemony of the receiving countries vision and international organizations (Delgado, Márquez and Puentes, 2010). From our perspective, on the other hand, we believe that these international migration approaches, suffer at least from four limitations that can affect our understanding of its causes and consequences in the contemporary global society, namely:

– Overvaluation of the impact of remittances. Although the role of migrants as agents of social and productive change is often pointed out (Portes, 2007), this role always ends up directly linked to the economic impact of remittances. Considering the magnitude and trend of remittances, they often represent one of the main fields of current transfers in the balance of payments in many developing or newly industrialized countries, constituting a real injection of economic resources in specific sectors of regional and local economies (Orozco and Wilson, 2005; Hugo, 2005). Also, and although it is recognized, there is no consensus on the meaning and magnitude of the social effects and economic impacts of remittances, at present a celebratory position around its possible effects on third world recipient economies tends to predominate.[3]

– The invisible contribution of immigrants. The overvaluation of remittances impact leads to avoiding or overlooking the social, economic and demographic costs of migration in the origin countries. Likewise, in the receiving countries, international immigration is seen as a social and political issue, which overlooks the contribution of immigrants to these economies and societies not only in economic terms, but also in demographic, social and cultural terms (Delgado, Wise and Márquez, 2007). Finally, it is common to underestimate the economic, social and familiar costs involved in a forced migration, either by political factors, or by environmental catastrophes, among others (Puentes, et al., 2011).

– The causes of migration have stayed out of the current debate. The debate and reflection about the structural causes of migration has remained relegated to the background, when not simply forgotten. Thus, for example, the blame is usually put on the conditions of underdevelopment and poverty in the countries of origin, as the main causes of migration, ignoring, however, the role that the prevailing conditions in the destination countries

---

[3] This is a more political than academic discourse, since it is clear that the aim is not so much to demonstrate or dimensioning the real contribution of remittances to economic growth or poverty reduction, as to promote and justify a government policy concerning them (Nosthas, 2006; Burgess, 2006).

have in the outbreak and causation of immigration, especially the changes in its economic and labor structure, as well as the dynamics of demographic change. Likewise, the widening of gaps and productive, social and economic asymmetries between the core countries and the peripheral economies are not considered, these are derived not so much from the absence of economic growth, as from the style and strategy of the development of peripheral countries, which in almost all cases are impositions coming from international organizations and governments of core countries (Canales, 2011).
– Distortion of the question of rights. One consequence of the invisibility related to immigrants contribution and their structural causes in the destination countries, is the distortion generated in the analysis and politics design oriented towards the defense and respect of immigrants human and labor rights. The debate usually focuses on the economic issues, simultaneously consolidating a vision that considers international migration as part of national security agenda in the destination countries, all of which has resulted in proposals and laws that tend to criminalize undocumented migration (Martínez, 2008). Although it is extensively accepted that any State has a right to limit and to restrict the non-nationals entering the territory, it does not authorize them to control and regulate the access of these populations to their fundamental rights. On the contrary, it is an obligation and responsibility of any modern and democratic State, to ensure the equal access and respect for the fundamental rights of all individuals (Martínez, Reboiras and Soffia, 2009; Wickramasekara, 2008).

To face these hegemonic visions of the Migration–Development relationship, diverse voices and proposals have been raised in those same forums and publications that, along with questioning its conceptual and empirical validity, raise alternative proposals with regard to both, the analysis and understanding of the phenomenon Migration-Development, as with regard to the design of politics and action programs in the field of Migration-Development (Puentes, et al.; 2011; Castles and Delgado, 2007; de Haas 2005). In particular, civil society organisms and many academics question these new approaches, arguing that essentially remittances are private transfers between individuals, which therefore, cannot replace the State's responsibility and market action in the promotion of economic development and welfare of population (Cortina, et al., 2004; Martínez, 2003; Lozano, 2005; Canales, 2008).

Considering the theoretical and political scopes of this debate, in this chapter we are interested in contributing by providing analytical and conceptual elements that help to sustain, from an academic perspective, a critical position with regard to this hegemonic vision of the Migration-Remittances-Development relationship. In this sense, we present not only a review of this debate from an academic perspective, but we are interested to identify the most important conceptual gaps of the debate, which allows us to progress in more substantive theoretical and methodological proposals.

## 1 Migration and Development: the Pitfalls of a Misleading Discourse

One of the major inconsistencies of Migration and Development debate, is the clear dissociation in the form and scope that arises in the migratory debate depending on the situation that prevails in the countries of origin or of destination (OIM, 2006). On the one hand, in the destination countries, migration is problematized according to the social, political and cultural problems. On the contrary, in the countries of origin, the same migration is evaluated and promoted according to the supposed benefits and opportunities it would have for development.[4]

### 1.1 *The Immigration Issue in Host Countries*

In the case of the receiving countries, this vision conceptualizes migration as a problem, at least from three perspectives:
− On the one hand, as a social and cultural problem, in terms of the social tensions generated by the massive immigration, as well as for the absence of integration – assimilation processes in migrants host societies. In this regard, perhaps the most important intellectual expression is that of Huntington (2004), for whom the Mexicans and Latin Americans, in general, are not the necessary and desirable type of immigrant for the United States, since in their life horizon neither their assimilation nor their Americanization is present, i.e., the adoption of the American way of life, which, given the massive character of contemporary immigration, does nothing but put national identity of North America at risk.
− On the other hand, it raises the question concerning the economic costs of immigration (social security, education, health, tax burden, among others) that the State must assume to maintain this immigrant population which is much higher than the economic benefits they generate (Borjas, 2001; Smith and Edmonston, 1997)

---

4  It is curious, to say the least, that in both cases the interest focuses on the effects and impacts, and not on migration causes and determinants. In fact, it reflects what we have already indicated, that the interest in the process Migration-Development is mediated more by political interests than academic concerns.

– Finally, it is indicated that migrants have a double negative impact on the labor market. On the one hand, displacing native workpeople from their jobs, and on the other hand, keeping the wage levels depressed. In both cases, immigration (especially undocumented) deepen the social problems derived from unemployment and low wages (Borjas, 2001; Martin, 2002).

In any case, from this perspective, irrespective of the observed dimension, the question in terms of social, economic or political problems that massive immigration raises are emphasized, especially when one also considers the high proportion of undocumented migrants who settle illegally (Portes and de Wind, 2006). A consequence of this vision, is the opening of spaces for the emergence of extremist positions that support political proposals such as criminalization of irregular migration, the closing of borders, construction of walls in the old style of cities and castles in the Middle Ages, among other restrictive measurements.

As an expression of this conservatism, and in the context of the debate on temporary and low qualification workers programs (temporary), some authors have gone so far as to raise the migratory dilemma in terms of a virtual *trade off numbers vs. rights* (Martin, 2009; Ruhs and Martin, 2008; Martin and Abella, 2009). According to this model and in the current circumstances, the societies of destination would face the following conflict: either ensure the migrants respect of the fundamental human and labor rights, but reducing significantly the volume of migration (*rights*), or to accept the overcrowding of migration, but in the context of aberration and high social vulnerability and legal lack of protection, which makes difficult and hinders the respect to their rights, especially as concerns labor (*numbers*).[5]

According to Ruhs (2009), the formulation of this quandary would be sustained in the principle that the Nation-States would have the inherent faculty to decide at least on three questions in terms of its immigration politics: i) to regulate the number of immigrants, ii) to define the criteria of immigrants selection and iii) to determine independently what rights can be guaranteed to those immigrants.

Although the first two criteria can be debatable, it is undeniable that the third one is frankly unacceptable. Independently of its legal status and of its volume, the migrant workers have fundamental rights, for both their status of

---

5   Martin and Ruhs were not the first to pose this situation of risk of a large immigration. Before them, Samuel Huntington pointed to the threat Mexico might pose to the United States, placing the risk not only in cultural and identity terms, but especially in terms of its different demographics, with particular emphasis on the risk that, by the end of the 1990s represented the rise of Mexican and Latin American immigration in current contexts of the aging of the white population (Huntington, 2004).

human beings, as for being workpeople. These fundamental rights have been recognized and laid down in the most diverse acts, agreements and international treaties, as well as in diverse instruments of supranational organisms, such as the United Nations and the International Labor Organization and, therefore, cannot be ignored by any democratic State (Wickramasekara, 2008, pp. 1254).

However, this exposition in terms of a supposed *trade off numbers vs. rights*, not only corresponds to a concept of labor migrants as simple merchandise that are traded on international markets, but also it is an ill-posed debate, that seeks to legitimize and enshrine as "natural" social inequality structures. From our perspective, the real quandary is not of *numbers vs. rights*, but rights of some (the migrants) vs. privileges of others (the native ones, middle and high classes). Beyond the attributions that every State has on the subject of migration policy, the truth is that independent of their legal status and number, every migrant has fundamental and inalienable rights (including the labor ones) that no democratic state can ignore.

The fundamental problem is that, given the social and economic context, the respect and guarantee of labor migrant's rights implies a more equitable distribution of social and economic privileges between the native population (especially those of middle and upper social strata) and immigrants. But this is none but the old problem of inequality in the distribution of wealth, power, revenue, and in general, in the unequal distribution of material and symbolic goods that involve every society. Thus through this *trade off*, what they really want to do is to legitimize a particular structure in the distribution of power (political, economic, social and cultural), among members of a society. They seek to legitimize the unequal access to this power, based on the migratory condition of the individuals. To accept this proposal is to accept a framework of legitimacy to a situation of inequality and ethnic discrimination, when it corresponds to question it.

The base of human rights is the status of human being. This is a fundamental condition that transcends all the others. The status of human being is above any circumstantial condition. Based on this principle, it is not possible to accept that a human or labor right, as a transcendental right, is subordinated to a circumstantial condition, as it is the migratory status of a person, or its quantitative magnitude (of being "many"). Much less can we accept that it is a State, supposedly democratic, which tries to subvert this basic principle.

It is a morally unacceptable proposal, not only because it seeks the *reversal* of migrants labor rights (to reverse the rights they have achieved in previous decades), but what is even more serious, is that it is sustained in a *perversion* of the basic principle on which the approach of human rights is based on contemporary society. The universally recognized philosophical principle that all men are equal, becomes perverted and corrupted when over it are constructed politics that legitimizes the unequal access to fundamental rights.

Just to suggest that interests of a national State (much less from their ruling classes) might be above the fundamental rights of a sector of the population, regardless of its social and legal condition, is not only an aberration and an insult to Democracy, but just a veiled attempt of political reversal which leads to undemocratic forms which are at the borderline with authoritarianism, ethnic discrimination and fascism. The State, institution that supposedly must ensure respect for the rights of all individuals, ends up being an instrument of a sector of the population (native, middle and upper classes) used to limit the rights of others (immigrant and other ethnic minorities).

### 1.2   Is Migration a New Development Paradigm for Origin Countries?

In the case of origin countries, the argument is reversed, they no longer speak in terms of costs or problems, but in terms of effects and opportunities of economic and social development that migration could mean and generate for these countries (Straubhaar and Vâdean, 2005). On the one hand, it is indicated that migrants would act as agents of economic and social change, since they favor innovation, knowledge and technology transfer (Portes, 2007; de Haas, 2007). On the other hand, remittances they send would mean a great potential as an instrument to reduce poverty and promote economic development in their communities (Terry, 2005; Adams and Page, 2005; Ratha, 2003).

It looks like a new paradigm of Third World development is being promoted by international organizations, according to which migration and remittances would assume a preponderant role, substituting the previous schemes and paradigms of development that were assigned both to the State and to the Market itself and in some cases, to international cooperation (Kapur, 2004; Chami et al., 2003). In particular, we can identify two levels from which remittances and migration would have such an impact on economic development.

At the microeconomic level, and based on the approach *asset/vulnerability* developed by the World Bank (Moser, 1998), it is stated that the situation of vulnerability that migrants, families and communities face, might be countered with a suitable management of economic, cultural, political and demographic assets, and increased with migration (social capital), regardless of its scarce income and economic resources, and the conditions imposed by the structural context.

This approach is coherent with the principles that the new policies support for the development and fight against poverty propelled over the last decade (World Bank, 2004). Unlike the assistance-oriented policies found in the previous politics, this new approach moves the focus to the promotion of a correct *management* of the assets and resources of the poor so that they can face and overcome by themselves their situation of poverty and vulnerability. This approach is based on Hernando de Soto proposals (2002), who pointed out that the political and economic structures that characterize the Latin-American countries (corporatism, populism, patronage system, public and private monopolies, among others), do nothing but to slow down and hinder this suitable management and potentiality of economic resources and social capitals of the poor.

In this new paradigm, remittances would shape a kind of economic capital, which, along with other social capitals linked to migration (familiar networks, familiar and community work, migrants' organizations, among others), would constitute privileged resources for the communities that might help to overcome the conditions of social vulnerability and economic instability, even if the conditions of the structural environment in which they live are not favorable. In any case, they just need to learn how to use and manage them properly. Measures such as *empowerment*, self-employment and the utilization of the social capital in poor communities would constitute privileged mechanisms to solve their vulnerable situation. In this sense, the following diagram illustrates this approach in the case of migration and remittances.

Thus, among the strategic guides to development, both from national governments and international organizations, features prominently the need of directing remittances towards the creation of small and medium-sized enterprises, as well as towards another type of expenses that encourage the formation of productive and human capital (Ratha, 2003; Shannon, 2006). In the case of Mexico and Central America, this thesis is already part of the official programs of the government, in which self-employment and promotion of family business financed with remittances are offered as alternatives to unemployment and poverty.

At macroeconomic level, this optimism is based on a series of arguments that elevate the impacts and effects of remittances in the economic dynamics of origin countries migration. In particular, at least four forms are indicated through which these positive effects of remittances would be channeled.

– First of all, it is indicated that even if remittances are used fundamentally to finance the household consumption, their volume towards productive investment in agricultural properties and to the formation of companies and familiar business in urban areas is often underestimated, resulting in an underestimation of the impact of remittances in the promotion of local development.[6] Based on these findings politics of promotion and support

---

6  On this matter see the works of Durand (1994), on footwear manufacturing in San Francisco del Rincón, Guanajuato; Jones (1995), on the peach production in Jerez, Zacatecas, as well as the application of econometrics models that Durand, Parrado and Massey (1996) have used

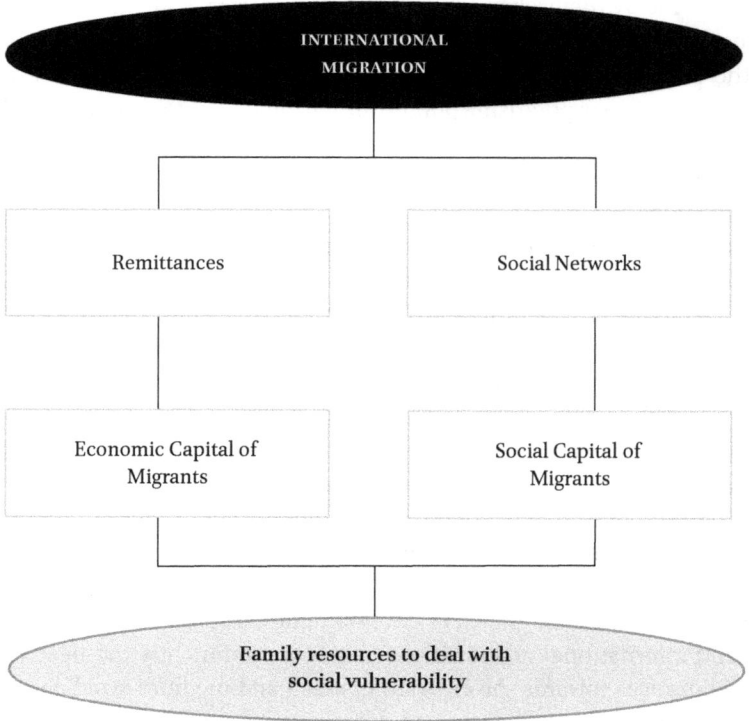

FIGURE 1    Asset/vulnerability approach applied in international migration

both of the productive investment of migrants, as of investment in social infrastructure of communities have been developed. Such is the case of the 3×1 programs that are based on the concurrence of funds between diverse governmental instances and the migrants themselves, to finance social and productive projects in the origin communities. These types of programs have been consolidated in the last decade, especially in the regions of greatest migratory tradition in Mexico, as well as in Central America and the Caribbean (ECLAC, 2000; Fernández, 2006; Moré, 2005).

- Secondly, diverse authors draw attention to the multiplier effects of remittances.[7] Not only the productive investments but also consumption

---

to estimate the level of remittances investment in local areas. In other geographical contexts, Russell (1992) presents similar examples for the case of intensive agriculture in communities of high emigration of the Sahel, Turkey and Zambia.

7   The multiplier effect is defined as the set of increases that take place in the Gross Domestic Product (GDP) as a result of an increase of external origin in the consumption, public expenditure or investment (Pino, 2004). In this sense, remittances constitute an external

expenditures, which are financed with remittances, speed up the national economy, since the increase in the demand for consumer goods stimulates the local market and favors the formation of new companies, pushing forward the generation of new jobs (Durand, Parrado and Massey, 1996, and Stahl and Arnold, 1986, for the Asian countries). On the basis of social accounting matrices, estimates have been made measuring more precisely the multiplier effects of remittances (Taylor and Wyatt, 1996; Zárate, 2007). These works are sustained in macroeconomic approaches of Keynesian type which describe and explain the multiplier effects that this type of transfers could have on the income and internal economic activity of the host countries. In this regard, in the case of Mexico, a pioneering work was that of Adelman and Taylor (1990), who at the end of the eighties of the last century, estimated that the multiplier effect of remittances in the local and regional economies was 2.9. This is, for each additional dollar entering the Mexican economy from remittances, the gross domestic product increased another 2.9 dollars.

- From the official perspective, encouraged by national governments and international organizations, it is said that remittances help to improve the living conditions and welfare of the receiving population, and in this way, to reduce the incidence of poverty. On this matter, four arguments are indicated: i) On the one hand, the volume of the remittances far exceeds the level of income that could be generated with any other local or regional economic and productive activity. ii) On the other hand, its effectiveness in poverty reduction is greater than in the case of another types of transfers, since they flow straight towards those who most need them without being held up by bureaucratic filters (Wahba, 2005). iii) For his part, Jones (1998) argues that in a first moment, when there are few families that have been incorporated to the migratory flow, the effect can be an increase of inequality in the community, nevertheless, as the emigration spreads inside the community, the inequality usually diminishes, because increasingly, there are more families and homes that are inserted in the circuit of sending and perception of remittances. iv) Finally, based on probabilistic models, other authors have thought that remittances usually have a positive impact on income distribution, especially at the regional and local level (Taylor, 1992; Djaji, 1998). In this way, it is said that remittances, more than any other types of transfers, have a clearly positive effect in the reduction of the economic inequality, generating a more equitable income distribution, especially in

---

resource that finances household consumption, and by this means, it generates multiplier effects on the national economy.

the case of those countries where the most benefited are rural households living in condition of poverty (World Bank, 2004).
- Finally, the contribution of remittances to the macroeconomic stability of the recipient countries is emphasized. Compared to other traditional currency sources, remittances show a greater dynamism and stability, what turns them into a more reliable income to overcome crisis situations. In fact, the historical series shows that in times of economic crises a massive flight of foreign capitals and national savings usually occur; remittances, on the other hand, are incremented by demonstrating a countercyclical and inflexible falling trend. Such was the case with Mexico in 1995, Indonesia, in 1997, Ecuador, from 1999 or Argentina, after 2001 (Ratha, 2003; Canales, 2008).

Based on these arguments, in recent years a series of studies about the analysis and statistical estimation of migration and remittances effects in diverse dimensions of development have been disseminated. These studies are focused on the situations in migration origin countries, giving little importance to what happens in the migrant-receiving countries. Likewise, it is a question of eminently empirical studies, which seek to measure and evaluate the impact of one dimension of migration (remittances principally), on selected indicators of development or economic dynamics (generally the GDP, the income distribution, the incidence of poverty or the formation of human capital, among others) (Adams and Page, 2005; Acosta et al., 2006; Alleyne, et al., 2008).

Now, perhaps nothing illustrates more appropriately the theoretical and conceptual deficiencies of this hegemonic approach on the relation Migration-Development, than the fact that the main results to which this type of studies arrive, is not in terms to describe the causes and mechanisms of why remittances have this or that economic impact which, certainly, is an academic and scientific knowledge goal, but rather, to obtain estimates and measures such as the amount that poverty or social inequality would diminish with a given increase in the volume of remittances, objective undoubtedly, nearer to an economic policy strategy with the set of interests and priorities involved.

Thus, for example, Adams and Page (2005) estimate that an increase of 10 % in the rate of emigration (with its consequent remittance increases) generate a reduction of 2.1 % in the poverty rate of each country, measured as the proportion of population living on less than a dollar a day. On the other hand, an IMF survey (2005) found that an increase in the relation Remittances/GDP of 2.5 percentage points is statistically associated with a fall of 0.5 % in the poverty rate. In addition, Acosta et al. (2006) extends these ways of estimating the magnitude of remittances impact according to the level of development and poverty in each country. In particular, these authors found that an increase of 10 % in the participation of remittances of GDP of every country, would imply a reduction of the poverty level between 0.4 % (poor countries) and 0.5 % (rich countries).

It is equally interesting, and paradoxical, to state that these findings are used to argue in favor of the role of remittances as an instrument for reducing poverty, when in fact they show exactly the opposite. In the case of the work of Acosta, et al., for example, with the same information, we estimate that the elasticity of poverty compared to the relative importance of remittances is only 0.04 points. This means that to reduce poverty in 4%, it would be necessary that remittances practically doubled the proportion of GDP. It would be too costly for an insignificant achievement on fighting poverty. Undoubtedly, it will be possible to find many other instruments of economic and social policy that result in increased efficiency and efficacy in the fight against poverty.

As mentioned elsewhere (Canales, 2008), in these studies, it turns out to be more important to prove (or to refute, as the case may be) the empirical validity of a political hypothesis, than to unravel the theoretical and conceptual bases that might explain the same hypothesis concerning to Migration-Development relationship. In particular, one of the most striking gaps, is precisely, the absence of a theoretical frame from which to develop a conceptual definition of migration and remittances as well as their relationships to the development processes from the diverse dimensions that include this complex social process. In fact, the conceptualization and theorization of the Migration-Development relationship, is reduced on the one hand, to the simple description of a series of mechanisms and forms in which it is assumed (without proof) it could operate, and on the other hand, to the formulation of econometrics models that allow to estimate the direction and statistical significance of remittances impact on selected indicators of economic development.[8] Beyond the statistical validity of these empirical results, from our perspective we think they are not enough to demonstrate the significance and meaning of a social process (Migration and Development) not only complex and multidimensional but also with unknown causes and theoretical conceptualizations.

## 2   Migration and Development: a Critical Perspective

From a critical perspective, alternative approaches have developed that not only question the empirical validity of these arguments, but also their theoretical

---

[8] Paraphrasing Nair (2006), we can affirm that the knowledge generated by this type of analysis is often more valuable to better understand the underlying political interests, than to understand and dimension the impacts of remittances.

and political foundations. In particular, the clear reductionism and ideological bias when addressing the issue concerning the Migration-Development relationship is questioned. It is undoubtedly suspicious that international migration turns out to be problematic and negative to the receiving societies and, at the same time, beneficial and a unique opportunity for the society of origin.

From this critical perspective the supposed negative consequences of immigration in the destination countries is questioned, to which the fact that this vision turns migrants' contribution invisible to these societies, not only in economic, but also in demographic, social and cultural terms is countered (Delgado, et al, 2011; Puentes, et al. 2011). In addition, it is argued that immigration is not only caused by the underdevelopment in the south, but also, in its unleashing, a transformation and modernization of the economic structure and labor markets has a fundamental role in northern economies, which, to maintain and gain world competitiveness in a globalized economic space, must be supported by a demand for cheap, flexible and deregulated labor force, which is provided to a large extent by international migration (Sassen, 2007; Zlolniski, 2006).

The supposed benefits of migration are also questioned in the countries of origin. In fact, it is indicated that there is not enough empirical evidence that sustains these optimistic and encouraging visions of migration and remittances (Newland, 2007). On the contrary, it is indicated that the empirical evidence corroborates the thesis that migration has very limited effects both on the promotion of development and on reduction of poverty (Lozano, 2005; ECLAC, 2006).

In particular, in a recent study on the Mexican case, we have identified a series of myths in regards to the supposed economic benefits that remittances would bring (Canales, 2008):

- In the first place, the macroeconomic effects are diluted to the extent that remittances represent less than 3% of the Mexican gross domestic product (GDP).
- Similarly, its contribution to the economic growth, is not only marginal, but also statistically non-significant, especially compared to other macroeconomic variables, as domestic investment or the manufacturing of exports.
- In the third place, the effects of remittances in income distribution and poverty reduction are really minimal, especially if they are compared to the impact of other macroeconomic variables. In fact, for Mexico as for many Third World countries, the thesis that the best politics against poverty is economic growth is still valid.
- Finally, at the level of receiving households, even though remittances represent almost half of its current income, it is not enough to make most of these

households overcomes the poverty line defined by governmental agencies. In an ECLAC study carried out in eight Latin American countries, it is demonstrated that the level of remittance perceived per capita in households, is far below the level of income per capita that every country determines as the income poverty line (ECLAC, 2005).

Other authors point out that although migrants could be agents of social change, given the structural contexts of marginality and social exclusion, this is not enough to generate an impulse towards economic development in societies of origin. Beyond the intrinsic capacity of migrants and remittances potentialities, both will never replace the role of the State and Market (private capital) in the promotion of productive modernization and structural transformations that, according to diverse international organizations, are necessary conditions to stimulate economic development in our countries (Castles and Delgado Wise, 2007).

De Haas (2005), based on results coming from the debate generated on the remittances- developments relationship, concludes that the fundamental question is not whether migration has positive or negative effects on development, but how and why in some contexts and communities, migration has a certain kind of effect, while in other contexts and communities the effects go in the opposite direction. In this sense, the debate should be oriented to determine and analyze which are the social, economic and demographic factors that help explain these differences (Ghosh, 1992; Taylor, 1999).

In this regard, Jones (1998) illustrates how remittances have different impacts on reducing poverty and social inequality according to the social history of the community, and the migratory stage in which it is found. Also, in the case of remittances, it is necessary to design an approach that allows to articulate the effects at the micro level with which they are identified at the macroeconomic level, which does not necessarily have to coincide and correspond in every single case (de Haas, 2007).

To these arguments, from our perspective, it would be necessary to add another two elements.

- In the first place, we think that the way in which the discussion has been raised, does not succeed to identify and apprehend the substantive and essential elements of the relationship between Migration-Development. Beyond the reductionist view of Migration and Development and beyond the need to appeal to more complex and comprehensive approaches, the main weakness is that they are based on a mistaken approach of the problem, where the initial question is one that needs to be reformulated.

  In the debate on the relationship between Migration and Development, both terms of the equation are often used as abstract and independent categories, without assuming that it is a question of historical and mutually related categories. In other words, when debating on the relationship between Migration and Development, before positioning in one or another academic and political trench, the question arises as to what migration and development we are talking about. Meanwhile in each position and approach outlined, both categories, migration and development seem to be concepts of equal conceptual, historical and empirical dimension, when in fact, it is a question of concepts at very different levels of analysis, as well as of different dimensions and degrees of abstraction. It is not possible to match the explanatory power and the fields that each one of them cover, where there is no doubt that migration refers to processes on a much smaller theoretical and historical scope with regard to the multiplicity of dimensions, social fields and analytical development that Development involves. Meanwhile, before taking sides in the debate on the relationship between Migration and Development, we must start from at least one conceptual definition of each of these terms, a definition that would allow us to situate and locate the historical scope and depth of the social process that we want to name and discuss with each term.

– Secondly, and consistent with the above, what we are really discussing here concerning each of these positions, are not the possible impacts, effects or consequences of migration, but the implications and opportunities for the development process. To criticize or defend one position or another, is not with regard to the role of migration, remittances or other phenomena related to migration, but a disguised defense and critique of the development process, and in particular, to the style and development strategy implemented in each country.

Thus, for example despite the fact that we are wrongly called "pessimistic", we are not really critical of migration or remittances and their limited and reduced impacts, but really, of the development model that is behind it, and in particular, we are critical of a policy that seeks to transfer to migration the responsibility of solving our countries developmental problems, causing that both the State and Market (capital and capitalists) ignore them. Similarly, in the also misnamed "optimistic", the meaning of their discourse is not an apology for migration and remittances, but rather, the aim of that discourse is to hide the defense and apology for the development model that generates them. In other words, the debate on the relationship between migration and development is nothing but a disguised excuse to reproduce an old debate concerning the process of development in a capitalist society, in this case, in relation to issues concerning capitalist development in current times.

In this sense, and without denying the validity of the arguments of each approach, we believe that the debate needs to be reworded by placing at the center not migration itself, but the process of capitalist development in contemporary society, and in that framework, to discuss both their consequences and effects, as their interactions and interdependencies with different dynamics and migration pathways. In other words, to have a full understanding of the relationship between Migration and Development, we must start from a wider perspective of the problem. In particular, we must proceed from the idea that the analysis and understanding of the consequences and effects of Migration on Development are not independent from the structural causes that from Development drive Migration.

In this regard, we uphold that it is not possible to understand and evaluate the impacts and effects of Migration on the Development process in the absence of a conceptual framework that allows us to understand and evaluate the causes and determinants of the migration process. In particular, it is not possible to have a theory, approach or perspective of the relationship between Migration and Development without a theory of contemporary development in which to frame migration in contemporary society.

In this regard, we think that it is a serious methodological error to circumscribe the relationship between Migration and Development to what happens in sending or receiving countries. On the contrary, in contemporary society, the relationship between Migration and Development refers to a global phenomenon. With this, we want to affirm that what happens in regard to the relationship between Migration and Development in sending societies is not independent of what happens in the receiving ones, and *vice versa*. Migration is a process that, along with many others, at the same time contributes to the development in both countries of origin and those of destination, it promotes the development and structuring of globalization itself. In a globalized world, through migration not only the places of origin and destination are linked and integrated, but also through this integration, it is possible to contribute to the reproduction of both. Migration and Development is a process which, along with others, also contributes to the reproduction of globalization.

Considering the above, we think it is necessary to point out a couple of premises that we must not forget when a deeper process of analysis and understanding concerning the Migration-Development relationship as a phenomenon of global capitalism is continued.

– On the one hand, there is no single process of capitalist development but there are options and variants in the styles and models of development that each economy and each country may adopt. Basically, the development is not confined to an economic determinism, but it is an issue open to variants

and vicissitudes of politics. Consequently, we can say that it is the result of a struggle between interests and ideologies in a power relations system which is not always fair.
– On the other hand, it is essential to consider that capitalism, everywhere and anytime, has always developed and strengthened the unequal social structures. We refer to class, regional and economic inequalities, among many others. What is relevant is that capitalism, far from moving towards a convergence, generates and reproduces this system of inequality.

Considering these premises, it is clear then, that when we talk about migration and development, we refer to a complex relationship in the sense of the two premises already identified. Finally, and perhaps the most relevant, is that these premises enable us to understand and put migration into context as a social and demographic factor, which along with many others, participates not only in the reproduction of capitalism, but particularly in the reproduction of its structural heterogeneities as well as its economic, social, territorial and demographic inequalities.

## 3 Conclusion: Three Theses and a Corollary on International Migration

While there seems to be no consensus on the meaning and nature of the relationship between Migration and Development (de Haas, 2007; Binford, 2003), a celebratory position around the possible effects of Migration on Development tends to predominate, especially focused on economies and communities of origin. In effect, after the fact that in the seventies and part of the eighties the prevailing tendency was a critical view of migration and remittances, which emphasized the barriers and distortions they generated to local and regional development (Reichert, 1981; Wiest, 1984; Mines, 1981), in the nineties there is a radical change in this perspective of analysis, prevailing an approach which moved to show how remittances and migration could constitute a preferential option for the development and structural transformation of communities (Massey and Parrado, 1994 and 1998; Russell, 1992).

Covered by this approach, studies that analyzed the effects of migration and remittances on various dimensions of development, proliferated. In general, these are studies focused on migrant's home countries situations, giving little importance, in parallel, to what happened in migrant-receiving countries.

Similarly, most of the time, these studies correspond to eminently empirical studies, which seek to measure and assess the impact of one dimension of migration (remittances in most cases), on selected indicators of development or economic dynamics (usually the GDP, or the incidence of poverty). More than trying to prove this or that theory to explain the relationship between Migration and Development, in these works what they are looking for is to give econometric support to a pre-established political discourse through various empirical measures on the role of migration and the impact of remittances in this or that macroeconomic variable.

In this regard, we consider that the celebratory vision of migration and remittances, is more a political-ideological position on Migration and Development than a theoretical-conceptual position on this social phenomenon. As an academic and theoretical discourse, this current perspective prevailing today contains serious and important conceptual and methodological weaknesses that we'd like to list.

- It is at least politically suspect the way that the discourse on international migration is constructed. It proposes migration as a development option for the sending countries, and in turn proposes it as a social and political issue for the host countries.
- It is equally suspect that the same institutions that advocate and proclaim the need for the globalization of the capital in all its forms (financial, productive, etc.), do not advocate nor proclaim in the same direction for the globalization of migration, this means, towards the free movement of the population and labor force at the global level.
- With regard to the causes of migration, these tend to focus on the problems of poverty, inequality, and underdevelopment that prevail in the countries of origin, without entering into the analysis of the structural conditions that development in the countries of destination generates in favor of immigration.
- A theoretically valid explanation for why remittances and migration could constitute a strategy of development policy in the countries of origin which could lead to a possible solution to the problems of poverty, vulnerability, insecurity, inequality and underdevelopment they confront, has never been given.

From other trenches, the hegemonic and celebratory approach on migration and development is refuted principally based on two kinds of critiques:

- On the one hand, it is noted that there is not enough empirical evidence that supports and corroborates the supposed impacts and positive effects of migration and remittances in the communities of origin.
- On the other hand, and, in the opposite direction, it is argued that this celebratory vision, does nothing but hide the different contributions of immigration to the economic and social development in the countries of destination, in terms of their demographic contribution as a labor force, to the GDP to the economic growth, to domestic savings, the financing of social security, among many other aspects (Puentes, et al., 2011; Delgado, et al., 2010).

In this regard, we would like to present three general theses on migration at the present time which return to these critiques, and contribute to the formation of a global and comprehensive approach of these phenomena. It is an approach that seeks to integrate in the same analysis model, the causes, consequences and conditions of origin and destination.

*Thesis 1. In a globalized world, migration and development must be understood from a global perspective.*

If, in the past, from the methodological nationalism that prevailed in the various analysis along with the academic and political discourses, migration was regarded as a flow that came from the outside, therefore as an external factor to society, nowadays, in this era of social and economic globalization, migration has stopped being a phenomenon exogenous to society and has become an internal process. It is not just that migration, as a social process is internalized as an intrinsic dynamic typical of societies, but in addition, it is society itself the one that has expanded its social and territorial limits and has been globalized. In so far as the globalization extends and covers the whole world, it is society itself which is becoming global. In this sense, we can no longer think of migration as a problem that comes to us from outside, but rather as a social phenomenon that is generated by the same factors which structure global society.

Again citing Giddens (1986), we can say that in a global society, migration constitutes a component, a factor that contributes to the structuring of society, and therefore to its dynamic and movement in a double process, for its reproduction sustenance, on the one hand, and its transformation, on the other.

*Thesis 2. Each model of capitalist accumulation has its own model of international migration.*

Paraphrasing Marx's famous Law of Population, we can state that at every stage of the development of capitalism, there is a corresponding migratory system, with its own tendencies, dynamics, and specific issues determined by history. In this sense, under capitalism, both international migration and the internal mobility have always been part of the capital reproduction and accumulation processes. It is a question, then, of identifying at each stage of capitalist development, which would be the role of migration in that development process, as well as the contradictions and tensions that might come up in them.

In colonial times, the forced migration of African slaves to the Americas had a clear sense of labor provision to the *Haciendas*, mines and other extractive activities. In the capitalist expansion era (end of the nineteenth century and first half of the twentieth century), international migration allowed the complementation of two different situations. On the one hand, the demographic excess generated by the capitalist expansion in Europe was taking place right in the middle of a demographic transition. On the other hand, there was a lack of population and labor force in many different countries experiencing a capitalist expansion process, and that required large demographic contingents to incorporate new territories to the dynamics of the capitalist accumulation. This is the case of the United States, Canada, Argentina and Australia, among others.

In current times, international migration allows to complement or articulate three different situations.

– On the one hand, the developed countries (Europe and the United States, mainly) experience a substantial reduction in their fertility and birth, as a result of the advent of the so-called Second Demographic Transition, and the ageing of its native population. This generates important demographic imbalances which can be seen in the fact that the demography of these countries can no longer generate the necessary population and labor force to cover the increasing supply of jobs that this economy growth generates.
– On the other hand, the sending countries, mainly from the Third World, are still passing through the last stages of the first demographic transition, which in some cases, is manifested in high population growth, and in others, in what has been called as the presence of a *demographic bonus* or *demographic dividend*, i.e., a great population growth in active and reproductive age.
– Finally, the economic model of globalization, generates a polarization in the developed countries structure of occupations. Along with the rise of employment and high–status jobs, also low-level occupations which are in situations of precariousness, flexibility and deregulation proliferate.

In this context, the current immigration model contributes, in some way, to fill the population scarcity generated by the demographic scheme of developed countries while being an escape valve for the population growth in the underdeveloped countries. In addition, this demographic mobility also helps to fill the jobs that the economic growth generates in developed countries, contributing in this way to the reproduction and accumulation of capital.

However, this demographic and economic complementarity, does not imply that the migration model is exempt from tensions and contradictions. In the meantime, a fundamental aspect is that in these same demographic conditions, massive immigration brings with it the possibility of a transformation of the population ethno-migratory composition in the destination countries. A process which some of them are already living, as is the case of the United States for example, where the Latino population represents more than a 17% of the total population.[9]

---

9   These changes in the population's ethno-demographic composition were much in evidence in the United States presidential elections of 2008 and 2012, when the so-called *Latino vote* was the basis for the electoral victory of Barack Obama at both times.

*Thesis 3. The structural causes of migration are not the lack of development, but the style of development and integration into the global economy.*

It is common to point out that poverty, underdevelopment, social inequality, and other evils faced by the Third World economies and societies, are the structural basis of the mass emigration towards the developed countries. While these evils are part of the emigration conditions, the structural bases are not in them but in the strategy and development styles that have been promoted and implemented in these countries. In fact, many Latin American countries are experiencing significant economic growth, especially since the nineties. However, this growth coincides with the rise in emigration from this region to the United States and Europe. This economic and emigration growth combination, tells us that the basic problem lies in the style of development and in the economic growth model that has been implemented in our countries.

In fact, the structural adjustment policies implemented since the eighties have resulted in the dismantling of the economic-productive base, and have redirected them towards the global markets. Trade openness along with the market liberalization and the abandonment of the role of the State, among other policies, make up the bases for the integration of Latin American countries to the global economy. However, in most cases this is more of a return to *commodities* and primary products export models, than to the development of manufacturing activities and/or services directed to the global economy. Similarly, in those cases where a process of manufacturing exports has been promoted, there had been a rise of the in bond industry, that is, of product assembly for their re-export, at a very low level of generation of added value and of internal productive chains with the national economy (Cypher and Delgado, 2010). In this sense, we support that it is this model of development and integration into the global pattern of accumulation which generates the international migration growth, and where this migratory model has an important role for the global economy to function, contributing their bit to the capital accumulation mechanism at a global scale.

In synthesis, contrary to what is usually proclaimed, the structural origin of contemporary migration, lies not so much in the conditions of poverty and marginalization that prevail in the origin countries as in the prevalence of a style of development that emphasizes social inequalities and economic asymmetries between countries and regions (ECLAC, 2010). In this sense, the solution is not in the promotion of development policies purely and simply, but in the implementation of other strategies and styles of social and economic development that directly combat the regional and international inequalities.

## 3.1 Corollary: Towards a Global Model of Understanding Migration

Undoubtedly, the debate on international migration and its impact is definitely badly addressed. What should be placed for discussion, are not the costs, impacts or consequences of migration, either in terms of development options, or the generation of social and political conflicts. On the contrary, the debate should focus on the development model, and in particular, on the model of globalization that prevails today.

Given this situation, our interest is not only to propose a new perspective of analysis that contributes to the debate, critique certain positions and returning to others. It is a question of advancing towards a more radical critique, in the sense of changing the axes on which the debate has been constructed. In this sense, our critique is not only theoretical (related to the causes and explanations of migration and development), neither is it only political (related to the positions and interests in conflicts), but it is essentially methodological and epistemological.

What we are proposing is not only a change in the answers (academic, political, social, etc.) that are in debate and confrontation, but a change in the questions that originated the whole debate. In this sense, the challenge is twofold. Along with the urgency for new answers there is also a need for new models that give meaning and consistency to those questions and answers. In other words, what we need is a wider analytical and comprehensive framework concerning migration and development which enables us to understand all the processes we have already mentioned, as well as their different articulations.

In this book we offer some theoretical and conceptual elements that allow us to arrive at a global and comprehensive view of migrations in contemporary society. This model of analysis is based on a conceptual premise from which we conceive and understand current migrations as a component of the *constitution* of societies in this era of globalization. In this regard, what we propose is to analyze and understand international migration from the *Society Reproduction* approach.

Although the object of observation is international migration, we must consider that it is above all a *mediation* to reach an understanding of society as a whole. The question is not only about migration itself, but about its role in the *constitution* and *reproduction* of society. In this sense, we propose three fields in which migration assumes a relevant role in the reproduction of contemporary society.

- First, in a class society, such as ours, social reproduction is necessarily the reproduction of this class structure, that is, the inequalities that differentiate and oppose social classes. In this context, the question is how migration

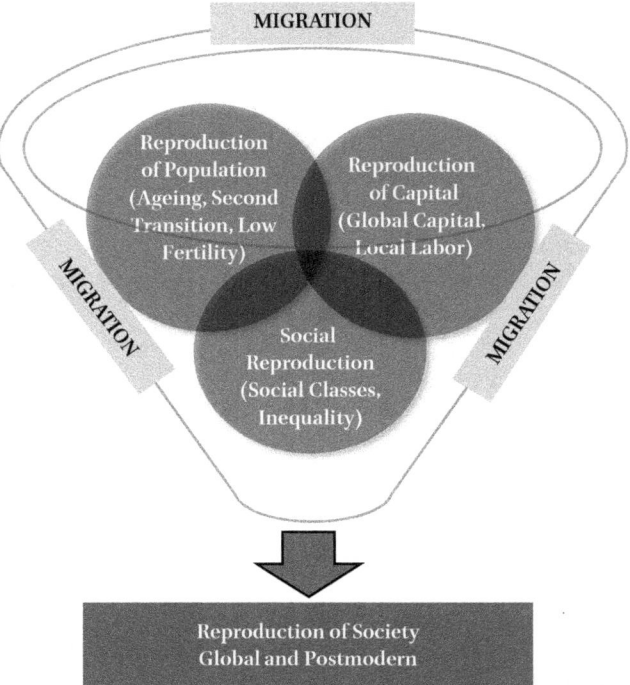

FIGURE 2  The migration-society-reproduction relationship from three levels of analysis

contributes and is part of the reproduction of the class structure and social inequality in the global society.
- Second, at an economic level, we analyze the role and function of migration in the simple and expanded reproduction of capital (accumulation) in global societies.
- Thirdly, at the demographic level, the question is about the role of migration in the configuration of a global regime of population reproduction, i.e. a system that articulates the patterns of demographic reproduction (births-deaths, migration) in both origin and destination countries.

We integrate these three levels of analysis into one conceptual model. This allows us to arrive at a global and comprehensive view of the role of migration in the reproduction and transformation of contemporary society. This is especially true in advanced societies, where immigration is contributing to the transformation of the ethnic and demographic composition of its population. In the following chapters, this migration approach as an integral component of the reproduction pattern in the global society, will be presented with more details.

CHAPTER 4

# Migration and Reproduction: Beyond the Critique of Methodological Nationalism

> *Oh! Comadre Lola, if you knew*
> *What it is to be divided, not knowing what your land is*
> *Ana la Chola, in the chase like a mouse without a tail*[1]
>     The Rose of the Winds
> MAKIZA/ANITA TIJOUX

∴

The current debate on Migration and Development seems to be affected by a series of ideological biases as well as methodological inconsistencies of great importance. Among the first, perhaps the most obvious is the ease with which the positions in debate are often classified and differentiated between the so-called "optimistic" and "pessimistic", depending on the particular position with regard to the role of migration and remittances in development processes of the sending countries (de Haas, 2008 and 2005). Beyond the mistake to call upon this type of categories to classify the debate, we think that this one is not only fallacious, but distorts and channels it to merely formal and rhetorical aspects, without venturing into a serious and purposeful reflection on the debate itself.[2] Also, the symbolism involved against a critical and alternative thinking, with regard to the official discourses that predominate in international agencies and local governments is obvious. Meanwhile, this conceptualization of the debate falls prey to the hegemonic vision according to which Migration is part of the Development *issues* only in the case of the sending countries

---

1 "¡Ay! Comadre Lola, si usted supiera, lo que es estar dividida, no saber cuál es su tierra. Ana la Chola, en la volá como ratón sin cola". Original in Spanish.
2 This type of (dis)qualifications only illustrate the creativity and inventiveness of those who proposed them, but in no case they prove or refute the consistency of ideas and theoretical, methodological or even political arguments that sustain every position. We think that nothing can be gained using this type of adjectives concerning the debate which, among other things, remains unfinished due to the lack of conceptual and methodological proposals that enrich it.

contributing to hiding and disqualifying the analyses that attempt to locate Migration as a factor of Development also in the host countries.[3]

In addition to this ideological bias, we identified an even more serious weakness in many of the positions in debate and that, therefore, becomes more important for our discussion. We refer to the *methodological nationalism* underlying them which results in serious distortions and biases when analyzing international migration. According to Beck (2000a), in modern society the thought and social theory were sustained by the principle of correspondence between State, Nation and Territory. This meta-theoretical perspective permeated the social sciences, particularly in the scientific observation as well as in the construction of the object of study. Thus, sociology became the science of modern society. In fact, the historical moment in which sociology arises, and in general, the modern social thought, coincides with the advent of Modernity, which meant that, as a modern social science, it was directly influenced by this principle which allowed that national societies could be established as an object of study and studied as independent units (Goic, 2007:105).

With the advent of the global and postmodern society, these approaches stay outdated since they do not fully comprehend the new dynamics and forms that the social processes assume. In light of this, the challenge for social sciences is to explore new approaches, concepts, categories, that allow to think about the world as a global society, and more precisely, in terms of *globalized societies*. It is not only a change in the analysis of the territorial scale. In other words, it is not purely and simply a matter of moving from a national scale to another global one, as it is not a problem of aggregation or abstraction levels of analysis, but something more complex and profound. As Beck pointed out (2000a), with the critique of *methodological nationalism* one of the fundamental assumptions about Modernity was put on questioning, which was that the spatial contours of society had been considered coincident with the territorial contours of the national states. In this sense, it is not only a theoretical rupture, but also epistemological, to the extent that the questions raised are not only new concepts, categories and social theories, but new perspectives from which contemporary societies are observed and studied.

In this regard, Ianni (1996) presents an interesting thesis. According to him, globalization signifies first and foremost, an epistemological challenge, i.e., the

---

3   Meanwhile, one can be optimistic or pessimistic (as the case may be) only in front of the consequences and impacts of migration in the countries of origin, keeping a suspicious silence with regard to the vision (and qualification of that vision) concerning the consequences in the destination countries. It turns out to be undoubtedly suspicious that the so-called "optimistic", adopts a "pessimistic" attitude when speaking of migration in the destination countries.

need to generate, and to invent as necessary, new categories that account for these space-time transformations of social processes, crystallized in a deterritorialization and reterritorialization of social relations. Just as the classic paradigms of modernity (on both the left and the right) were sustained by a certain conception of the national society,[4] the emerging paradigms should develop and mature based on a renewed conception of global society. Meanwhile, "society" in this case has to refer to a multitude of "societies". In general, the categories corresponding to traditional paradigms (modernity and national society, for example) must be used but with an epistemological turn leading to cancel out or relocate their conventional space-time connotations.[5]

In a world where societies are becoming globalized and where the social, economic and cultural processes daily reach across national borders, it has become anachronistic to keep on assuming that the nation-state is the natural social form of the contemporary world (Wimmer and Glick Shiller; 2002). In this context, we support that, as well as in the past, the scientific discourse on Modernity resulted in a social science that limited its object of study to the social and territorial limits of the nation State. The challenge has now become the social-scientific delimitation of the research field and the problematization of its object of study. We must overcome and cut across the Nation-State borders to think about the problems in terms of its globalization.

In this context then, it makes sense to wonder how to analyze processes that are only meaningful in a global sense whose categories are created to represent national levels. Or what is the same, how to analyze processes in which the national categories are insufficient to apprehend them simply because such processes are not contained in the national issue but have overcome and fragmented that level of analysis. This seems to be the challenge in the case of international migration and its links to the development processes. In a globalized world, based on economic models and global patterns of accumulation, there is no doubt that migration as well as development must also be thought

---

4  Either in a perspective of its conservation (right), or transformation (left), or of the infinite number of intermediate positions, the various paradigms of modernity shared a same substrate: the national society, its development and modernization. On this point, see Wallerstein, 1995.

5  As Ianni indicates, "the reflection on the global society opens up fundamental epistemological issues: space and time, synchrony and diachrony, micro and macro, singular and universal, individualism and holism, small story and great narration. These are issues dealt with on the basis of a global society recognition as a complex and problematic whole which is articulated and fragmented, integrated and contradictory ... These are forces that feed inclusive and fragmentary tendencies and sign up to nation and nationality, group and social class, regionalism and provincialism, localism and cosmopolitanism, capitalism and socialism" (Ianni, 1996:168).

of and analyzed in global terms. In fact, each term of the relationship by itself is incomprehensible if it is not part of a vision that locates them as components of globalization, i.e., as processes through which the global nature of contemporary societies manifests itself on a daily basis.

However, this critique of methodological nationalism implies a double challenge. On the one hand, it has to depart from a more comprehensive perspective, where the sending countries conditions providing labor force are not the only issues of interest, but also and especially, the situation of countries receiving this labor migration. On the other hand, the analysis must be based on categories and indicators that account for this integral and global vision of the migratory phenomenon in contemporary societies. In this regard, in this chapter we want to present a theoretical and methodological proposal which contributes to achieve progress in the design of a comprehensive framework of migration and development in a contemporary global society. To do this, we start from an examination of the globalization approaches and paradigm of transnationalism, both of which correspond to a first and necessary openness towards new ways of understanding the migration process in the current times.

Considering the above, we will start with a brief revision of the central features of the analytical model of globalization, and then in the following section we will do the same with those of the transnational communities. This allows us to identify some of the theoretical-methodological challenges and demands that these models imply for the purpose of knowing the way of addressing the study of international migration in contemporary societies. Rather than presenting an evaluation of such models,[6] we have selected some important points of discussion that turn out to be particularly relevant to our proposal of analyzing migration as a factor that contributes to the reproduction and transformation of contemporary society.

## 1    Globalization as a Critique of Methodological Nationalism

In the social sciences a wide and unfinished debate has opened on globalization. However, there is still no consensus on what is meant by that category. It seems that Mires is right when he says that "globalization is what everyone

---

6  For such type of evaluation, see, Beck, 2000a; Wallerstein, 1995; Stiglitz, 2002; Castells, 1996, in the case of globalization and its consequences; and Khagram and Levitt, 2007; Glick Schiller and Levitt, 2006; Portes, Guarnizo and Landolt, 2003 and Wimmer and Glick Shiller; 2002, in the case of transnationalism.

understands by globalization" (Mires, 2000: 18). This author points out that this confusion and distortion of the scope and meaning of this concept are due to the confusion of two different albeit interconnected issues. When discussing globalization it would be necessary to specify if we want to characterize the natural and logical tendency of capitalism, or rather we want to refer to the description of the current state of capitalist development. As a trend, capitalism has always been global. However, only in the last time we can speak of a globalized capitalist structure. What is new and distinctive of this age or stage of capitalism?

The English historian Eric Hobsbawm gives us a thought-provoking answer. He notes that trade has always made possible the articulation of distant productive fields, configuring economic spaces that transcended the territorial limits of production. Capitalism did not do more than promote this translocal vocation of trade. In this sense, the distinctive element in the current times is that for the first time in human history the new communication and transport technologies allow not only trade but also the production to organize in a transnational way. As this author indicates, "whereas in the past, the global division of labor was limited to the products exchange between specific regions, today the production is possible by crossing continents and States borders. This is the real difference between the already existing global economy in the past and the current ones" (Hobsbawm 2000: 84).

From political economy, globalization refers to the new paradigms of territorial organization of the world-economy, where the rules of oligopolistic competition and the international division of labor are substantially redefined (Oman, 1994). This change has been driven by the development of new technologies and ways of organizing work process by which have been reformulated local, regional and national productive specializations, as well as patterns of economic exchange internationally. Globalization implies moving from a scale of national production and international exchanges to a scale of production and economic exchange that is fully globalized or global.

Until recently, the production process, the firms, the factories and industries were essentially *national* phenomena. In this context, the international division of labor, prevailing until a few decades ago, was the expression of the spatial form that international trade took which developed mainly as an exchange between national economies (Amin, 1996). The international division of labor and trade was literally a matter of economic relations *among* nations.

Today, on the contrary, we are witnessing an entirely different process. Improvements in communications and transportation technologies allow that the geographical scope of any industrial plant to be amplified at a global scale. Alongside this, new forms of organization of the production process (automation, division operations, etc.) have allowed the separability of the parts and segments constituting the production system. This implies more flexible patterns of spatial localization of different workplaces according to their best options, without necessarily depend on you location criteria other work units facing different locational requirements (Storper and Walker, 1983).

It is, ultimately, a question of a new logic of location, where the principles of urban agglomeration, that gave rise to twentieth century large industrial cities, are disrupted by the telecommunications and informatics development (Sassen, 1998).

This new modality of localization, has ruled out one of the supposedly unshakable premises of the industrial societies work system. "There is no longer need for the operators to work together in a specific place to produce certain goods and services. Now the jobs can be exported" (Beck, 2000a:39). What earlier was manufactured in the same space, today it is *deterritorialized*, it is spatially fragmented, and its segments are located in different local spaces, articulating directly in a world system (*supra-national*), local and regional economies which are territorially separated and distant. We are witnessing the emergence of the *global factory* through which *geographic dispersion* process of production, productive forces, capital, technology, labor force, the planning and of the market is intensified and generalized (Ianni, 1996).

This dispersion is not synonymous with disarticulation. Rather, there is dispersion because the space of production has expanded, has deterritorialized dislocating its former international configuration. As Mattelart points out, a global factory is an "organic structure in which each party must serve the whole. Any failure on interoperability between the parties, any obstacle to the free exchange of flows, brings the risk of collapsing the system" (Mattelart, 1998: 83).[7]

In this context, Castells (1996) argues that the structure of the global economy is deeply asymmetric. Not in the simplistic sense of a center, a periphery and a semi periphery, as proposed by the center-periphery approach of the world-system theory. On the contrary, it is an extremely variable geography that has involved the dismantling of national and international basis upon which is built the world economy. Globalization is itself a process of deterritorialization (Appadurai, 1990), in terms of the disarticulation of national spaces, of national economies.

Considering the scope of our discussion, what is relevant is that globalization of social and economic processes raises a methodological requirement in

---

7  A global factory is an "estructura orgánica en la que cada parte debe servir a la totalidad. Cualquier fallo en la interoperabilidad entre las partes, cualquier obstáculo al libre intercambio de flujos, trae el riesgo de colapsar el sistema". Original in Spanish.

terms of the need to formulate new concepts and categories to see and understand social processes. As Wallerstein indicates (1995), for some decades we have been undergoing an era of change, the emergence of new historical horizons that reveal the social sciences shortcomings and limitations in terms of its commitment with a very particular world view that has been called Modernity. In this framework, the social sciences have to be reformulated, not only in terms of their theoretical principles, but also in terms of their methodological and epistemological ones.

With the advent of globalization and the information age, we would have also reached a breaking point with the models of analysis that we still have and use for thinking about society and for understanding migration, which are imbued and constructed under the premises of methodological nationalism. According to Beck (2000a), the methodological nationalism is an inheritance from social thinking of Modernity, according to which the economies spatial boundaries were considered practically in accordance with the territorial boundaries of the national states. Thus, from the spatial point of view, global society was built based on the aggregation and interaction between the national territories and national States. It is not only that there was no global space per se, but rather, there was no way of thinking about society in terms of global spaces because the categories and concepts used were permeated with such *methodological nationalism*, which hampered the vision and conception of a social and economic process based on spatialities that were not those of the Nation-State.[8] The global processes that go beyond the Nation State borders were analyzed and categorized as international relations, i.e. between national states, and must not be regarded as a global space in itself, i.e. , as a unit and category of analysis in itself.[9]

If globalization implies a radical change in the way social life is organized in all fields, it is necessary to wonder what to do when the social processes that makes up this new social reality (such as international migration, for example), can no longer be apprehended by the existing social theories, not because of "theoretical" weaknesses as such, but because its configuration obeys purely

---

8   Not without reason, the Nation-State is one of the institutions of modernity that is becoming increasingly questioned (Ohmae, 1995). Thus, for example, in contrast to the nineteenth century liberal ideologies that promoted the concept and practice of national sovereignty, our orthodox neo-liberalism by the end of the century, however, seeks out its fragmentation at a state and national level, displacing them towards global corporations and organizations.

9   The exception to this rule is the already extensively well – known and disseminated Immanuel Wallerstein's World System Theory. Or national economies, or national populations, or national class structures, etc.

and simply to *unthinkable* space-time parameters (Wallerstein, 1991). In this sense, a glimpse of the social reality from its globalization raises then, the need of a break with the methodological nationalism that is imbued with these ways of observing the national societies.

With globalization, society itself is influenced by a system of networks and local-global interconnection relationships, as well as processes, transnational and translocal actors and social forces. The old economic, social, demographic, and political geographies have become extremely variable as a result of the destructuring of national and international bases on which they had been built in the modern state and society. Thus, globalization expresses the emergence of new territorial units such as the *State-region* (Ohmae, 1995), the *global city* (Sassen 1991), or the *transnational community* (Smith, 1995), among others.

This is a matter of socio-economic spaces and geographical units that can equally be located within the nation borders as conformed by regions and/or cities of more than one. The fact of being spatial is rather a historical accident.[10] What is relevant is that these are the territorial units on which the global space are set up, and no longer the national states.[11] In this sense, the global even though might well be understood as a *supra-national* or even *trans-national* phenomenon, it is not, however, assimilated nor reduced to the *international phenomena*.

Thus, globalization refers to a network of interconnections and interdependencies that have arisen among multiple regions and that seem to end in a deterritorialization context of social life (Appadurai, 1990). In these times of globalization, the world becomes a territory that belongs to the world. Everything is deterritorialized and reterritorialized, in a process in which borders become irrelevant, superfluous, and are constantly ignored and fragmented. However, it is necessary to consider the warning that Beck points out when he says that global society "world society is thus not a mega-national society containing and dissolving all national societies within itself, but a *world horizon* characterized by multiplicity and non-integration which opens out when

---

10   As an example, we can name the Sillicon Valley, the transboundary region of San Diego-Tijuana, Tokyo and its surrounding areas, among many others. However, these territorial units should not be confused with large megalopolis, such as Mexico City, Sao Paulo, Calcutta, Los Angeles, etc. A large city can form a global region in itself, but it is neither necessary nor sufficient. What matters is that these territorial units are oriented towards the global economy, and not to the national states that host them. This, for example, is the main differentiating factor between a global city and a simple megalopolis. On this point, see Ohmae, 1997; Sassen 1998 and 1991; And Borja and Castells, 1997.
11   Or national economies, national populations, national social classes, and a large etc.

it is produced and preserved in communication and action" (Beck, 2000a:12. my emphasis).

The global issue rather alludes to a social process dimension, this is, to a form of space-time organization at a global level. Strictly speaking, there is neither *one* time nor *one* global space. In Milton Santos words, "all the times are global, but there is no single world time. The space is being globalized, but it is not global as a whole but as a metaphor. All the places are global, but there is no single global space. People and places are the ones who are becoming globalized" (Santos, 1994:31).

In a literal sense, no one can produce *globally*. Any company, both traditional and the most globalized, must rely on relationships and *local* pillars. The global rather alludes to the idea of being "in many places simultaneously", and consequently, does not exclude the local. On the contrary, the local is an aspect of the global, as well as global is a synonym of *translocal*. The local goes hand in hand with globalization. In this regard, Robertson (1992) raises the neologism *glocalization* to understand and specify this *global-local* duality in contemporary society.

In summary, neither the global space nor the global village, as such, exist anywhere, they are only metaphors. What do exist are *globalized spaces*, this is, globalized villages and communities. The global space, as a heuristic and analytical construction, in fact is composed of an infinite number of globalized local and regional spaces.

The challenge for the social sciences, then, think of the world as a global society, and more precisely in terms of globalized societies. It is not just a problem of change in the territorial scale of analysis. That is, it is not about moving from a national scale to another, purely and simply, while not a problem of aggregation or abstraction levels of analysis, but something more complex and profound.

In this context, we understand the scope of Beck's critique to *methodological nationalism*. It is not only a question of a theoretical rupture, but also of an epistemological one, to the extent that what arises is not only the need for new concepts, categories and social theories, but above all, for new perspectives from which contemporary societies can be observed and studied.

## 2  Transnational Communities and Transnationalism

In spite of the fact that population movements have their most deeply rooted causes in structural factors, it must also be taken into account that they are the outcome of an aggregation of individual migrations by people who make decisions on the basis of what is happening in their immediate environment. Most of these individual migrations are in practice determined by the existence of family and community networks, specifying an itinerary and geographic destination (and often labor) of emigration. It has always been documented that members of the same community usually emigrate and settle in the same place, commonly constituting a micro-society in the host country that reproduces the same community from which they come. At present, however, this phenomenon reveals a greater complexity.

Currently, international migration is a diverse process, which not only involves a flow of people and workers but also an important flow of material and symbolic goods. Migrants activate and consolidate social, cultural and family networks on the basis of which a complex system of exchanging and circulation of people, money, property and information is supported, which articulates and integrates migrant settlements on both sides of the border in a single large community scattered among a great number of locations.

Various authors allude to this process in terms of the *transnational communities* configuration as a way of referring to the *density* of movements and social bonds that extends from the community of origin to all the places where their migrants are located (Smith, 2006). Through migration, various factors and processes of articulation are activated in the cultural, social and economic field, between distant and geographically separated communities and social institutions. It involves a dislocation and disruption of the traditional concept of "community", especially in terms of its spatial and territorial dimensions (Kearnay and Nagengast, 1989). This virtual "deterritorialization" of origin communities makes that reproduction be direct and intrinsically linked with reproduction and migrant labor in their different settlements located in urban neighborhoods and rural villages of the receiving countries (Rivera, 2004).

For over two decades, various authors have raised the concept of "transmigration" and "transmigrants" to refer to these new modalities and forms of population mobility at a global level (Smart, 1999; Portes, 1997; and Glick Schiller, Basch and Blanc-Szanton, 1992; Moctezuma, 2016). The transmigration differs from the classical forms of migration in that it involves the consolidation of new social spaces that go beyond the origin and destination community. It is about a transnational expansion of the community's space through social practices, artefacts, and transnational symbol systems. Unlike temporary migration, transmigration does not define a transitional situation but reflects the consolidation of "plurilocal" spaces and transnational communities where, in addition, the migrant status becomes completely transformed.

Emigrating is no longer necessarily a break with the community and family of origin. On the contrary, migration becomes a way to expand and extend family and community relationships. Immigrants do not travel alone but they take their community with them, not in a metaphorical sense, but in a real and literal sense (Levitt, 2011). Emigrating is no longer a synonymous of *leaving something behind*, it becomes *bringing something with them*.

Unlike the migratory flows that existed at the beginning of the twentieth century, current migration has allowed the creation of a transnational field of reproducing meanings and collective actions. It is the material and imaginary construction of communities beyond their original spaces which enables to confront both the processes of social breakdown and social life individuation characteristic of postmodern societies, as well as the economic and social exclusion which are also essential features of contemporary societies in this age of globalization (García Canclini, 2014).

Just as adopting a perspective on globalization implies having a theoretical and epistemological rupture with the scientific paradigms of Modernity, so adopting a transnational point of view of migrations presents an equally radical methodological challenge. To start with, it obliges us to come to an understanding of migrations and of social processes from a global, transnational perspective whose epistemic basis is in its "questioning of the classical model of scientific knowledge, structured and basically thought of within the geographical limits of the so-called Nation State" (Cavalcanti and Parella, 2013:14).[12] Nevertheless, this view of migration as the construction of transnational social spaces is not exempt from being questioned and criticized itself.

In the first place, there has been a wide-ranging debate of Methodological Nationalism covering its historical and even theoretical and methodological aspects, related to the difficulties of measuring and analyzing transnational social processes empirically (Chernilo, 2011). This particular author, for example, points out how hard it is to advance a critique of methodological nationalism without having defenders of the "methodological nationalist" point of view to argue against. Basically, and without being ironical, this is really about a critique of the underlying foundation of modern thought, and precisely for this reason not a premise that has been discussed, conceptualized and formalized within this philosophical matrix. This is not to minimize the critique of Methodological Nationalism but to contextualize it, and to understand it as another epistemological principle which requires adopting a position, a way of seeing and observing social phenomena, rather than being a finished, formalized,

---

12  "cuestionamiento al clásico modelo del conocimiento científico, estructurado y pensado básicamente dentro de los límites geográficos del llamado Estado-nación". Original in Spanish.

theoretical and methodological construct. Fundamentally, to recognize the z-axis is to become conscious of the point of view of the observer in the construction of objects of study and in theorizing about them and measuring them (Zemelman, 1992).

We should also remember that the transnational perspective covers not only migration, but all the social phenomena that occur in the contemporary world. While migrations do have the considerable advantage of themselves being a process that crosses national borders, we should not forget that they form only one of the many areas where applications of this critical view of methodological nationalism can be made, and that the latter has its origins in critical analysis of the processes involved in globalization and post-modernism, where the social construction of spaces is sustained by de-territorializing social processes and re-territorializing them on the basis of global, trans-local and transnational logics (Appadurai, 1990; Rouse, 1991; Beck, 2000a).

The term "transnational" came into use a long time ago, and from the very start suggested an epistemological point of view requiring processes to be observed from a global perspective, as the world system model does. In economics for example, the concept of "transnational" was used to critique classical and neo-classical theories of international trade, which have tended to circumscribe and conceptualize the world economy as a system of exchange and economic relations *between* nations (i.e. *inter*-national). Yet it has been pointed out ever since the writings of Marx up to the most recent developments by Wallerstein of the theory of a World System, that capital does not respect the logic of national borders. It has always had a global, transnational vocation, which seems obvious to us now in the light of contemporary globalization of the economy.

From a transnational point of view of global and local economic processes, these are not restricted to exchanges between nations, or to processes within nations. National economies do not exist as such, but are components of a worldwide, transnational economic system, that is, one that transcends local and national frontiers.

At any rate, what is relevant here is that there has always been a dispute between those who analyze and conceptualize social processes of the Nation State as an area confined to the limits outlined on a map, and those who analyze and conceptualize these processes from a global perspective, regarding them as the political, economic and cultural relations of a world system. A transnational perspective on migration evidently brings new elements to this discussion. But it would be wrong not to recognize that there are epistemic elements underlying the discussion that link it to other visions of transnationality that come from critical thinking about society.

In concrete terms, a methodological problem of considerable importance arises in transnational studies of migrations, deriving from a confusion of terms and their misapplication. The concept of "transnational" tends to be used indifferently as a synonym for international, multinational and sometimes even postnational (Suarez, 2008). So for example, any practice of migrants may be confused with a transnational practice. All migrants, at all times, have kept up links with the communities they emigrated from and these links imply a continual flow of information, news, merchandise and economic resources. All migrations create spaces for the reproduction of the migrants' national identities in the places they have immigrated to, whether through starting football clubs, restaurants serving typical food, everyday communication by telephone and suchlike with their families in the places they emigrated from, sending remittances, taking trips back to the community and family feasts, and many other activities. But these practices by the migrants are not always transnational practices. There is however a moment when migration does become transnational, and this has to do with two aspects that need to be taken into account.

Firstly, there is the density of these practices and the degree of involvement in them of the population and communities in the places migrated from and the places migrated to. And secondly, we find the reproduction and formation of spaces of identity and belonging that surpass national boundaries, at both ends of the migration (Smith, 2006). In other words, the formation of a *transnational social field*, as a point of reference for identity and belonging, beyond the national (or state, or region or even community) fields of the places migrated from and to.

In line with this analysis, and taking it to a more practical level oriented towards measuring and theorizing about the transnational phenomenon, Portes, Guarnizo and Landolt (1999) establish three criteria for when the particular and characteristic activities of any migrant qualify for being referred to by the term transnational: a) they have to involve a world of relevant people, both from the place they come from and from where they now live; b) their practices must be established and have existed for some time, and not be transitory or sporadic. And they must be activities that are repeated on an everyday basis, not something exceptional or extraordinary; and c) they should represent original practices whose transcendence cannot be captured by categories, processes or conceptualizations that already exist (Cavalcanti and Parella, 2013).

If transnationality comes with an epistemological requirement, in terms of how to observe and understand social processes, it also makes a demand for theoretical and conceptual rigor (Dahinde, 2017). Transnational studies of migration cannot be content with generic and abstract definitions of the term that lead to the use of superficial categories with very little theoretical content, and are therefore not much use for analysis. We require a theory and a methodology that is more profound so the term can really help us to identify the social, political and economic practices of the migrants. Thanks to their density, massiveness, recurrence, stability and rootedness in time, they now form transnational social fields. So we can differentiate these from other migration practices that are the same in concrete terms, but occur in contexts that do not make them transnational social fields, and merely imply the reproduction of situations and conjunctural or circumstantial conditions that the migrants experience.

Another point of discussion has to do with the social and political transcendence of transnationality in migration. We must consider whether transnationality implies the constitution of a social and political subject, the *transnational migrant*, or merely refers to social practices. Some scholars such as Portes, say that "immigrant transnationalism is not driven by ideological reasons but by the very logic of global capitalism" (Portes 2001, 187). Whereas Al-Ali, Black and Koser (2001:12) state that "transnational communities can wield substantial political, economic and social power".

Accordingly, there is an interesting proposal by Moctezuma (2016), who makes a conceptual and political distinction between the idea of *transnationalism* and that of *transnationality*. While transnationalism focuses on migrants as individuals and covers their communities and the intense activity among them, transnationality is a theoretical proposal focusing on the activity developed by migrant organizations. This distinction makes it possible to establish a theoretical and practical difference between the transnational conduct of the community, and the social involvement of migrant organizations; a difference which is larger when these assume the character of social subjects. In this sense, the distinction that the author makes between the organized action of migrants and the categories of actor, agent and migrant subject is fundamental and is the key factor for understanding the different categories.

In this context, transnationality as a conceptual proposal refers to the set of organizational practices undertaken by migrants both in the country of origin and in the country of arrival. It is about different forms of transnational involvement in which substantive or practical citizenship are exercised. Transnationality focuses on social subjects, that is, on migrant organizations when they have acquired the rank of associations; it also includes the simplest manifestations of migrants' organizations, as seen in social clubs, and even covers the leadership of individuals, but in this case migrant associations continue to be the migrants' *cohesive structures*, hence the unit of observation.

## 3 Migration, Social Networks and Transnationalism

However, to think about migration in terms of transnational community's formation, implies to think about it in terms of the social networks and community configuration. Transnational communities make up a dense system of social networks that cross political boundaries which are created by migrants in their search for social recognition and economic progress (Portes, 1997). These networks arise from the linkages, friendship and family relationships, but above all, from community identity. In addition, the configuration of these networks is based on relationships of confidence, reciprocity and solidarity that characterize the nature of the relationships within the communities.

In particular, the social networks serve to recreate, although in a transformed way, the community of origin in the settlement sites, and in this way to reproduce it in the context of its transnationalization. The communities of origin are also transformed as a result of both their close dependence with the labor markets dynamics in the United States and the strong links with the migrant's social and daily life within the places of settlement. This is an on-going adaptation process concerning both their lifestyle and economic and social structures. Alarcón (1992) defines this process as the *norteñizacion* (northernization) of origin communities to the extent that the social, cultural and economic reproduction of these communities is not only oriented towards the "North", but in addition, increasingly disjointed from the "South". For these communities, the relationship with migrant's settlement locations in the "North" is more intense than the relations they have with their neighboring communities (Lindstrom and Muñoz Franco, 2005). For their reproduction, the flow of goods and symbolic material that comes from their twin communities on the other side of the world is more important, than the interactions they maintain with the rest of the communities in their country of origin.[13]

In this sense, Rouse (1991) notes that migrants end up becoming experienced exponents of a bi-focused culture, participating in a daily tension and conflict between two very different ways of life. This situation has also been taken up by Portes (1997), who points out that, through the translocal networks, migrants have a dual life, they are often bilingual and move between two cultures, they keep their home in both countries and get involved in relationships that require their physical and symbolic presence in both spaces.

---

13  Just to illustrate, we can say that in the case of Latin America, migrant remittances constitute between 40% and 50% of receiving household's income. This gives some idea of the transmigration and remittance importance in the social and daily reproduction of migrant households. For more details, see Canales, 2008.

One of the more transcendent consequences emerging from this approach about transnationalism is its critical view of the classical assumptions concerning immigrant's integration and assimilation in host societies. At present, assimilation models are not only being abandoned but also considered as inadmissible, since a justified suspicion of racism falls on them (Izquierdo, 2011). However, the alternative integration models have also failed. In contrast, Wievorka (2011) raises the need to abandon the so-called *inclusion sociology* to seriously consider the point of view of migrants themselves, as they are people immersed in a globalized world.

Along the same line, Telles and Ortiz based on a longitudinal study which included intergenerational trajectories, found that "economic integration, the most desirable aspect of assimilation, becomes stagnant after the second generation" (Telles and Ortiz; 2008:80), simultaneously that the assimilation at other levels (social, cultural and political) takes place so gradually that sometimes, it is questionable whether it is a real progress or not.

Considering this virtual failure of assimilation and integration models, one of the most analyzed and deepened aspects, from the point of view of transnationalism, is that it increases the ethnic, cultural and linguistic diversity into the host countries, which absorb some of the characteristics of the emigrant's sending countries. This is completely contrary to the so-called "paradigms of sovereignty" (Smith, 1995) by means of which it was thought that migrant became a citizen through its assimilation or "Americanization" (Rumbaut, 1997).

The East neighborhood of Los Angeles (better known as East L.A.) illustrates this situation. This area of Los Angeles, currently brings together the largest population concentration of Hispanic origin in the United States. In fact, its population is almost exclusively of Mexican origin and Spanish is practically the only language spoken by people. What is relevant, however, is that this part of the city is not just something similar to a piece of Mexico grafted into the United States, but rather configures a type of neighborhood that is reproduced with similar composition and characteristics in many other cities in the country. In other words, East L.A. is not only a " Mexican neighborhood ", but at present, it is essentially, a typical North American neighborhood, as native and representative of what is now Los Angeles, as any other neighborhood in the city (Hollywood, Beverly Hills, Malibu, among others).

At present, this type of neighborhoods defined by their immigrant origin do not constitute only an ethnic enclave, a picturesque singularity to promote tourism, but an intrinsic characteristic of the global cities, a space of identity and belonging which provides substantive aspects for the city operation and reproduction, not only in demographic terms, but also in terms of their economic-productive activities, labor force, cultural life, political processes, social movements, urban-territorial conflicts, tensions and so forth.

In this context, the question arises of the sense of belonging and the construction of transnational identities, says Smith (1995). It is a sense of belonging to imagined communities that coexist with many different other forms of belonging, residence and citizenship characteristic of the political communities created by the national states. Migrants develop social and cultural links along with economic and labor ones. As a result, many of them "imagine" themselves as part of a United States community, but not any community, a migrant translocated one that reproduces and recreates the cultural patterns and symbolic forms of their origin communities (Chavez, 1994).

This imaginary construction is based on a set of all kinds of relationships and transactions that are within the framework of a transnational system of social networks and cultural capital. These networks make up the individual interpersonal niche, and contribute to its own recognition as an individual and to his self-image as a community member, as a subject of a basic social fabric. According to Goldring (1997), a transnational community differs from the transnational migrant circuits to the extent that it refers to a social field where the links *density* and social ties makes possible the construction of a relationship and sense of belonging of migrants in terms of the community.

In the case of transnational communities, the "belonging" defines a very different situation and condition from that of citizenship. The transnational community defines and constructs a sense of belonging and dependence with it which is stronger and deeper than the respective national states involved with migration. It is a question of configuring a sense of belonging to this which is before but also beyond citizenship. As Smith indicates (1995), the "membership beyond citizenship" refers to the transnationalization of the community sense beyond national borders both of the Nation State of origin, but also of the Nation State of destination. Thus, according to this author, Mexican migrants living in the United States maintain and increase its importance and links with their communities of origin even after their stable and definitive legal settlement. For them, the possible social citizenship i.e. the construction of a sense of belonging with the American State, when it happens, does not imply, however, a break with their sense of belonging with their communities of origin. The belonging to these is deeper and more vital than the politically constructed belongings. Meanwhile, in many cases, the citizenship is not but a way to defend and maintain these community links.

In the case of the transnational community, the membership has a different sense and meaning to that of political communities. Membership is defined by migrants themselves and it is based on the territorial expansion of their social networks, which are transnationally structured through their practices (Smith, 1995). In this sense, this membership becomes substantive, and not only declarative, to the extent that it allows to undercut the sense of physical and contiguous presences for imagined and symbolic presences. In this framework, we can point out the practices, privileges and benefits enjoyed by migrants in their communities, even after their settlement in the United States. Example of this, is the capacity of influence and power that migrants can exert on the decision-making process concerning various aspects that affect the origin communities. The physical "absence" is countered by the imagined "presence" that becomes real and concrete by means of the information and power flowing through the social networks built by migrants and facilitated by the telecommunication development.

## 4  Migration and Reproduction

Regardless of how many attempts made to systematize reality, it will always be a step ahead. This is the case of international migration, where the growing integration between countries caused by globalization has made many of the theories and concepts from which the phenomenon had been addressed have become obsolete. The main critique refers to the methodological nationalism that lies behind them which prevents them from arriving at an overall view of all contemporary migration. A first break with these visions happened through the rise of the transnational approach that has led to important conceptual and methodological advances, many of which have been shared and outlined in the previous section.

Transnationalism is not just an emerging social phenomenon but it also stands as a paradigm that enables us to interpret the international migration peculiarities in this age of globalization. From this approach, we recover an angle of analysis which requires an overall view of the migratory phenomenon. In a global world, the understanding of international migration, as well as other social phenomena, cannot be confined to the national contours we have inherited from the modern social thought that are present in many of the concepts, categories and indicators we usually use for analysis and apprehension.

To this vision we want to add a second order of rupture and analysis. Taking up the theory of the structure (Giddens, 1986), our thesis is that from various fields and levels, international migration contributes to the *structuring* of contemporary society. To understand this process, we intend to analyze migration from the reproduction approach that is, analyzing migration as a reproduction factor of society, and by this means, of its transformation. Let's take a look at this in more detail.

Following the critique to the methodological nationalism, today's society is no longer limited to the territorial contours of the Nation-State, but it has extended and expanded beyond them, as has its globalization been extended and expanded. What is happening in the origin places is not exogenous to the destination places, and vice versa, since through migration (and other globalization phenomena), both societies (origin and destination), extend and expand, configuring transnational social fields. Not only the communities of origin become transnationalized, but through them, are created the communicating channels that articulate origin societies with the destination ones. When we say destination society, we are not restricted to migrant communities in the destination places, but to the whole society that receive them, this is, to all the native population and their social, economic, cultural and political dynamics that make up society.

This approach poses a double challenge. On the one hand, the object of observation is no longer limited to international migration only, but it extends to the society as a whole. It is through the observation of contemporary society that we can problematize and contextualize the meaning and significance of the current migratory processes or, which is to say, not to lose sight of the fact that the study of migration has as an ultimate meaning, the understanding of society. There lies the importance and significance of its study. Through migration, we want to understand some of contemporary society's problems.

On the other hand, this perspective of society and migration analysis requires concepts, categories and indicators that account for these processes. These are analytical categories that while giving account of the current international migration vicissitudes, enable us to make the leap to the understanding of contemporary society's vicissitudes. As well as transnational community and transnationalism are analytical categories which make it possible to understand contemporary migrations, we need categories that allow us to refer not only to migration, but also to contemporary society. In this regard, terms such as *Globalization, Cosmopolitanism* (Goic, 2007; Robertson, 1992), among others, contribute to this purpose.

In this sense, our interest is to add other categories and other levels of analysis that give an account of various migration aspects and dimensions within the framework of these more comprehensive concepts and approaches. In particular and following this analytical perspective of globalization, we are interested in the analysis of the international migration role in the contemporary society process of *reproduction*.

In methodological terms, international migration includes different levels from which it can be analyzed, namely:
- On a first level, migration is, first of all, a movement of people from a social space to another. This is the first form in which any migration is manifested. Here, it is important to define who the persons migrating are (their demographic and socio-economic profiles among others), as well as which forms of migration are chosen by each individual or social group (temporary, circular, seasonal, definitive, pendulous, by stages, irregular, forced migration, among many others).
- A second level, corresponds to the analysis of the causes and consequences of migration. This level of analysis allows us to understand migration not only as a flow of people, but also as a labor force mobility or displacement for political reasons (refugees, exile), or natural disasters, among many other categories that can give an account of the nature of each particular migratory flow. Likewise, it also enables us to understand and estimate the demographic, social, economic, political and cultural impacts of these different types of movements of people.
- On a third level, we can give a new twist by looking at migration (as well as its causes and consequences, forms, profiles, etc.) as a component of a greater social dimension process. At this level, we understand migration as part of society reproduction and transformation processes, all of this viewed from the most diverse dimensions: economic, demographic, social, political, cultural, historical, and generational, among many others.

Commonly, the analysis and conceptualization of international migration is restricted to one of the first two levels of analysis that we have pointed out. In particular, the debate on the Migration-Development process, focuses precisely on this second level, where the causes and migration consequences are being analyzed. In the best case scenario, the analysis of migration consequences on the development process is derived from the analysis and understanding of the causes that, from the development, originate these migration processes (to some extent is what we have already described in previous pages). In other cases, the causes and consequences are maintained separated from each other.

Here we have some of the current predominant analytical proposals in which migration and remittances are proposed as a factor of economic and social development in the origin countries but without a conceptual framework to account for the causes of that same international migration. In these cases, the consequences attributed to migration, arise from migration itself and not from a structural framework that, on the one hand, explain the conditions that cause that same migration, while, on the other hand, accounts for the conditions that could either limit or enhance such consequences attributed to them.

However, without denying the importance of these two first levels of analysis, our proposal seeks to move forward in this third level of analysis, so as to arrive to a comprehensive model of international migration, which goes beyond its description as well as its causes and consequences.[14] We refer to the analysis of migration role and meaning in the *reproduction and transformation* of global society, i.e., in the reproduction of inequality and social differentiation structures that characterizes globalization.[15]

In terms of society reproduction, one of the immediate consequences for the understanding of international migration is that, through it, some mechanisms are activated that articulate and integrate the conditions and dynamics of social reproduction in the origin countries with the ones in the destination countries in a same process (Canales and Montiel, 2010). In other words, the socio-economic and socio-demographic structures of the hosting countries of immigration are becoming more open to the outside world not only because the migratory flow contributes to its evolution but also because, through it, the social dynamics of the countries of origin have a direct impact on the internal dynamics of the recipient countries. Conversely, the social structures of reproduction in the origin countries become more open to the social dynamics of their migrants destination countries.

However, we have no doubt that the reproduction of any society involves multiple dimensions, components, and various levels from which this matter can be analyzed and theorized. In our case, we have chosen to discuss only three of them, in which, we think, international migration has a relevant role. We are referring to the role of migration as a reproduction factor of populations, capital and social inequality structures.[16]

It is clear that much of what we want to raise with this model is only a return to what many authors have said before. Each of these levels or reproduction fields, include in itself a broad theoretical and methodological background which has resulted in many research and particular findings. Our contribution

---

14  This third level does not imply to deny the findings and analysis of the previous two, but to incorporate them in a broader and more comprehensive analytical model that allow the understanding of migration as a complex social structure component.

15  To avoid misunderstandings, it is worth pointing out the following. The reproduction of social inequality structures occurs through several mechanisms and social processes. Migration is not the only one, but only one of these many mechanisms and social processes.

16  A fourth form might correspond to the shape of a symbolic and cultural relations system that is activated with international migration. Likewise, a fifth form would be the one referred to the political relations and political power distribution. And so on, shapes, dimensions and levels can be added to this process of society reproduction based on local-global processes of articulation that can be activated by contemporary international migration.

in this regard is rather, to give them both a general overview and a close view of parts and gears of this great puzzle that reproduction represents in today's society from which we derive the position, function, and contradictions that correspond to each of these three great moments in society reproduction: demography, economy, and social classes.

However, beyond the analytical and conceptual richness of each of these levels or moments of international migration, they are partial and insufficient in themselves to understand the role of migration as a component and architect of the reproduction in the globalized society. In this sense, what we propose is to move beyond the traditional limits of each level and moment of the analysis of migration to configure a level of second-order, constructed from the combination and integration of the previous three. It deals with transcending the meaning of migration in each level, to reach a new order and level of understanding migration.

– On the one hand, from a demographic point of view, we can understand how this translocal reproduction of migration, is also a translocal reproduction of populations, shaping a global system of demographic reproduction. It is the articulation of different demographic reproduction patterns, apparently independent, but that, through migration, partially integrate into a scheme of demographic complementarity. In one case, migration constitutes an escape valve in front of a demographic bonus that the local economy is not able to transform into cash. On the other hand, migration and migrants themselves, allow to fill the demographic gaps that the population ageing and reduction of fertility leave with the advancement of the second demographic transition.

– On the other hand, from economy, we can also understand the meaning of this demographic reproduction, at least from three complementary perspectives. On the one hand, the analysis of economic globalization tells us that this is not migration of people purely and simply, but essentially it is a labor migration, and by this means, a mechanism to provide labor force to capital. Likewise, it is not a worker migration purely and simply, but that of a socially and vulnerable group of workers inserted in precarious, flexible and unstable jobs. Finally, migrant remittances, are a way used to transfer the salary and ensuring their families reproduction, closing, in this way, the capital reproduction circle on having sustained the articulation of the local reproductive moment (of the labor force, through their communities and families of origin) with the global productive moments (work and labor insertion in economies of destination).

– Finally, it is not only a question of reproducing the population or the capital, but of social subjects, and in particular, of people inserted in certain positions within the social structure. On the one hand, through the insertion in occupations related to social reproduction at the destination end, migrants contribute to sustain the reproduction of middle and upper class population, enabling not only its material reproduction, but above all, a life style reproduction, a pattern of social behavior (individuation, women emancipation, quality of life, among other aspects). On the other hand, migration itself and remittances undoubtedly, make up a reproduction strategy of migrants, families and their communities. But let's be clear, these are strategies that allow survival and reproduction in precarious conditions and social vulnerability, but that does not necessarily imply a solution or exit strategy of these structural conditions. In this sense, what is important for our discussion, is that migration sets up a kind of hinge, which links the reproduction of socially different and geographically distant subjects in what we can call as the configuration of a global and transnational reproduction system of the class structure and social inequality, characteristic of contemporary society.

The vision from all these three levels, allows us to understand that migration is not a people displacement phenomenon in abstract, but through this

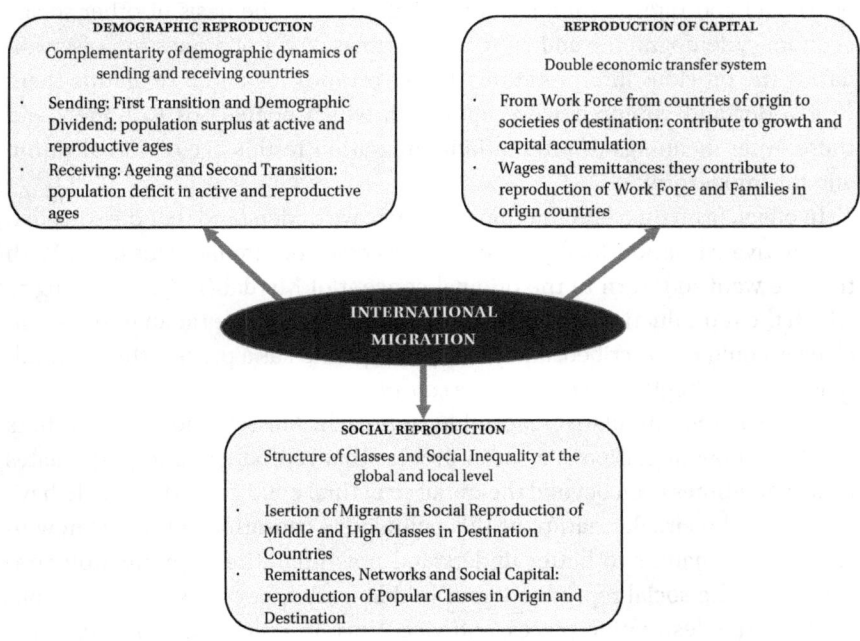

FIGURE 3   The three components of the Reproduction Model

phenomenon, a complex system of complementarities and transferences of all types is set up, which involves people in certain social, economic and labor positions. Or in other words, it is not just a system of demographic reproduction, but that through it, the economic and social system reproduction is permitted and made possible at least in terms of polarization and segmentation of labor markets, and by this means, of the social inequality forms in this era of a globalized economy.

In summary, the integrated vision of these three international migration dimensions or moments (demography, economy, social classes) enables us to achieve a new level of understanding international migration, as a component and architect of the contemporary global society reproduction. In the following diagram we tried to illustrate migration role in the reproduction of society, through its role in the reproduction of capital, population, class structure and social inequality.

From this perspective, what is relevant is that this local-global articulation happening through international migration, does not only refer to economic categories (labor, labor force, remittances, production, reproduction, among others), but also, and fundamentally, it is the articulation and opposition of social subjects, classes, groups and social strata, as well as of their unequal positions in a social structure. This gaze from the society reproduction enables us to read and interpret international migration on the basis of other social, economic, demographic and cultural meanings. It is not a question of invalidating the previous interpretations, but of recapturing and articulating them in a wider and comprehensive approach, which enables us to understand these other meanings of international migration in this age of globalization and postmodernity.

In effect, from this reproduction approach, we understand that the so-called cumulative causation finally becomes, processes of circular causation. With this, we want to return to the original concept of Myrdal (1957) according to which the reproduction of social and economic inequalities at an international level, could be described, analyzed, and explained as a process that is simultaneously of circular and cumulative *causation*.

Through the cumulative causation approach, Massey and other authors taught us how migration is a social process that reproduces and perpetuates itself, sometimes even beyond the initial structural conditions that would have triggered. The circular nature of this cumulative causation, allows us now to extend this analysis to better understand how migration reproduction contributes to the social reproduction of middle and upper classes native population in the destination places, and vice versa. In other words, through this approach of the circular causation we can understand how reproduction and perpetuation of migration (through the social networks system) and the social reproduction of the middle and upper classes native population, are also reciprocally caused.

Just as in the past, Myrdal used this concept of *cumulative and circular causation* to analyze and explain the reproduction and perpetuation of economic unequal structures at an international level, today we can use this approach to understand how in current times, migration and migrant labor, constitutes a privileged social field to observe and analyze the reproduction process in the society at least from these three levels: population, capital, and the class structure reproduction along with social inequalities. This thesis is what we want to expose in the following chapters.

CHAPTER 5

# The Role of Migration in the Global System of Demographic Reproduction

*I am a citizen of planet earth*
*A human being who does not believe in borders*[1]
    The Rose of the Winds
    MAKIZA / ANITA TIJOUX

∴

## 1      Thesis

Through international migration, a global system of demographic reproduction is configured, based on the complementarity of the population dynamics of the regions of origin with the dynamics in the countries of destination. In the sending countries, the Demographic Dividend generates a surplus of the active population. In receiving countries ageing and declining birth rates, generate gaps and deficits in working-age population. Both regimes complement each other and through migration are integrated as a global system of demographic reproduction. The corollary is that in migrant-receiving advanced societies this global system of reproduction is expressed as a process of demographic replacement.

## 2      From Demographic Transition to a Global System of Reproduction

The interest in population reproduction is as old as humanity itself. However, the way in which this concern has been delimited and reinterpreted in each society is substantially different, and expresses the fears and the worldview own of each historical era. Thus, for example, in the modern-industrial society, the most developed and widely accepted formulation is the one that

---

1   "Yo soy ciudadano del planeta tierra. Ser humano que no cree en las fronteras". Original in Spanish.

conceptualizes the population dynamics as a process of *Demographic Transition* (Thompson, 1929; Landry, 1934; Notestein, 1945; Davis, 1945).

According to this model, the demographic change would express itself as the transition from an agrarian and traditional society, characterized by high levels of fertility and mortality, to an industrial and modern society characterized, on the other hand, by low and controlled levels of such demographic variables (Thumerelle, 1996; Kirk, 1996). Similarly, this transition would be interpreted as the demographic face of society's modernization process that along with the change in the structure of values and attitudes, the industrial development and our society's urbanization would also lead to the modernization of the population reproduction practices, household formation, women labor insertion, among other components of demographic dynamics (Germani, 1981).

On the other hand, Livi Bacci (1994) interprets this demographic *modernization* as a gain in terms of a greater "demographic efficiency", which is manifested in a reduction in the levels of "demographic chaos", and a transit towards the "demographic order". In particular, this author indicates that

> (in traditional societies), growth was slow and took place with a big 'demographic energy' dissipation: women had to give birth to half-dozen children in order to be replaced by the later generation. Each newborn's generation lost between a third and half of its components before they reached the reproductive age. The *old regime* societies were, therefore, inefficient from a demographic point of view.... In addition to its inefficiency, the old demographic regime was characterized by the demographic 'disorder'. There were high probabilities that a child died before their parents were subverting the *natural order* .... We can say that we use the expression 'demographic transition' to define the complex process that represents the transition from order to disorder, and from waste to economy: this implies a decrease from high to moderate levels of mortality and fertility.[2]
> 
> LIVI BACCI, 1994:13–14. My emphasis

---

2 "(En las sociedades tradicionales) el crecimiento era lento y se producía con una gran disipación de "energía" demográfica: las mujeres debían dar a luz media docena de hijos para poder ser remplazadas por la generación posterior. Cada generación de nacidos perdía entre la tercera parte y la mitad de sus componentes antes de que estos alcanzaran la edad reproductiva. Las sociedades del antiguo régimen eran, por consiguiente, ineficientes desde el punto de vista demográfico.... Además de su ineficiencia, el antiguo régimen demográfico se caracterizaba por el "desorden" demográfico. Eran notables las probabilidades de que un hijo muriese antes que sus padres, subvirtiendo el orden natural de la procedencia de las generaciones.... Podemos decir que usamos la expresión "transición demográfica" para

Based on this vision of demographic change as a *transition* from one demographic state to another, different "stages" were identified in which we can locate the different national populations or societies.[3] It would be a transition path by which all societies would have to pass, but in different rhythms and times as the different moments or stages of modernization process were developing in every society. However, what is relevant is that in all of them are established an earlier drop in deaths than births, thus creating the demographic conditions for an increase in the population growth rates, which in some cases, would even become "explosive".[4]

In summary, the Demographic Transition constitutes what would be a modernist perspective of population. It is Modernity, as a world view, what has given significance and transcendence to the contemporary demographic discourse, expressed both in the concept of population in itself and in the process of Modernization as its matrix of significance. In effect, as it is clearly illustrated in Livi Bacci's thought, the demographic transition model was constructed based on the principles and meta-narratives that historically

---

definir el proceso complejo del paso del desorden al orden y del desperdicio a la economía: este tránsito implica un descenso de los niveles altos a niveles moderados de mortalidad y fecundidad", Original in Spanish.

This quote is interesting, and we reproduce it extensively since, in a way, Massimo Livi Bacci applies the modernization theory to the analysis of demographic change, with virtually the same terms, analysis criteria and status for the used categories. His discourse not only expresses analytical aspects of the modernization theory, but also the ideological background of his position, which is expressed in the ideological force of various categories used (efficiency, order, former regime, among others) that allow him to sustain the superiority of a modern demographic regime above a traditional one, superiority based on an increased rationality in the use of demographic resources. For a broader and more complete review of these author's theses, see Livi Bacci (2012).

3 Thus for example, in various works, the Latin American countries are grouped according to the degree of progress in its demographic transition. This classification can spread throughout the world, as it becomes evident that in general, the core countries appear in more advanced stages of transition than peripheral and dependent countries. Regarding this classification of countries, you can consult various papers presented at the IV Conference of Latin American population. The demographic transition in Latin America and the Caribbean. Mexico. IUSSP-PROLAP-ABEP-CELADE-SOMEDE.

4 Such would be the case of some Third World countries, where this period of transition in the demographic dynamics would be marked by an "explosive" growth of its population as a result of different rhythms and patterns of response of each demographic component, to the transformations in the social structure, generated by the economic development and social modernization. In particular, the improvement of health conditions, services and medical infrastructure would have allowed a rapid fall in mortality. However, fertility tended to stay high responding with some delay, due to the fact that the "modernization" of the cultural patterns that affects the reproductive behavior, both at the individual and family level, has been more gradual and slower (Benitez, 1994).

arise with a modern, consolidated vision of the world and society. The ideas of social progress, the centrality of the reason in the developmental ideology, the secularization of social practices, among other aspects, underlie the whole demographic thinking of the first modernity. In this context, it is not surprising that the *Demographic Transition* ended up being the frame of reference par excellence for the purpose of understanding the population dynamics in modern societies. Beyond the critique it received in terms of its theoretical and political scope,[5] what is true is that this population analysis model filled with meaning the practice of demographer.

However, the discourse on Modernity, along with giving full potential to the analysis and understanding of population dynamics in relation to the social and historical changes of modern society, has also produced its own epistemological limitations and biases. In this sense, there is no doubt that the Demographic Transition approach is, among other things, also prey to the methodological nationalism embedded into the whole discourse of modernity.

In effect, the Demographic Transition approach was built on the basis of an abstract model of closed populations. This is expressed in that all the demographic transition models, have always referred to the combined analysis of birth and death dynamics, but the migratory processes have always been left out the analysis. Contrary to what the classical compensation equation says – one of the basic tenets in Demography – the migration flows have always been excluded from the demographic transition model, nevertheless being a fundamental component for the demographic reproduction of any population, especially at national and subnational levels.

The biases are evident in the fact that the first formulations on the demographic dynamics that gave birth to the demographic transition model (Landry, 1934, and Thompson, 1929), were fulfilled at the same moment in which, for several decades, millions of people emigrated from Europe to various countries of the new world, especially, the United States, Canada, Argentina and Australia.[6] The question remains why and how it was possible that this migratory phenomenon remained absent in the demographic transition models since then, when the impact on the population growth and reproduction dynamics was evident.

This critique is particularly important and relevant in the face of the increasing importance of international migration in a reproduction system

---

5   For a critical view of the demographic transition, see Patarra, 1973.
6   Tapinos and Delaunay (2000) point out, in this regard, that this migratory flow at the end of the nineteenth century and early twentieth century was, in relative terms, even more important and quantitatively larger than that of the present time.

configuration at a global scale. At present we are not only witnessing the end of the demographic transition as an historical process, but also to its obsolescence as an analysis model of population dynamics in modern society, at least in a double sense:
- On the one hand, there is no doubt that the demographic, social and structural changes that have been developing since the end of the twentieth century, inaugurate a new historical era that requires revisiting the very foundations on which, the demographic discourse in particular, and, the modern social sciences discourse in general, have been built.
- On the other hand, the population dynamics itself is opening to new issues, trends, and structures that radically break with the patterns that the demographic transition model had established. We refer to the emergence of new demographic processes, some of which are derived from the end of the first transition, but also from other dynamics that are typical and characteristics of the global and postmodern society. In the first one we can locate a tendency towards a demographic ageing, which raises a previously unimaginable transformation of population structures. In the second case we locate both the rise of a great new migratory wave at an international level, and the configuration of a second demographic transition.

There is no doubt then, that from the demographic transition approach, it would be impossible to progress towards a new model that analyses the reproduction of population and society in an era of globalization and modernity. In this regard, the thesis we support, differs. Although demographic dynamics of origin and destination countries (advanced societies and peripheral countries) are structurally heterogeneous and differentiated through international migration, they combine and complement each other, setting up a global system of demographic reproduction where each set of dynamics and particular population structure have a particular meaning and specific function.

Through migration, the demographic dynamics of the origin countries become relevant factors in the demographic development of the destination countries in such a way that in practice, they become endogenous factors of these dynamics. All this implies that the demographic structures of the hosting countries are becoming more open to the outside not only because the migratory flow contributes to its evolution, but also because, through emigration, the demographic dynamics of the origin countries have a direct impact on the internal dynamics of the recipient countries.

In the case of the destination countries, for example, immigration is not only a complement of natural population growth, but for most of these countries, it is an intrinsic part of its population reproduction system. This contribution is not limited to the population increase that immigration generates directly, but it is also necessary to consider the subsequent contribution made by immigrants and their descendants to the population's natural growth.[7] In the case of the origin countries, something similar happens, but in the opposite direction. Emigration is not only a proportion of its population, but also a way of moving to the outside, part of their population reproduction.

Thus, we find ourselves in the presence of a structural situation of demographic complementarity between sending and receiving countries. Following this line, we could also say that international migration has always played a role in the configuration of a global or international demographic reproduction system, although historically the current actors are not the same as those of the past. This would have happened, for example, in the migratory wave of the late nineteenth century and the beginning of the twentieth century. At the at time, a complementarity of the demographic surplus that the first stages of demographic transition generated in the framework of capitalist industrial development in several European countries displayed the need for extensive population contingents and labor force generated by the capitalist expansion and the incorporation of vast territories to its form of exploitation. This was the case in the United States, Argentina, Canada and Australia, mainly.[8]

In this sense, and viewed as a component of the population reproduction, contemporary international migration not only constitutes displacement, but, through it, different demographic reproductive processes are articulated in terms of their patterns, magnitudes, forms and space-time dimensions. It involves a global system of demographic reproduction that is based on this interrelationship between the population dynamics of origin regions with the dynamics in the destination countries.

This model of interrelations and complementarities is based on the demographic change that occurs in both the advanced societies as in the underdeveloped countries. It is a matter of a unique conjunctural configuration in history, combining on the one hand, the gaps and demographic shortcomings

---

7 The demographer Anna Cabré (1999) develops this thesis from the case of Catalonia, which during a century received immigrants from the rest of Spain and currently from other parts of the world. Based on her calculations the author concludes that, in the absence of such continuous immigration, the Catalan population would have been 2.4 million instead of the slightly more than 6 million that were recorded towards the end of the nineties of the past century.

8 In simpler terms: the population surplus of some regions, was the demographic base for the colonization and settlement of other regions. International migration, was the mechanism by which this complementarity operated at that time and it is the mechanism that still operates according to the current international demographic imbalances.

of the current reproduction regime in core countries, with the population surpluses that are currently generated in peripheral countries.

## 3   International Migration and Demographic Change in Sending and Receiving Societies

In view of the above, in this section we refer precisely to the processes of demographic changes that are currently evident both in societies of origin and destination. These are two population regimes completely different in their dynamics and trends as well as in their demographic structures, but nevertheless they show a high complementarity which becomes clear when analyzing the role of international migration in each of these demographic reproduction patterns.

In the case of the destination societies, it involves the conjunction of two different but complementary demographic processes: the ageing of the population and the advent of the Second Demographic Transition. As for the origin societies, this would be the configuration of a unique demographic juncture in history, which precedes the stage of ageing, and that is characterized by a large and systematic population increase in the active age, producing what has been called as demographic dividend. In this regard, our thesis is that international migration is a mechanism that enables the linking of both structures and demographic dynamics, generating a system of complementarity between them.

### 3.1   *Ageing Population and the End of Demographic Transition*

For more than two centuries in developed countries, the population dynamic was framed in what has been termed as Demographic Transition. In the last decades of the twentieth century, however, such a transition is nearing completion as they have arrived at a situation characterized by low and controlled population fertility and mortality levels. The direct consequence is that in these societies, along with the almost total brake on population growth, a substantial change would be taking place in the age structure and composition, in what has been termed as the population ageing (Teitelbaum and Winter, 1985).

The ageing population process, has been extensively treated in texts, political forums and academic seminars. In general, it is often pointed out that ageing corresponds to a demographic process that operates on three simultaneous and complementary levels: on the one hand, at an individual level as such, on the other, at a demographic aggregate level, i.e. the population as a whole, and finally, at the society level (Canales, 2001).

- At the individual level, the ageing corresponds to an extension of life expectancy per individual. This increased longevity enables not only the survival at older ages and acceptable health conditions, but also generates the creation of new stages in the individual life course. Consider, for example, the difference that implies a life span of 40 years in relation to another of 80 years. This supposes the appearance of new stages in the life course, in which specific and concrete demands and needs are stated.
- At the level of the whole population, the basis of ageing rests on the reduction of the fertility and birth levels, that at a medium-term turns into an age structure transformation, by means of reducing the specific weight of children and young people and increasing, on the other hand, the relative weight of adults and the older population. If at an individual level ageing supposes the appearance of a new phase in the life cycle, on the population scale, ageing is manifested in the emergence of a new demographic stratum, that is, a new social and demographic category with demands, needs, responsibilities and capabilities, characteristic of a specific population group and different from those that prevail among adults, young people or adolescents.[9]
- Finally, at the level of society, the ageing process is also manifested in a profound transformation of the previous intergenerational demographic balance (Lee, 2003). In this sense, the population ageing does not only refer to a change in the quantitative balance, but also in the social structure on which the intergenerational differentiation system is set up. Thus, the ageing is also reflected in a third level of analysis, which corresponds to society itself. In this context, there are those who even raise that it is society itself the one that is "ageing", in the sense that its extension, magnitude and intensity will cause substantive changes in the society model in which we will live in the near future (Rodríguez, 1994).

In summary, the *population ageing* is ultimately a result of the fact that most people survives up to old age. This is what has come to be called as "mass maturity" or "democratization of the old age" (Pérez, 2002), which would indicate that an advanced stage in the process of modernization was reached. The immediate consequence of this process is that the population age structure is modified.

---

9 In this sense, one of the problem in contemporary society, is that many of the cultural, social, economic and political categories of our society correspond to a growing young demographic structure with shorter life time horizons.

The age structure shows the proportion that the age and gender of individuals represent on the whole population and is graphically represented in the population pyramid. In fact, the name "pyramid" comes from the classic demographic regimes which took that typical geometric shape characterized by a wide base which is the result of high rates of fertility and birth, and a low and narrow peak, as a result of high levels of mortality. With the progressive population ageing, on the other hand, the age structure of the population begins to acquire an oval or ogival shape, characterized by a base in constant narrowing, derived from birth reduction and a top that simultaneously rises and widens, as a result of mortality reduction, and the increase in people's life expectancy.

For example, in countries like Germany, the population pyramid shows the narrowing of its base next to its peak broadening, thus reflecting the transition to an ageing population. In some cases, such as Germany and Italy, the process shows a greater advance compared to what it presents in Spain and the United States. In the first two cases, the median age is 45 years, while in the United States it is 41 years, and 40 years in Spain.

Likewise, the shape of the pyramids tells us how quickly this phenomenon has progressed. While in the European countries the decline of the child and juvenile population occurred in an accelerated way, in the United States has been somewhat more gradual. This is reflected in the shape of the base of the pyramid that in the case of European countries, shows a clear mismatch between the young and the child population with respect to the adult population. A mismatch that in the case of the United States is shown in a smoother way.

In any case, what matters is what this imbalance between the elderly and adult population shows about young people and children, clear evidence of progress in the process of population ageing in all countries, and how it has progressed in the past four decades.

In the case of Spain, for example, the proportion that the population aged 65 and above represents, has begun growing systematically since the seventies, from representing less than 10% of the whole population in 1970 to almost 17% in 2015. Also, the child population (under 15 years), shows the opposite tendency, going from almost 28% in 1970, to only 17% in 2015. In the United States, something similar happens. While older adults increase their participation, from 8% in the fifties, to 17% in 2016, the child population repeated Spain's behavior, going from almost 30% in the fifties, to about 16% in 2010.

In Germany and Italy, the same phenomenon occurs, although more intensely. In both cases, more than 22% of the population during the 1970s was younger than 15 years, and only 11% and 8% were over 65 years. At present, these relationships have been reversed, and in both cases only 13% of the

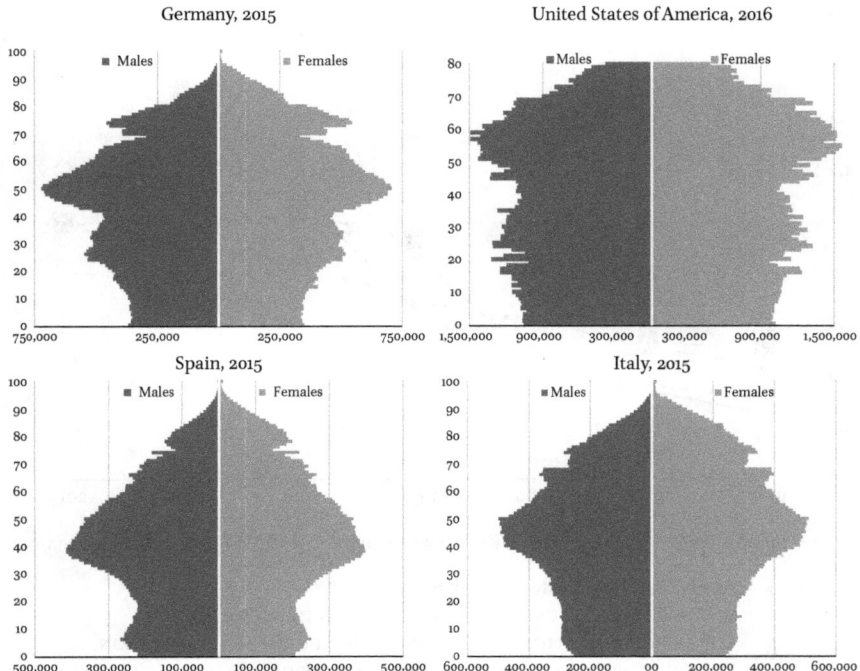

FIGURE 4    Population pyramid, selected receiving countries
SOURCES: US CENSUS BUREAU, CURRENT POPULATION SURVEY, ASEC 2016; EUROPEAN COMMISION, EUROSTAT, POPULATION DATA, HTTP://EC.EUROPA.EU/EUROSTAT/WEB/POPULATION-DEMOGRAPHY-MIGRATION-PROJECTIONS/POPULATION-DATA

population is less than 15 years old, while the elderly represent more than 21% of the population.

The combination of the two tendencies have virtually the same effect in all these countries and are expressed in the systematic growth of population ageing index. In the case of the United States, for example, it goes from a ratio of more than 3 children under the age of 15, for each adult of 65 years or more, in 1950, to practically a relation of parity between both age groups today. In the case of Spain, this change is more intense, because in less time, this relationship has not only reduced, but it has even been reversed. If in 1970 the child population exceeded those of the older adults in a ratio of nearly 3 to 1, at present it is the older population that exceeds the child one, by something more than 20 %, a tendency that is expected to continue increasing in the following decades.

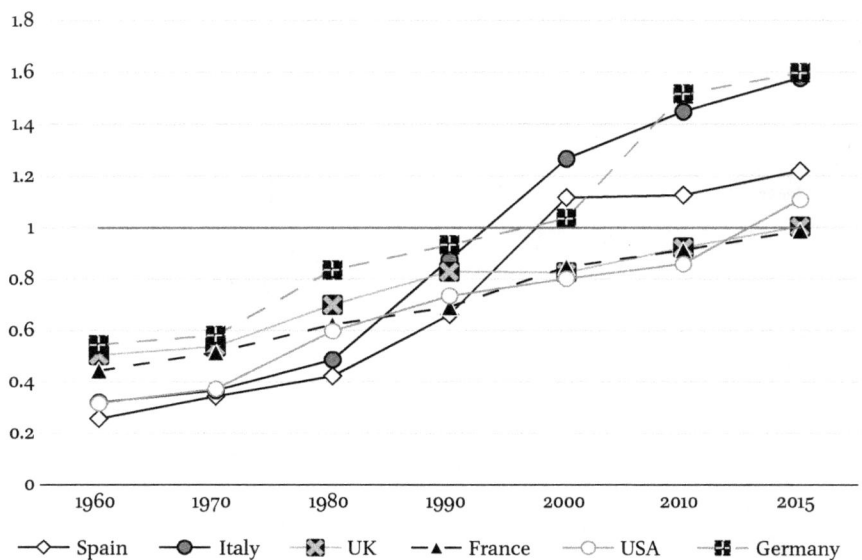

FIGURE 5   Ageing index in selected receiving countries
SOURCES: US CENSUS BUREAU, POPULATION CENSUS AND CURRENT POPULATION SURVEY, ASEC 2015; EUROPEAN COMMISION, EUROSTAT, POPULATION DATA, HTTP://EC.EUROPA.EU/EUROSTAT/WEB/POPULATION-DEMOGRAPHY-MIGRATION-PROJECTIONS/POPULATION-DATA

In Germany and Italy, This process is even more intense, reaching today a relationship of ageing where the elderly is nearly 60% higher than the population of children under 15 years[10]

In synthesis, the demographic ageing is a systematic process that, in the long term, manifests in the population age structure. Historically, its development starts with the modernization of the demographic dynamics, which involves the birth and death rates control. As such, the ageing process is the result of the Demographic Transition itself although it should not be interpreted, in a reductionist way, only as its final stage. In a broad sense, the demographic ageing might also be understood as a turning point in the demographic history of humanity.

– On the one hand, it indicates that the Demographic Transition would have been finally completed arriving to its final stage, with the advent of modern

---

10   In France and the United Kingdom, although aging is slower, it follows the same pattern as in Spain and the United States, currently reaching a peer relationship of older adults and children.

patterns of reproduction that are based on the efficient control of the population fertility and mortality levels.
– But on the other hand, it is also the initial stage of a new "transition", that is to say, of a new demographic regime, based not only on new population dynamics, but also on new social and cultural principles that define conditions and reinforce them. In this regard, we frame what has been termed as the Second Demographic Transition.

### 3.2  The Second Demographic Transition

It is a model proposed by van de Kaa (1987), to explain the demographic dynamics in European societies at the end of the twentieth century that would experience a continuous decline in fertility levels, reaching in some cases even below the levels that would ensure the demographic reproduction.[11]

Until the middle of the twentieth century, the developed countries would have completed their first demographic transition, which was basically to reach a demographic context with low mortality rates, high life expectancy and low fertility rates (Coale, 1973). However, in the last decades of the twentieth century, a new demographic transition model set in. Although in quantitative terms, it was to continue the decline in fertility and birth, this was now based on very different social principles. As van de Kaa (2002) put it, if the first transition could be classified as altruistic, the second one undoubtedly has to be catalogued as individualistic. Likewise, while the first demographic transition is associated with the nineteenth century and the first half of the twentieth century modernization of European societies, this second demographic transition is associated more with the advent, in those same countries, of a postmodern and global society. This is a situation that re-defines the

---

11   In Demography, population fertility and reproduction are measured based on the women reproductive behavior, and not on men, then it is said that a population reaches its reproduction level, when each woman at the end of her reproductive life has given birth to at least one girl, this is, to have reproduced herself as a woman. This situation is measured through the Gross Reproduction Rate (GRR), which is defined as the average number of daughters that a woman (or a group of women) would have during their lives if they are adjusted to the age-specific fertility rates for specific years during their reproductive period (Leguina, 1981, Livi Bacci, 1993). When the GRR is equal to 1, it is said that the population would have achieved this level of demographic reproduction. Rates less than the unity, would indicate that the fertility levels are not sufficient to ensure the population reproduction, and inversely, levels superior to 1, would indicate the opposite. Since in human populations the constant is when proportionately are born more boys than girls (to a total of 105 boys for every 100 girls), for the reproduction gross rate to be equal to 1, it is required that the global fertility rate is equal to 2.05, approximately.

system of values and population behaviors in what Bauman (2000) refers to as liquid societies.

In effect, in the first demographic transition, the tendency towards a fall in fertility was sustained in a concern for the descent in the family, and led to a family strengthening as a social institution (Aries, 1980). In the second demographic transition, on the other hand, the decline in fertility is based on a tendency towards the individuation of the social and family processes particularly, (van de Kaa, 1987). In this way, the second demographic transition involves a virtual weakening of the family as an institution, and a strengthening of the individual, their rights and their fulfilment at various levels of the social, economic, political and cultural life, which transcend the traditional and strong family circles.

The causes of these changes in the demographic and, in particular, reproductive behavior, lie in the individuation process that has prevailed in these post-materialist and post-modern societies. In fact, in opposite of traditional family values of industrial capitalism (transcendence through the offspring, the children and the family, for example), in contemporary and postmodern societies (Europe and America), tend to predominate the values of personal fulfilment, freedom and individual autonomy. Beck and Beck (2002) point out the female emancipation as an important component of this individuation process, which has resulted in the promotion of a context with greater gender equity, opening various spaces for women's participation in public, labor, social and educational life, as well as in the re-composition of gender roles within private spaces of the home, family and daily life.

There are two types of demographic consequences of this phenomenon. One involves a change in the composition and dynamics of households and families, and the other, a continuous decline in birth and fertility levels. In the first case, the traditional nuclear family model, has become outdated, imposing instead a variety and diversity of family patterns and couple unions which also have an evolution and change of great dynamism. In the face of the decline of traditional nuclear families, prevails the increase of people who live alone, as well as single-parent households, reunited families and traditional households. The divorce and cohabitation rate has also increased, and the rate of marriage has reduced (Herrera, 2007).

In the second case, both Europe and the United States experience a steady decline in birth and fertility. In Europe, the crude birth rate fell from 19 births per thousand inhabitants in 1960 to 12.4 in 1990 and 10 in 2015. Also in the United States birth rate fell from 24 births per thousand inhabitants in 1960 to 16 in 1990 and only 12 today. This reduction in crude birth rates is mainly explained by the decline in the total fertility rate of women in both cases.

MIGRATION AND GLOBAL DEMOGRAPHIC SYSTEM            115

In this regard, the data for the Germany, Italy, Spain and the United States are clearly illustrative. On the one hand, all of these countries go from a global fertility rate superior to the 2.5 children per woman in 1960, to levels that are below the replacement level in 1990. A tendency that keeps downward, reaching currently a level lower than the 1.76 children per woman in the case of the United States, and less than 1.5 children per woman in the case of Germany, Italy and Spain.

These decline in birth and fertility rates owes not so much to the impact of the use of modern methods of contraception (which are already widespread throughout the population), as to social factors that have changed the behavior and attitude in relation to having children and descent, and that is made manifest in a greater delay in the age to the first son, but above all, in the increased number of mothers with one child or couples and women who do not wish to have children (Bongaarts, 2001).

It should be noted that the second demographic transition is expressed not only in this decline in general fertility, but also and particularly, in the reproductive behavior by mother's ages. In this regard, the data for Spain and the United States are equally eloquent. By 1970, in both cases, a pattern of early fertility prevailed, this is where the highest fertility rate was among young women

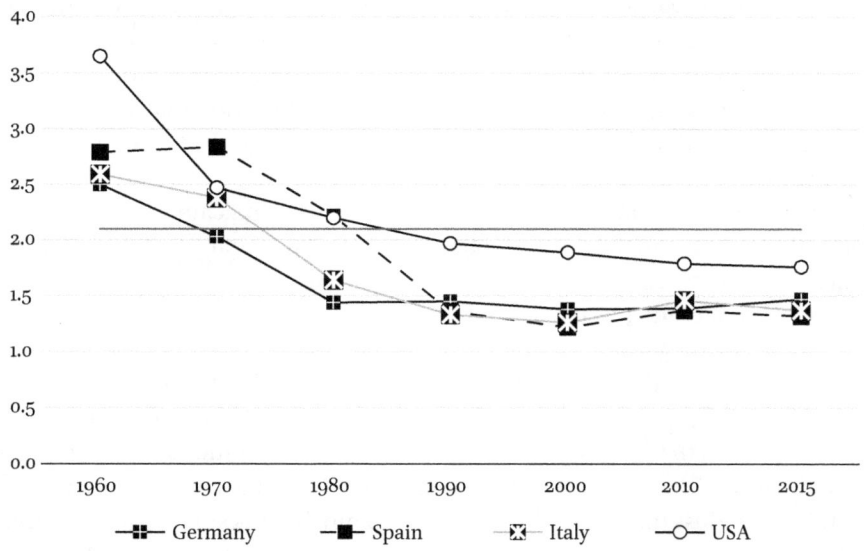

FIGURE 6     Total fertility rate, selected receiving countries
             SOURCES: MARTIN, ET AL., 2017; AND EUROPEAN COMMISION,
             EUROSTAT, POPULATION DATA, HTTP://EC.EUROPA.EU/EUROSTAT/WEB/
             POPULATION-DEMOGRAPHY-MIGRATION-PROJECTIONS/POPULATION-DATA

aged 20 to 24. However, currently the highest fertility rate is given among women aged 30 to 34, in the case of Spain, and of 25 to 34 years in the case of the United States. This delay in fertility reflects the individuation processes, which in the case of women has involved a radical change, especially in terms of the greater importance the personal fulfilment acquires (study, work and leisure) over the traditional values of motherhood and family.

This would explain this dual process of, on the one hand, reducing the number of children and, at the same time, delaying their birth, from early stages of life cycle, to intermediate stages, getting ahead instead, the completion of studies, the insertion into the labor market, and other behaviors that strengthen their participation and integration in society as independent individuals (Herrera, 2007).

### 3.3 The Demographic Dividend: Dynamics of Population in Origin Countries

In the case of the origin countries, especially in Latin America, we are witnessing the last stage of the demographic transition, prior to the population ageing (Guzman, 2002). In this sense, the current times correspond to a particular historical period, which is unlikely to be repeated in the future. Since the end of the last century and in the coming decades, the demographic dynamics in the peripheral countries will be crossed by various structural tendencies which arise from the conjunction of different demographic transition stages. On the one hand, the resulting from the culmination of the mortality transition, and on the other hand, those arising from the fertility transition that would be in its final stage, and that will tend to impose new patterns in the demographic dynamics.

In the case of Latin America, for example, the data indicates that we would already be in the final stage of the Demographic Transition. On the one hand, already in the seventies the mortality transition would have completed, reaching by then a crude mortality rate below the 10 deaths per thousand inhabitants, and reaching its lowest point at the beginning of the last decade with less than 6 deaths per thousand inhabitants. Since then, a slight increase in deaths began resulting from the change in the age structure of the population.

For its part, the crude birth rate has maintained a continuous decline since the fifties and sixties, going from a level above the 42 births per thousand inhabitants, to less than 20 births per thousand inhabitants at present. Likewise, although it is estimated that this decline will continue in the coming decades, it would be more gradually. Undoubtedly, the basis of this crude birth rate behavior, is the continued decline in the total fertility rate, which would have passed from almost 6 children per woman in the fifties and sixties, to only 2.2

children per woman at present, a tendency that if maintained, very soon will imply reaching the demographic replacement level.[12]

These tendencies of the demographic change components involve major changes in the population age composition. Indeed, on the basis of most recent estimates and demographic projections that CELADE, Population Division of ECLAC has made,[13] we can observe that the population, according to large age groups, presents three different tendencies that will alter the demographic dependence relations, balance and intergenerational exchanges.

- On the one hand, the children population (under 15), has already reached its peak in the year 2005, with a volume of 165 million of boys and girls. Since then, a continued and sustained process of reduction has initiated to achieve in 2050 a similar volume to the one it had by 1975.
- On the other hand, the elderly population (65 years or more) shows the opposite tendency, that is to say, of continued and sustained increase which will be maintained throughout all this century. In fact, the population that in 2050 will be over 65 years has already been born, and are the ones that currently are over 35 years which were born in a historical context where high fertility and birth rates were still common. In other words, the fertility drop, that would explain the absolute and relative volume reduction of child population, will take, however, almost a century to be reflected in an absolute decline of the older population. In this way, the absolute increase of elderly persons is a structural trend that will define the nature of the demographic dependence relationship in all this century.
- Finally, the working age population (15 to 64 years) presents a peculiar trend. In the coming decades it is expected to sustain its current level of absolute and relative growth. A tendency that will only be reverted from the second half of this century. In fact, estimates indicate that the working age population would reach its maximum volume in the five-year period from 2040–2045, and only since then it would begin a continuous and sustained decline throughout the following decades. This is due to the fact that, again, the fertility reduction effect will take time in manifesting as a result of demographic inertia we have already discussed. In other words, the effects of high fertility and large number of births took place between the decades of the fifties and eighties of the last century and maintained until the middle of this century, moment in which a fertility reduction, started in the

---

12  Estimates based on data taken from Cepalstat, database and statistical publications. ECLAC, http://estadisticas.cepal.org/cepalstat/WEB_CEPALSTAT/Portada.asp.
13  Estimates based on data taken from Cepalstat, database and statistical publications. ECLAC, http://estadisticas.cepal.org/cepalstat/WEB_CEPALSTAT/Portada.asp.

seventies of the last century, became evident on the volume of the working age population.

This peculiar trend of the population age structure is the basis of a unique situation in terms of relations of dependence, which starts in the eighties and will be maintained until the twenties of this century. In fact, until the seventies the high crude birth rate and infant mortality reduction caused an increase in the dependency relationships, as a result of the increasing absolute and relative weight of the child population. The Dependency Ratio[14] reaches its maximum value in 1970, when the population in inactive ages accounts for nearly 90% of the working age population. Since then, the general relation of dependence starts a downward trend that will continue until 2020 approximately.

This demographic tendencies combination causes a single historic juncture. During the first fifty years of this century the demographic dependence levels will be low. This means that the burden the inactive population represents will be far lower compared to those of other historical junctures. That is why this peculiar situation has been called *Demographic Bonus* or *Demographic Dividend*, since it wants to emphasize the favorable situation, in terms of relationships of dependence and economic burden that this reduction of inactive

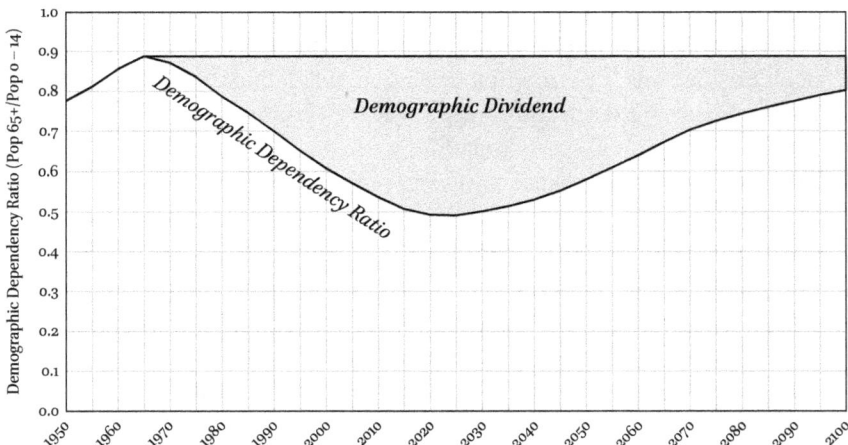

FIGURE 7   Latin America, 1950–2100. Demographic Dependency Ratio and Demographic Dividend
SOURCES: ECLAC, CEPALSTAT. HTTP://ESTADISTICAS.CEPAL.ORG/CEPALSTAT/WEB_CEPALSTAT/PORTADA.ASP

---

14   The Dependency Ratio is defined as the quotient between the population in inactive age (0 to 14 years and more than 64 years) with regard to the Active Population (15 to 64 years).

population implies (Brenes Camacho, 2009; Redondo and Garay, 2012). Never before, and perhaps never after, a demographic situation like this one, in which the economic burden that the inactive population represents is so low will be presented. Therefore, it is a unique opportunity in terms of the full use of the productive forces that demography would be generating.[15]

## 4  Demographic Change and Migration: Towards a Global Model of Population Reproduction

These demographic trends existing in both the origin and destination countries, shape a particular stage in the demographic history characterized by a high complementary of population dynamics and structures. In this context, our thesis is that international migration is a process that in the same way that helps linking and articulating these structures and complementary dynamics, also constitutes the demographic base for the setting up of a global system of the population reproduction. Let's take a look at this in more detail.

In the first place, in the case of the developed countries, both the second demographic transition as the population ageing process, constitute a peculiar demographic situation characterized by an unfavorable relation of demographic dependence. Both the increase in absolute terms of the third age population (which in some cases already reaches 20% of the total population), as for the fertility decline, that has reduced the number of children, already manifests itself in a continuous and systematic population deficit in active and reproductive ages resulting in a situation of high demographic instability at least in two directions, namely:

– On the one hand, to the reduction of the native population fertility levels (in some cases, even below the demographic reproduction level), the absolute reduction of population in reproductive age could be added, resulting in a decline of the crude birth rate which compromises the natural reproduction of the native population.
– On the other hand, the population deficit in active age, also compromises the economic reproduction capacity of the population, to the extent that the labor force tends to be reduced, especially in young ages under 50 (Cooke, 2003).

---

15  However, we must not forget that, in the Latin American case at least, we are almost in the middle of this demographic change process and its effects have not been noted so far. The fact is that even though this is a demographic opportunity, its realization requires social and economic conditions and, above all, favorable policies.

In this context, international migration, and in particular, its massive proportion (such as Latin American migration to the United States and Spain, for example) contributes precisely to fill this age-active population gap, that is generated both by the fertility reduction, as by the ageing population in developed countries (Domingo i Valls, 2006).

In the case of the United States, for example, between 2000 and 2013 the child population under the age of 15, grew by 780 thousand children approximately. However, by differentiating the growth according to ethnic and migratory origin, it is found that it is directly based on the Latino population. In effect, while the white non-Latino child population in those years dropped by 5.6 million children, which represents a decline rate of the order of 1% annual average, the child population of Latino origin grew at an average rate of 3.5 percent annually, which represented an absolute increase of nearly 4.5 million children.

Similar tendency occurs in the case of the 15 to 49 years population, which corresponds to the full productive and reproductive age's population that is the bulk of the working age population and people living in conditions of demographic reproduction. In this age group, there is a total increase of 5.5 million people. However, once more, by disaggregating this growth according to the ethnicity and migration of the population, it is noted that while the non-Latino whites natives were reduced by 6.1 million people, the Latino population increased by 7.7 million people. The difference is given by the immigrant population coming from other countries, mainly Africa and Asia, as well as other ethnic minorities.[16]

Also, in the case of Spain, the situation is almost the same.[17] Between 2000 and 2013, the population in this country increased by 6.63 million people, of which only 22% corresponded to people born in Spain, and the 78% to immigrants from abroad.[18] In the case of the population from 15 to 49 years of age, we have the United States situation reproduced. While those born in Spain

---

16 Calculations based on information from the March supplement of the United States Current Population Survey for the respective years.
17 In the case of Spain there are no statistics to estimate the population volume according to the origin of parents. This prevents us from estimating the volume of the child population that having been born in Spain is the daughter of immigrants. In the case of the over 15 years population, this problem is corrected in part because there are available statistics by country of birth, making possible to identify the immigrants volume by both age and sex.
18 It should be noted that in Spain, only 25% of the immigrants come from European Union countries, except Romania, while the rest comes mainly from Latin American countries (30%), Africa (17%), Asia (7%) and Romania (16%). Author's calculations based on INE, Statistics of the Continuous Register as of January 1 of 2013, Spain http://www.ine.es/inebmenu/mnu_padron.htm.

were reduced by 1.95 million people, the international immigrants in those ages increased by 3.74 million people.

These data illustrate how in the United States, Spain, and in a similar manner in other developed countries of Europe, immigration from peripheral countries clearly contributes to fill the gap left by the current dynamics of their populations. This is a shortage of people, particularly in active and reproductive ages, which to the extent that it is maintained over time, and nothing seems to indicate the opposite, it could lead to a virtual demographic replacement of the native population by immigrant population and their descendants (United Nations, 2001).

Here there are two tendencies that combine and enhance this process.
– On the one hand, the decline in the fertility rate of the native population, coupled with the ageing of this population, leads to a systematic reduction of its birth. Along with reducing the average number of children that each native women has, it is also reducing the female population base at reproductive age.
– On the other hand, the immigrant origin population presents the opposite dynamics. They consistently show a higher fertility, and they also show a continuous increase in the population at reproductive ages.

The effect of both behaviors is directly reflected in the descents and births that this migrant population generates, something that we can directly observe in the case of the United States. Between 2000 and 2010, an average of around 4 million births each year were generated. Of these, only half, approximately, corresponded to babies born from non-Latino white mothers (which nevertheless represented more than two-thirds of women in reproductive age). On the contrary, 25% of the births corresponded to babies born from Latino origin mothers, while the other 25%, to mothers from other ethnic and migratory origins (African, American, Asian, aboriginal people, and immigrants from other regions of the world) (Martin, et al., 2017).

That is to say, at present in the United States, only half of the new Americans correspond to children of the current demographic white majority, while the other half corresponds to children from various ethnic and migrant minorities. Among these, the case of the Latin origin population is emphasized, which, by itself, contributes with one of every four new American children by birth. We can directly observe at the base of the age pyramid, the effect of this reproductive behavior on the ethnic composition of that country population along with the reduction of the native infantile population, and the increase in that of migrant origin, which will make this demographic replacement process intensify in the coming decades, when expanding to other age groups.

With regard to the other part of the binomial, this is what happens in the countries of origin. Migration also plays an essential role as a population control mechanism, by helping to reduce the demographic pressure on the economy and local labor markets. As we have pointed out, in the countries of origin, especially in Latin America, we are witnessing the last stage of the Demographic Transition, prior to the ageing of its population. In this phase, there is an absolute and relative volume reduction of the child population, as well as an absolute and relative increase of the active population. Likewise, the older population, even when growing in absolute terms, is maintained in low demographic amounts. This difference in the demographic dynamics of each age group is expressed in a significant reduction of the demographic dependency ratio, this is, in the relationship between population in active and inactive age.

For quite some years and in the coming decades, the burden of the inactive population will be much lower in relation to that of other historical junctures. This peculiar situation has been called *Demographic Dividend*, because it wants to emphasize the favorable situation, in terms of dependence relations and economic burden implied in this reduction of inactive population. In this context, international migration constitutes a way to export this demographic dividend towards the First World countries, which also undertake a particular juncture of young and active population deficit.

In the case of the Latin American countries, for example, it is estimated that between 2000 and 2010, the active population (15 to 64 years), would have increased in 60 million people, approximately. Of them, however, it is

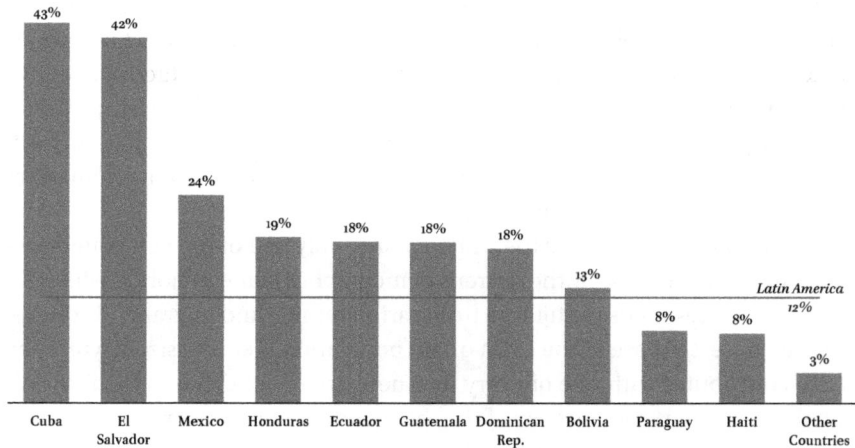

FIGURE 8  Latin America, 2000–2010. Export of Demographic Bonus by country of origin migration rate of working age population (%)
SOURCES: US CENSUS BUREAU, CURRENT POPULATION SURVEY, MARCH SUPPLEMENT, 2000 AND 2010; SPAIN, INE, ACTIVE POPULATION SURVEY, 2000 AND 2010; AND CEPALSTAT, HTTP://ESTADISTICAS.CEPAL.ORG/CEPALSTAT/WEB_CEPALSTAT/PORTADA.ASP

estimated that 5.4 million emigrated to the United States, at the same time that another 2.0 million emigrated to Spain, main destinations of Latin American emigration. In other words, in only 10 years, slightly more than 12% of the demographic dividend generated by the population dynamics in the region would have been expelled (Canales, 2011).

But this is a regional average, the situation is even more serious in the case of those countries with higher emigration. In the case of Mexico, for example, it is estimated that the loss of this demographic dividend, will reach 24% in that decade, i.e., in these years Mexico has lost almost a quarter of the growth of its population in active ages. A similar situation would happen in Honduras, Ecuador, Guatemala and the Dominican Republic, where emigration would represent something more than 18% of the population growth in active age. The extreme cases are those in El Salvador and Cuba, where it is estimated that more than 40% of their demographic dividend has emigrated to the United States and to a lesser extent to Spain.

These data and analysis presented here, support the thesis that through international migration, a global system of demographic reproduction, based on the articulation and connection of these different local and national population dynamics is set up. Although it is a question of demographic dynamics locally placed, through international migration they acquire a global sense and meaning that transcends their national borders. In effect, through migration, the transfer of part of this *demographic dividend* coming from peripheral countries is promoted, which contributes in turn, to solve the active population deficit generated by the population ageing in developed countries. Finally, this is about the configuration, at a global level, of a demographic complementarity system, which allow to support the population reproduction, both in destination and origin countries of migration. The following diagram allows us to illustrate these relationships.

In the first place, the demographic change in developed countries is radically transforming its population age structure, creating a gap or population deficit in active and reproductive ages, which if it is not adequately covered, can lead to serious demographic instability problems in these societies.

For its part, in the origin countries a converse situation has been observed. Here, the demographic change is aligned with earlier stages of the first demographic transition, which is generating an active population surplus which the economic dynamics of these countries is not capable of absorbing. This is what in literature is called the demographic dividend.

These tendencies constitute an international context of demographic imbalances. In this context, it should be noted the role of international migration as a mechanism that allows to link these different and complementary population dynamics.

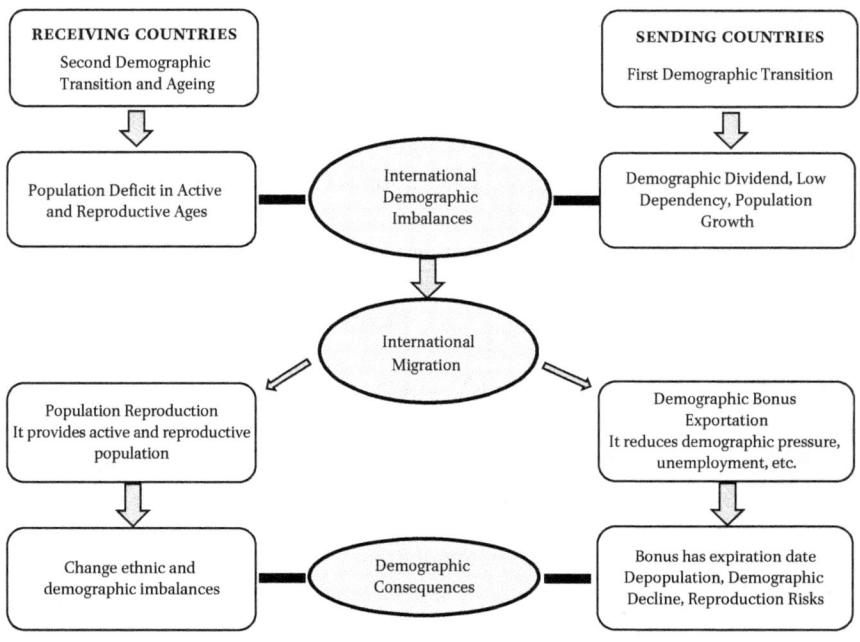

FIGURE 9   International migration and global regime of demographic reproduction

In this context, international migration has emerged as a process which at the same time is helping to unlock, in part, these demographic imbalances and, in that same process, it contributes to the reproduction of the population, both in the places of origin and destination. In one case, supplying the necessary active population to cover the deficit in the developed countries, and on the other hand, constituting a form of exporting the demographic dividend from the countries of origin thus contributing to reduce the demographic pressure on the economy and labor markets.

## 5     Migration and Demographic Change: the Contradictions of the Model

Although it is a demographic system that displays an important carrying capacity, it is not exempt from tensions and conflicts that sooner or later, could cause a lack of viability generating an instability framework with unsuspected demographic consequences, both in the origin and destination countries.

In the case of the countries of origin, there is no doubt that in the short term, the massive character of emigration has helped to reduce the pressure that the *demographic dividend* generates on the economy and labor markets.

However, in the medium and long term when this demographic bubble, generated by the active population growth, tends to deflate, the effect may be counterproductive and seriously affect the demographic conditions of population reproduction, and by this means, reproduction of society itself.

In effect, as any dividend, the demographic one has also an expiration date which can vary in each country, but that undoubtedly will expire in the coming decades. In this regard, the data indicates that this situation is very close, and in some countries this would already be happening. In the case of Latin America, estimates based on CELADE[19] indicate that the working-age population growth would have reached its maximum in the nineties, when it grew at a rate of 3.1 million people a year. This would initiate a rapid and sustained decline from then on in such a way that by 2040 growth will not only slow down completely, but will initiate an absolute reverse decline cycle of active population, the same one that would imply a net loss of nearly 2 million people a year.

This tendency in the growth and subsequent reduction of the population in active and reproductive ages of Latin America has a double effect
- On the one hand, it implies that the demographic dividend could no longer operate as a mitigation framework of the mass emigration demographic effects, directly affecting the population evolution and growth. Such is the

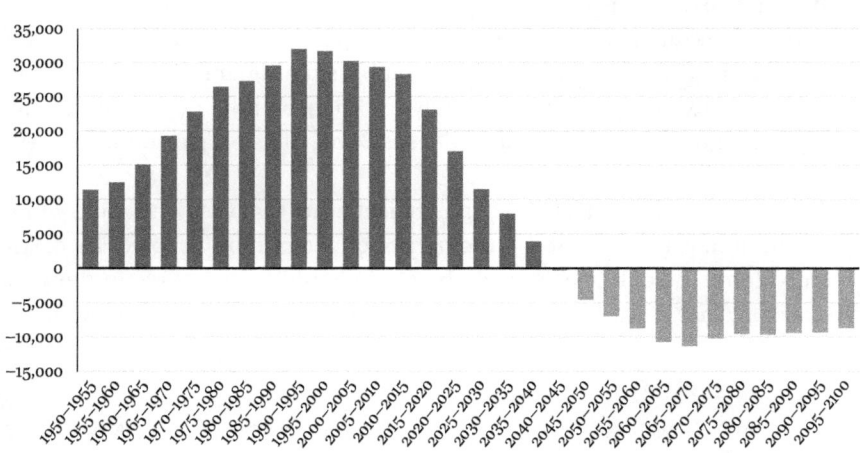

FIGURE 10  Latin America, 1950–2100. Working age population growth (thousands)
SOURCES: ECLAC, CEPALSTAT, HTTP://ESTADISTICAS.CEPAL.ORG/CEPALSTAT/WEB_CEPALSTAT/PORTADA.ASP

---

19  CELADE, Population Division of ECLAC, CEPALSTAT, *Databases and Statistical Publications*, http://estadisticas.cepal.org/cepalstat/WEB_CEPALSTAT/Portada.asp.

case of Mexico where, according to the most recent population demographic projections of CONAPO,[20] it is estimated that in the 2020–2025 period the emigration to the United States would exceed the active population growth, thereby bringing forward the times in which this growth bubble, generated by demographic dividend, finishes. This is a highly complicated situation, since it would begin a cycle where the emigration would no longer be only an escape valve of a surplus population, but would become an absolute and net loss mechanism of active population.

- On the other hand, the reduction of working-age population result in the medium-term in a birth reduction to which, if we add the fertility reduction already being experienced in Latin America, then we would be in a situation in which is compromised the reproductive capacity of the demographic population and society itself. This is the case of Cuba, for example, which is one of the countries in the region to progress most in demographic transition and where the total fertility rate during the past two decades has been below the minimum level to ensure the reproduction of demographic population.[21] Also, in the case of Mexico, the National Population Council (CONAPO) estimates that by the forties of this century, the loss by emigration to the United States, could perfectly represent almost half of the country's population natural growth.

In the case of destination countries, the most important consequence perhaps could be the change in the population ethnic and migratory composition which could result in a virtual demographic replacement of native population by immigrants. This is a complex demographic situation on which various hypotheses are expressed, as evidenced by the change in the population ethnic composition that the United States Census Bureau has projected for the next five decades.[22]

In this regard, the first data to highlight is the fact that the non-Latino white population never would exceed the barrier of 200 million people. The maximum volume it would reach would be of 199.6 million of people in the year 2024. From that point forward, a trend of demographic decline would begin

---

20  CONAPO, Population Projections 2010–2050. National Population Council, Mexico. http://www.conapo.gob.mx/es/CONAPO/Proyecciones.

21  Already in the eighties, the total fertility rate in Cuba fell to only 1.85 children per woman, and has continued to fall, reaching currently only 1.5 children per woman. (Data taken from CEPALSTAT, ECLAC portal of statistical information for Latin America and the Caribbean, http://estadisticas.cepal.org/cepalstat/WEB_CEPALSTAT/Portada.asp).

22  The results of the projections, as its methodology, can be viewed on the following link: http://www.census.gov/population/projections/data/national/2012.html.

and would reach in 2060, less than 180 million people. This is less than the volume that this same ethnic group already had in 1980.

On the contrary, the Latino origin population will tend to experience the opposite trend. In this regard, it is projected that by the year 2044 the mark will reach 100 million, to continue growing to reach a volume of nearly 130 million people in 2060, a figure that would represent 31% of the total population. In this way, if currently the difference regarding demographic volumes between the Latino population and non-Latino whites, is nearly 150 million, obviously in favor of the latter, the trends projected by the census Bureau indicate that this difference will be reduced to only 50 million people by 2060.

Undoubtedly, it is a question of trends and relationships that lead us to rethink the traditional ethnic and demographic balance in the United States population. Meanwhile, a first relevant data is that, from the year 2043, the white population would cease to be a demographic absolute majority, to reach only 43% in 2060.[23]

This transformation in the United States population ethnic composition is even more clearly illustrated if analyzed according the population age strata. As can be seen in the below graph, according to the Census Bureau projections, it would go from a current situation, where the primacy of the

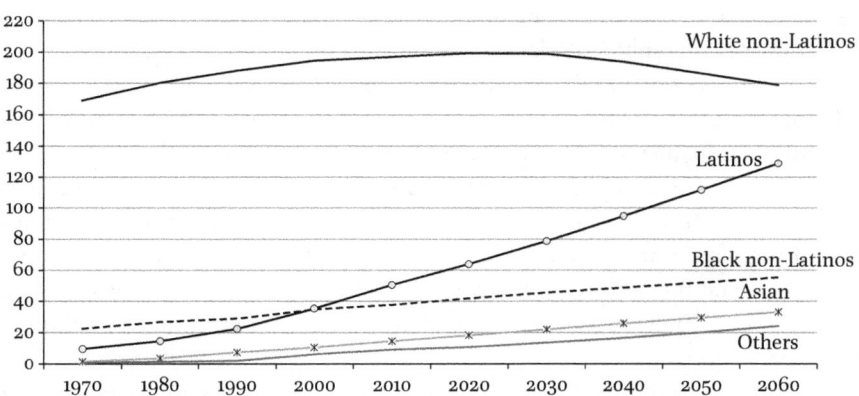

FIGURE 11   USA, 1970–2060. Population by ethnic origin (millions of people)
SOURCES: HOBBS AND STOOPS, 2002; US POPULATION CENSUS 2000 & 2010; AND US. CENSUS BUREAU. 2014 NATIONAL POPULATION PROJECTIONS

---

23   Coleman (2006 and 2009) shows similar trends in several European countries, a process which he conceptualized as the Third Demographic Transition. For more details on this thesis, see Canales 2015.

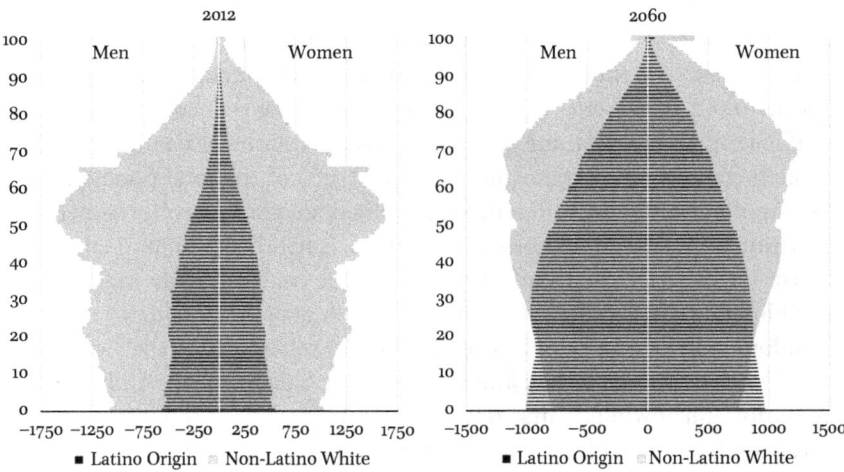

FIGURE 12   USA, 2012 and 2060. Population pyramid, whites and Latino population
SOURCE: US CENSUS BUREAU, *2014 NATIONAL POPULATION PROJECTIONS*

white population is virtually indisputable in all age groups, to a situation in the year 2060 where the white population would stop being the main ethnic group in the early ages, simultaneously that it would share its primacy in intermediate ages, and only retain its majority position in adult ages and older adults.

These demographic trends would indicate a peculiar dynamic in the ethnic composition of the population pyramid of the United States population. While the pyramid base (child and adolescent population) will tend to be predominantly Latino, at the peak (adults and older adults) the predominance will tend to continue being of non-Latino white population. Now, the key issue in this particular ethnic composition in an age pyramid is that while the predominant population in the top in fact corresponds to groups that are in the final stages of their life cycle, the ones which are located at the base of the pyramid, on the other hand, are those who will shape the thickness of the population in the near future.

Based on this observation we can say that we are witnessing a situation of ethnic-demographic replacement. In effect, by 2060, the projections from the Census Bureau estimated that among those younger than 40, the volume of Latinos would exceed the whites. On this date, the Latino population younger than 40 would be estimated at 73.5 millions of people, overcoming the 72.4 million, which would correspond to the non-Latino white population.

This would indicate that unless there was a reproductive revolution intervention that promoted the crude birth rate of the non-Latino white population, Latino supremacy would include the whole population under 80 by the end of the century, thus configuring the first demographic majority in that country. In this way, the replacement of whites by Latinos as the main ethnic and demographic group of the United States population, might well be a real demographic trend and not just a metaphor within a political and ideological discourse.

This situation, which could be taken as a script for a science fiction movie, is a reality that is experienced in several states of the American Union. Such is the case of California, Texas, Florida, New Mexico, Arizona and Nevada. In these states, until 1970 they followed the classical pattern of a large white majority vs. small ethnic minorities. In 1970 the white population accounted for more than 75% of the population, while Latinos accounted for only 11.5% of the population.

Today, however, this situation has changed radically. According to data from the American Community Survey 2015, whites are no longer the demographic majority, accounting for only 44.4% of the population, while the Latino population increased its stake to 35.2% far exceeding the other ethnic minorities. These data indicate that in these states, the trend that the Census Bureau is projecting for a few decades for all the United States is already foreshadowing.

The population pyramid shows the extent of these changes in the ethnic composition of the population. As can be seen, while the white population maintains its majority position in age groups over 40 years, Latinos are already a large majority in the younger groups, under 25 years of age. In the middle ages, there is an equal situation between whites and Latinos.

What is relevant is that while Latinos are the majority in the young groups, the whites are in the oldest, that is, they are already out of the population structure. This differentiated structure of the population pyramid of whites and Latinos, foreshadows that in the near future Latinos become the first demographic minority in virtually all age groups, relegating the white population to a second place. These data illustrate that we are in the presence not only of a demographic change, but of a true *ethnic replacement*, which will expand throughout the United States in the following decades, as it has already occurred in these states in the last four decades. In this sense, the current situation in California foreshadows the social and demographic future that is foreseen for the rest of the country (Hayes-Bautista, 2017).

## 6 Conclusion: Dilemmas and Contradictions of a Model

From the Demography point of view, migration is one of the population dynamics components, contributing not only to its growth, but also to the reproduction and transformation of its fundamental structures. This contribution can be analyzed in complementary ways.
– On the one hand, in the short term, they contribute directly when conforming a demographic contingent that either is added to the population (immigrants) or separated from it (emigrants). In both cases, its contribution is central to determine the growth dynamics and volumes evolution of the society population.
– On the other hand, in the medium and long term, they contribute, in addition, to the configuration and transformation of the fundamental demographic structures (age, sex, ethnicity, among others). It is a question of contributing through their offspring, which in many cases, has allowed the reproduction and population growth far beyond that which would have been achieved in the absence of the migratory flows (Cabré 1999).

This is what happened in the first major migratory wave of the modern society at the end of the nineteenth century and beginning of the twentieth century, as also happens at present with the resurgence of international migratory flows. What is relevant in any case, is that today international migration is not only a central component of the population dynamics, both in the societies of origin and destination, but that through this same process it contributes to make up a global system of population reproduction, articulating and integrating in a same dynamics the demographic reproduction patterns of the origin and destination places (Canales, 2015).

The population surplus that the demographic dividend generates in the countries of origin, is the other side of the demographic deficit generated in the destination countries attributable to population ageing and the advent of the so-called second demographic transition. In this context, international migration articulates both demographic dynamics, thereby contributing to the configuration of a regime or global system of population reproduction.

Now, what is relevant in this thesis is that contemporary migrations not only would be part of the population reproduction in the origin and destination societies, but also, through the same process, constitutes a factor that contributes to the contemporary society reproduction and transformation.

Undoubtedly, migration is not the only, nor probably the most important factor of social change. However, we have no doubts that it is a social phenomenon that also participates and contributes to the configuration of the dilemmas and contradictions of today's society, which lead to its necessary

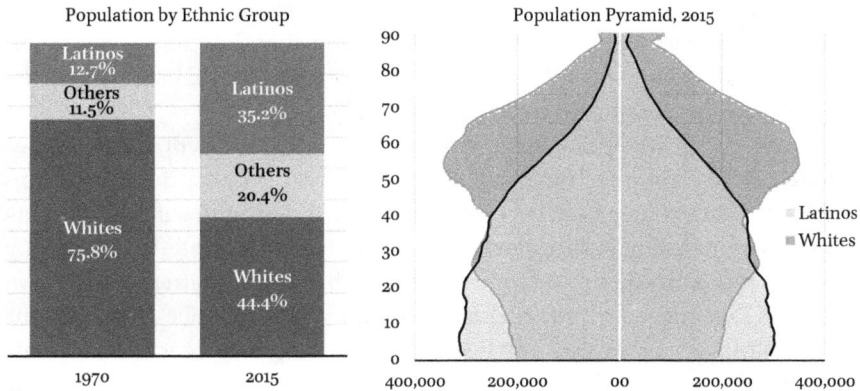

FIGURE 13  Arizona, California, Florida, Nevada, New Mexico and Texas. Population by ethnic groups, and population pyramid
SOURCES: CAMPBELL AND JUNG, 2002; AND AMERICAN COMMUNITY SURVEY, 2015

movement and transformation. This is especially true in the case of destination societies. Let's take a look at this in more detail.

Contemporary society faces many dilemmas and tensions. One of them that is of particular interest to our discussion, is the challenge posed by the current demographic change in advanced societies. These are societies with low fertility rates and in a process of changing its population age composition. This is an expression of both the second demographic transition, as the population ageing. As we have seen, this is not any change, but one that directly affects the local demography capacity to generate the necessary contingents and labor force to support its demographic reproduction.

In this demographic context, the populating immigration in active and reproductive ages, especially from peripheral countries, is an attractive option for those advanced societies. On the one hand, they provide the necessary population to maintain the levels of demographic reproduction, and on the other hand, they provide the necessary labor force, both to activities directly productive (construction, traditional industry, etc.), as in reproduction occupations (domestic service, health care industry, food preparation, cleaning and maintenance, etc.). Also, they provide relatively cheap labor, to the extent that part of its economic reproduction is based on the same social and family networks that these migrants weave between their communities of origin and their destination places settlements (Canales, 2013).

However, in these same processes, an important dilemma is enclosed at present. Both, the massive nature of contemporary migration and its particular social and demographic behavior, cause migrants to be no longer seen only as a demographic minority in the destination societies, In other contexts and moments, the dominant and hegemonic social patterns could have been taken and tolerated as acceptable culture deviations.

In contrast to what happened with European migrations of the late nineteenth century and the beginning of the twentieth century, the current immigration wave comes from very different social, ethnic and cultural contexts than those prevailing in their destination societies, which leads them in many cases to reproduce life styles, value systems, behavioral patterns, collective identities, among other things, that maintain and reproduce an important socio-cultural distance with the hegemonic and dominant positions in their destination societies. In particular, they set up new social components that, far from being assimilated to the dominant culture, contribute to the emergence of cultural, social and symbolic alternatives forms, and reinforce the status of multicultural societies, ethnic differentiation, and social inequality (Levitt, 2011; Rivera, 2004; Smith, 2006).

If we add the fact that because of its massive nature as well as for its reproductive behavior, we can see that these are demographic groups in continuous growth, which in some cases, may even get to question the traditional ethnic primacy of the native demographic groups. This gives a more complete picture of the complexity derived from the social, cultural and demographic changes that can be set into motion.

This seems to be the case, for example, in the United States, where today Latinos are an ethnic group with the largest population growth which is supported by both the direct effect of the continuous and systematic immigration and indirectly as a result of their offspring. In particular, and according to the most recent population projections made by the United States Census Bureau, it is expected that Latinos will not only compose the largest demographic minority of the United States, but might even question the primacy of demographic non-Latino whites.

In this regard, the data indicates that the non-Latino white population would reach its maximum volume towards the year 2024, then start a slow but systematic decline that would mean that by the year 2043 it will cease to be an absolute majority to represent only 49% of the United States total population, proportion that would be reduced to 43% towards 2060. On the contrary, it is expected that the Latino population will continue its growth trend, bringing the total number of 130 million in 2060, representing 31% of the population. This would indicate a substantial reduction in the absolute and relative distance that currently separates both demographic volumes, going from a relationship of almost one Latino origin person for every four of white-non Latino origin today, to a ratio of 3 Latinos for each 4 white non-Latino in 2060.

The consequences of such a change in the ethnic composition of the United States population are not fully knowable. Meanwhile, it is not difficult to imagine a change of such a magnitude in the present political balances which could involve a transformation that we can already see in the population composition according to its ethnic origin. In the end, it is a matter of questioning the social, political and cultural current white population hegemony in that country.

In this sense, the data indicates that today the United States, as well as a large part of the developed countries, are facing a demographic situation that poses dilemmas. Either it ensures the demographic reproduction process based on the adoption of an openness and tolerance policy on immigration, leading to, however, either a transformation in the ethnic composition of its population, or adopting a radical policy of control and stem massive immigration. But it does so at the risk of entering into an unsustainability demographic process that would risk not only the demographic but also the economic and social stability of this country.

In other words, it is a demographic dilemma, but that has important economic, social and political implications. Consider, for example, the impacts that a reduction of the active population would have on their economic and productive forces development. In other words, if this immigration and ethnic transformation of population is not maintained, the economy itself, along with the demographic dynamics reproduction of advanced societies, could be seriously compromised.

The emergence of a political figure like Donald Trump, along with the rebirth of groups of white supremacy, made sense in the light of this political and demographic dilemma that posits the eventual ethnic replacement of the current white majority by the emerging Latino minority. It would be a late attempt to reposition themselves to these changes that threaten its current hegemonic position, reestablishing a correlation of political, social and cultural forces that are favorable to their class interests. However, the dice have been thrown and are not at all favorable. Although they will be able to overcome with some success some conjunctures, they face in the medium and long term irreversible demographic processes that directly destroy the demographic bases of sustentation of its current social and political hegemony.

In a later chapter we present a more detailed analysis of the social and political implications of this demographic dilemma. There we discuss the tensions that this Third Demographic Transition in the United States are already generating. The main consequence is that it must pass from having been for more than three centuries a white country, to become in just a few decades a society of ethnic minorities where whites must share their current position of demographic primacy with Latin origin population, with all the social, political and cultural consequences that this implies.

CHAPTER 6

# Migration and the Reproduction of Capital

> *I am from North, South, West, East*
> *A traveler with no whereabouts, no name, no ID*
> *A Ulysses without Promised Land*
> *I have created my own modern Odyssey*[1]
> 　　The Rose of the Winds
> 　　MAKIZA/ANITA TIJOUX

∴

## 1    Thesis

Migrations are a double process of economic transfers. On the one hand, they are a transfer of labor from the communities of origin to the developed economies. On the other hand, remittances and other goods and services that send migrants constitute a reverse transfer contributing to the social reproduction of immigrants, their families and communities. This double system of economic transfers links the reproduction of the migrant labor force in the places of origin with the reproduction of capital and economy in the destination societies, thus contributing to the reproduction of capitalism as a global economic and productive system.

From the demographic perspective, we see migration as a system of demographic transfer that allows to sustain the population reproduction, setting up a global system of demographic relationships. From the economy, we can understand it as a dual process of economic transfers, which together contribute to the reproduction of the global economic system.
–   On the one hand, the essentially labor character of contemporary migration, allows us to understand it as a process of labor force transfer from the origin communities to the developed economies.
–   On the other hand, and as a counterpart to the labor force migration, a flow in an opposite direction is generated, that corresponds to the remittances that migrants send back to their families, which represents a system of

---

1   "Soy del norte, del sur, del oeste, del este. Una viajera sin paradero, sin nombre, sin carné. Una Ulises sin Tierra Prometida. He creado mi propia Odisea moderna". Original in Spanish.

salary transfers that is the basis of social reproduction for immigrants, families and communities of origin (Canales, 2008).

In the first case, as a labor flow, migration is involved in the production process, and therefore it is a component of its globalization. Here, its importance lies in that it represents a workforce whose contributions are manifested both in the labor market dynamics as in the production and economic growth of advanced societies, contributing to the generation of the economic surplus needed to sustain the extended capital reproduction.

In the second case, the remittances flow that derives from migration itself is part of the economic and material foundations that sustain social reproduction of migrants, their families and communities. In this regard, remittances are a wage fund whose function is to reproduce the necessary and available work force for the capital growth and accumulation.

What is relevant is that, through labor migrants flowing one way and remittances the other, the social and economic conditions of origin places are linked with the capital and the economy reproduction of the destination societies, the first one becoming an additional component of the conditions in which nowadays the reproduction of capitalism is given as an economic and productive system. In particular, remittances contribute to maintain the conditions of cheap and available labor reproduction for globalized capital. To understand this idea on the labor migration and remittances role in global economy, we will re-capture some analytical and conceptual elements, both of neoclassical economic theory as well as from structuralist and Marxist viewpoints.[2]

## 2   From the Circular Flow of Income to the Reproduction of Capital

In any manual to introduction to economics, it is stated that the economy works as a system, according to which each transaction always involves a dual

---

[2] It could be argued that migrations are always labor migration, and consequently, migrants will always be inserted in labor market in the places of destination. What we want to highlight here is rather the economic and social context of each migration. Thus, for example, in the last major immigration wave from the end of the nineteenth century and early twentieth century, the nature of migration was another. It was inserted in a land colonization process and places settlement, in a framework of a capitalist territorial expansion stage. With immigration it was sought to fill geographic gaps that the internal demographic growth, in the recipient countries, were unable to cover. Today, on the other hand, international migration is part of an intensification process of capitalist relations, in a world where capitalism has virtually covered all its spaces. In this case, migration is seeking to fill gaps that the population dynamics is leaving in developed countries and which are necessary for economic growth and accumulation of global capitalism.

flow. On the one hand, the seller that delivers a product or service, that has some value in use (utility) to the buyer. In return, he receives some form of money, which corresponds to the exchange value of the product or service sold that is estimated as the cost of producing it. On the part of the purchaser, the opposite happens, he delivers money in exchange for a product that it is considered has some utility for him. In this way, the seller disposes a value in use, receiving in return the exchange value of that good or service, and the purchaser does exactly the opposite.

From this principle, economic theory formulates the functioning of the economy as a two–way circulation system. On the one hand, the circulation or flow of material (goods and services), and on the other hand, the flow or money circulation (income, etc.). This model is called the circular flow of income or also, the circular flow of macroeconomic activity (Samuelson and Nordhaus, 2005). The combined gaze of both flows allows us to understand the functioning of the economy. Let's take a look at this, based on the simplest but more enlightening model, which corresponds to the economic exchange between two agents: the domestic units, on the one hand, and the productive units, or companies, on the other.

Domestic units are either families or persons who participate in the economic system in two ways. On the one hand, they are the owners of the production factors (capital, land and labor force), and on the other hand, they demand goods and services to meet their multiple needs. For its part, the companies are units where, with these productive factors, are produced the goods and services that are offered to families for their maintenance and subsistence.

In this way, through the market of production factors the families sell factors and get the needed income to access market in goods and services for purchasing those things that best meet their needs. On its part, the companies, with their initial capital, buy the production factors (inputs, technology, etc.), necessary for the goods production, and pay for them wages, rents and profits, depending on the productive factor they are purchasing. With these production factors, they return to the production process for manufacturing goods and services that they subsequently will offer in the corresponding market, recovering the initial investment.

This model can become more complex by adding new agents, markets and economic components of the system, such as the State, companies, consumers from the outside, the exchanges between companies, the production and circulation of inputs, capital goods, technology and distinguishing all this, according to the various production sectors (primary, secondary, tertiary, or any other classification that arises in every moment). Likewise, from a structuralist viewpoint, the domestic units are often disaggregated according to the production factors ownership, being able in this way to have an approximate model of the class structure and therefore of the income distribution (Castro and Lessa, 1991). Despite this increased disaggregation of the economic model, what is relevant is that it operates by the same principle of income movement which is acquiring various forms, depending on the actors involved: wages, rents, profits and earnings, taxes, subsidies, etc.

Based on this basic model in terms of the functioning of the economy, the basic elements of macroeconomic theory can be illustrated. In particular, the origin and composition of aggregate demand, the functioning and role of money and financial markets, the savings-investment system, the foreign trade (exports-imports), the conditions to illustrate and understand the different roles of State in the economy, among many other aspects.

Although from neoclassical economic theory, the model is used to analyze the flow of income, and through this, the conditions for the economic activity growth, as well as its distribution among the different economic agents, a structuralist perspective can use the same model of the functioning of the economic system, but for linking the consumption and production processes. We can understand the first as the work force reproduction process and the second as the capital reproduction process. Following the same scheme of the circular income flow, we can understand the economy functioning as the complementarity of these two different moments, namely:

– Productive moment: It corresponds to the production of both the means of production and means of intermediate consumption (machinery, inputs, raw materials, technology, etc.), as well as to the goods and services production for final consumption. In this process, the capital *consumes* the labor force, that is to say, it extracts what has value to the capital: the labor, in its double character. First, as *concrete* labor (utility-producing), i.e., the worker's ability to use other means of production, inputs, technology, raw materials, etc., in the goods and services production. Second, as *abstract* labor (value-producing), i.e. abstract time labor (basic unit of value) which is transferred to commodities in the labor process and by this means, make it possible to value the capital. In this latter capacity, labor becomes "a means to create wealth in general, and has ceased to be tied as an attribute to a particular individual" (Marx, 1971:210).
– Reproductive moment: It corresponds to the individual (and familiar) process of goods and services consumption previously produced. Through this process, people not only meet their needs (neoclassical perspective), but reproduce themselves, and by this means, reproduce its own labor force every day (structuralism perspective). But this is not a work-force for themselves,

but to be sold to others, in this case, the capital.[3] Thus, if for the individuals, this moment of individual consumption does not represent a productive act in itself, in the sense that it brings them back something more than the satisfaction of their needs; to the capital, on the contrary, it is a production moment, since it corresponds to the production and reproduction of the labor power, i.e. the only component of the work process that has the ability to generate wealth and valorize the capital.

Although at first sight it seems to be the same pattern of economic theory, this structuralist perspective implies an additional turn, in the sense that it does not only account for the process of capital accumulation (economic growth, profit, etc., in neoclassical theory language), but together with this, it allows us to analyze the capital reproduction both, in its material form (money, goods production, etc.), and in its form of social relationship, as opposed to the labor-power.

In fact, from this vision related to the functioning of the economy, the following would have been achieved:

– On the one hand, the production of goods and services of various kinds (means of production, inputs, raw materials, productive services, goods and services for final consumption, etc.) corresponds to what in national accounts is documented as economic activity, in their various categories, and that are synthesized in the production value, i.e. the Gross Domestic Product (GDP).
– On the other hand, the labor force reproduction for the capital, this is, people's work ability which is offered to the capital for its use (work), in exchange for a salary.
– The capital reproduction in expanded form is capitalism's *leit motiv*, what impels the capitalist to re-start repeatedly all this production and capital valuation circuit.
– Finally, the reproduction of the social relationship between capital and labor, as opposing economic entities, that are the foundation of the economic system functioning, by restarting, again and again the whole economic

---

3   This is characteristic of a capitalist society where the worker is a "free", person, i.e. they are free to sell the labor force, in opposition to non-capitalist forms where the worker is often tied to the land or masters, in the case of the feudal or haciendas system or in the case of slavery forms. However, although in capitalism the worker has achieved its freedom, the problem is that, as he is not the owner of nothing more than their labor force, that freedom is in fact, a restriction, a structural conditioning of having to sell their labor force to get the resources for their subsistence and reproduction. In that sense, in capitalism the time of consumption, is actually a field of labor force reproduction not for themselves, but for others, for the capital (Marx, 1967).

process of labor and capital valuation (accumulation), in an *ad infinitum* process, or until some crisis dictates to the contrary.[4]

However, this is a general model that describes the operation of the capitalist economy in abstract. What interests us in this case is to reconstruct this model for the analysis and understanding of contemporary migration role in the capital reproduction process in the current context of economic globalization.

In previous chapters we referred, in more detail, to the globalization processes of economy, with particular emphasis on how it would have influenced the contemporary international migration forms and patterns. In this section, we are interested in giving an additional turn to that globalization and migration approach. To do this, we are interested in illustrating how in this globalization context, international migration constitutes a mechanism that enables the linking of productive moments (of the capital valuation) in receiving countries with the labor force reproductive moments of labor force in sending countries, and by this means, it contributes to link the capital accumulation with the labor force reproduction.

In the figure below we illustrate this situation where the reproduction of the migrant labor force and capital are linked through international migrations, in a shared globalization process.

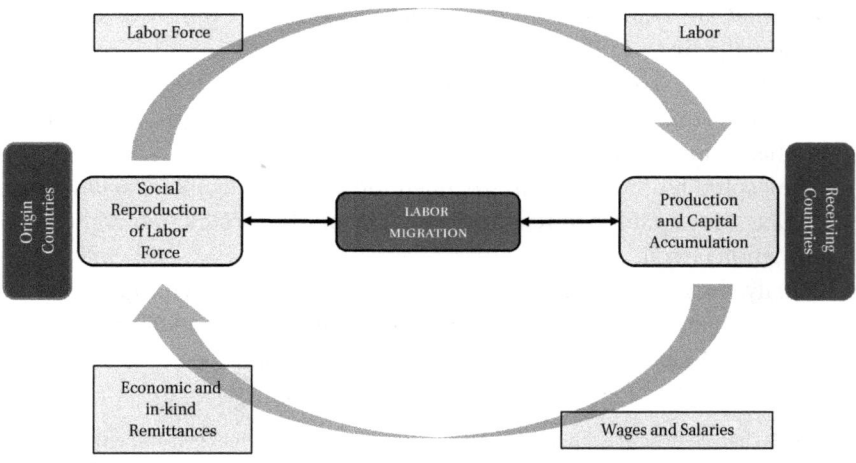

FIGURE 14    Labor migration and reproduction of capital

---

4   Although this sentence may seem a sarcasm, in fact it is something that has already been raised by great economists. For example, Marx argued that the same principle that moved capitalism and sustained the capital extended reproduction process, contains in itself, the germ of capitalist recurrent crises. From another perspective, Keynes raises something similar in that economic crises are the product of the markets functioning for which arises the need for their regulation through the State intervention.

Migrations are a two-fold process of economic transfers. On the one hand, they are a transfer of labor from the communities of origin to more developed economies. On the other hand, remittances and other goods and services sent by migrants constitute a reverse transfer that contributes to the social reproduction of immigrants, their families and communities. This two-fold system of financial transfers linked reproduction of migrant labor in places of origin with the reproduction of capital in societies of destination, thus contributing to the reproduction of capitalism as a global economic and productive system.

This link between productive and reproductive moments can be analyzed from the role of migration in shaping labor markets in the global economy. These are global labor force markets, where the spatial linkage between the reproductive moment of the labor force and the productive moment of capital is given (and sometimes exclusively) through migration and social and economic processes that activates in its development and continuous becoming. This peculiar territorial configuration allows that the reproduction of the labor force, on the one hand, and that of capital, on the other, develop each in different spaces and locations and distant from each other, with no greater link than those generated by one's own Migration of the labor force.

With globalization, capital has succeeded in relocating the reproductive moments of the labor force beyond national borders, and for this reason, it has made it possible to separate the social reproduction of the labor force from the entire social and political system. This is in contrast to Fordism and industrial capitalism that were integrated through the state, politics, and the most diverse institutions that structured the capitalist societies of the developed world throughout the twentieth century.

However, this disconnect between the two moments of capital accumulation is only apparent and conceals the true role of labor migration as an articulating device of both moments that sustains the accumulation of capital in the global economy.

In the following sections, we describe and explain these migration linkages with the global economic system reproduction.

## 3  Labor Migration and the Reproduction of Capital

In relation to the so-called productive moment, various authors highlight the changes that have been experienced in its spatial configuration from the advent of global economy. Without entering into the details of this globalization debate, we are interested in focusing our attention on those aspects that provide us with the understanding of international migration. In this sense, we are interested in the analysis of the changes that globalization has introduced in labor's organizational forms and labor relations, to the extent that this sets the context for the immigrants labor insertion in the global economy.

These changes in the employment and labor market structure and dynamics, are based on the new productive and organizational paradigms of globalization. We refer to post-Fordism, *just in time* production, the idea of a global factory, the economic deregulation of markets, the end of the Welfare State, the dramatic increase in labor flexibility and labor markets segmentation, among many other aspects (Mendieta, 2007; Hirst and Zeitlin, 1991; Amin, 2000; Koch, 2017).

With this, various social inclusion/exclusion mechanisms are configured, that, through the precarious employment situation and other modern forms of social segregation, affect mainly weakened social sectors due to the economic deregulation and labor flexibility, as it is the case of migrant workers in developed countries (Bauman, 1998). The globalization processes are not under any circumstances, geographically uniform, but heterogeneous and differentiated on the basis of which are created and recreated various forms of social, economic, and spatial inequality (Stiglitz, 2012).

These forms of differentiation and social inequality are based on new forms of population social stratification that have economic and demographic bases which we are interested in recapturing. In the meantime, if we consider that the social process of work is the basis of social stratification, then, it is expected that the changes at this level, reflect and direct impact on the structuring of society in class, strata and differentiated social groups. In this regard, it is necessary to refer to the transformations in the employment and occupations social structure, and in general, the capital-labor relationship.

For many authors, these changes make the most characteristic features of the transition from industrial society to a postindustrial or informational (Koch, 2017; Amin, 2000; Kumar, 1995). Based on this, it is pointed out that with economic globalization, the dynamics of the labor market are involved in two processes that complement and reinforce each other. On the one hand, the transformations in the labor matrix derived from the changes in the economic-productive structure. On the other hand, in the polarization of occupations and segmentation of labor markets.

### 3.1 *Deindustrialization and Tertiarization in the New Labor Matrix*

On these changes in the employment structure, there has been a broad debate among the various theories on post-industrial society. Initially, authors, such as Daniel Bell (1973), emphasized the making of a new social structure, based on the transition from an industrialized economy to one of services, and therefore, in the rise of the executive and professional occupations, along with the disappearance not only of the agricultural and primary-extractive work, but also and importantly, those of the industrial sector.

Others, such as Castells (1996), however, point out that the informational nature of contemporary societies, is not expressed so much in the decline of the industrial activities, as in the new character that occupations have. The emphasis is placed on the increasing number of information and knowledge required for the labor process, having, therefore, an impact on the occupations and employment structure. In this sense, Castells chooses to speak of *informational society*, and not so much of *industrial society*. What accounts for the informational nature of this new era, is that it is based no longer on the exchange and material relations, but in the exchange and processing of information, that is, symbols, which redefine the whole process of production and distribution of goods and services.[5]

Lash and Urry (1994) go beyond, and indicate not only the informational nature of the current processes of accumulation, but emphasize their reflexivity. For these authors, in the information economy, the accumulation process is not only *flexible*, but *reflexive* to the extent that it is based on self-regulation processes that transform the labor process in an object of itself. For these authors the concepts of flexibility, deregulation, postfordism, are inadequate and loaded with bias productivism that does not allow them to "capture all the extent that production and consumption have as its foundation a discursive knowledge" (Lash and Urry, 1994: 91).

These processes have provoked transformations to the dynamics of the economy and to the productive matrix of contemporary societies. Especially the process of de-industrializing and tertiarizing the economies of developed countries, one of whose features is based on the relocation of capital and productive processes from inside the core economies out to other regions of the world, in order to benefit from the advantages offered in terms of the price of labor, tax exemptions, flexibility with regard to environmental policies, and others (Castillo Fernández, 2016).

Figures for Europe and the USA are eloquent. Between 1995 and 2016, employment in the USA grew in net terms by nearly 28 million jobs. This growth, however, was not evenly spread over all economic sectors, but concentrated

---

5   As Negroponte (1996) points out, it is the transition from an economy of "atoms" to one of "bits". In the first exchange value is based on the material character ("atoms") of things that are exchanged, and therefore the material labor necessary to produce them. In the second, in the information economy it is no longer true. The value is not in function of the material, but of the information, it is not the hardware that is exchanged, but the contents and symbols. In some cases, even production materializes only in a virtual sense, never exists materially as such.

on specific activities while leaving others virtually stagnant with diminished production. The growth of employment in services, whether personal, social or professional, amounted to 34.5 million jobs in all. But in the case of the manufacturing industry and commerce, the number of people employed in these activities was reduced by 9.1 million.

In Europe something similar happened. Between 1998 and 2016, employment increased with 25 million more jobs than before. However, in the United States, this growth was concentrated in social services which increased by 13.7 million jobs, followed by services to businesses and personal services, where employment grew by just over 8 million jobs in each. Meanwhile, employment in directly productive sectors diminished considerably. In agriculture, livestock and fishing, the reduction was of nearly 2.5 million jobs, and in the case of manufacturing the number of jobs was reduced by 6.7 million.

The different dynamics of employment in different sectors reflects a substantial transformation of the labor matrix of the core economies. In the 1990s, commerce and social services accounted in almost equal proportions for 50% of all employment, while manufacturing industries accounted for around 18% of employment in the USA and 21% in Europe. Financial or professional services to companies accounted for another 16% of all employment in the US, though only 11% in Europe.

Today the composition of employment by sector has been significantly modified. First, social services are now far and away the main sector of employment, providing 30% of jobs in both the USA and Europe. And while services to companies have increased their share of employment by 3 to 5 percentage points, manufacturing has reduced its share by nearly 7 percentage points, both in Europe and in the United States. The contrast between the two dynamics is perhaps the maximum expression of the new orientation of the US and EU economy, where the direct production of goods has tended to be replaced by the creation of production services, as a result of the formation of an information economy and the consolidation of processes of reflexivity in the organization of work (Lash and Urry, 1998).

However there has also been a remarkable increase in personal service jobs (maids and housekeeping cleaners, care of persons, food preparation, cleaning and maintenance, to name but a few). These are jobs requiring little in the way of qualifications and which are highly precarious in terms of employment, and tend to attract workers suffering from various degrees of social vulnerability. Both in Europe and in the United States, activities of this type have increased their share of employment by over 4 percentage points, thus showing that it is work of greater importance in the dynamics of employment, which reflect

TABLE 1  United States and European Union (15 countries). Employment by major industry groups (thousands of people)

| | United States of America | | | | European Union (15 countries) | | | |
|---|---|---|---|---|---|---|---|---|
| | Volume of employment (thousands) | | Distribution % | | Volume of employment (thousands) | | Distribution % | |
| | 1995 | 2016 | 1995 | 2016 | 1998 | 2016 | 1998 | 2016 |
| Total | 122,859 | 150,608 | 100% | 100% | 152,662 | 176,951 | 100% | 100% |
| Agriculture, fishing | 2,582 | 2,508 | 2% | 2% | 7,700.2 | 5,227.8 | 5% | 3% |
| Construction | 7,265 | 9,891 | 6% | 7% | 11,794.7 | 11,691.0 | 8% | 7% |
| Manufacturing | 22,398 | 17,262 | 18% | 11% | 31,712.5 | 25,033.9 | 21% | 14% |
| Wholesale and retail trade | 30,900 | 26,886 | 25% | 18% | 33,114.1 | 36,136.5 | 22% | 20% |
| Social services | 19,441 | 31,256 | 16% | 21% | 43,348.6 | 57,120.5 | 28% | 32% |
| Financial, real estate and professional services | 30,537 | 43,803 | 25% | 29% | 17,303.4 | 25,636.2 | 11% | 14% |
| Personal services | 9,736 | 19,002 | 8% | 13% | 7,688.4 | 16,104.6 | 5% | 9% |

Sources: US Bureau of Census, CPS, 1995 & 2016; and European Commission, Eurostat http://ec.europa.eu/eurostat/data/database

tendencies towards polarization and segmentation in labor markets (Canales, 2017).

The tertiarizing of the economies of core countries has created processes of differentiation with regard to working conditions and the demand for labor. While the sectors of professional and social services have created a large demand for qualified labor, the sector of personal services, as of administrative back-up and assistance, has created a demand for unqualified workers. Also, de-industrialization has not affected all branches of industry equally, and has created further processes of differentiation with regard to demand for the labor force.

In this sense it is appropriate to analyze the patterns of insertion in employment by migrant workers, who are in a state of vulnerability and therefore tend to take less protected jobs which have a larger degree of labor flexibility. In the case of the USA, figures illustrate the point. In the year 2016, immigrants from the Third World tended to follow the process of tertiarizing and de-industrializing the economy, but in a particular way, preferring to take up places in those manufacturing and productive sectors that had been left behind in the process of global capitalist accumulation, or else in services requiring lower levels of qualification. In general, they take positions in activities with a smaller capacity for value added, with greater levels of productivity, and more labor flexibility.

We can also see that Third World immigrants have 24% of the jobs in agriculture, and 23% of those in construction. These are highly precarious and "flexible" jobs, where contracts are mostly for limited periods or day laboring.

With regard to the de-industrialization process, we can see that some of the most affected branches of industry are converting to the employment of migrant workers. This applies to the textile and footwear industries, food, drink and tobacco, and the production of furniture. Overall, Third World migrants account for 26% of employment in these branches of industry. By contrast, in branches of industry in a more competitive position, with more developed technology, such as microelectronics, automobile, machinery and equipment, metal mechanics and suchlike, the number of immigrants hired has reduced to being only 13% of the total.

Further, something similar to what happened with de-industrialization as mentioned above, has happened in relation to tertiarization. Immigrants tend to be relegated to the activities and services lagging farthest behind, which are very long way from forming the economic base of the information economy that explains the tertiarizing of the productive matrix. In concrete terms, Third World immigrants have 11.3% of the jobs in services proper to the age of information (professional services, financial services, services for businesses, etc.)

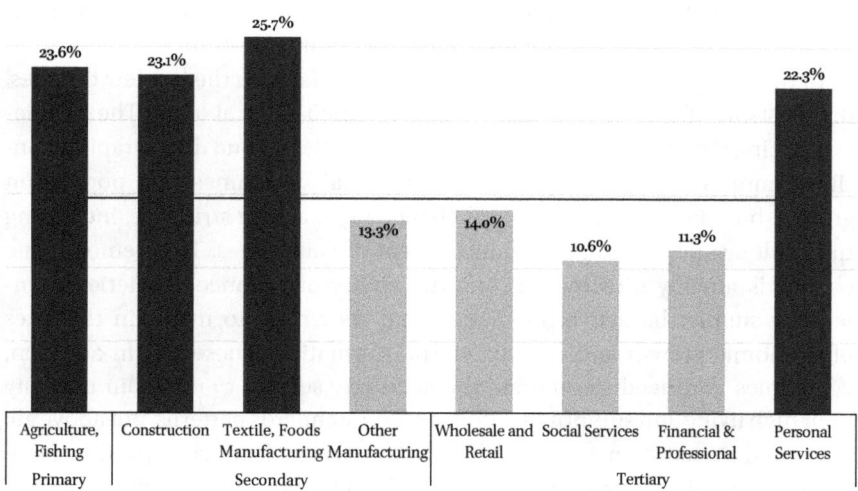

FIGURE 15  USA, 2016. Third World immigrants by major industry groups
SOURCES: CURRENT POPULATION SURVEY, ASEC, MARCH 2016. US CENSUS BUREAU

and only 16% of the jobs in social services (health, education, government). However, these immigrants have 22.3% of the jobs in personal services and administrative support, that is, in services requiring little qualification and therefore having high levels of labor precariousness and contractual deregulation.

### 3.2 *Immigration and Labor Deficit*

However, these economic conditions of polarization along with the demographic weaknesses already identified, configure the structural framework that allows us to understand the role of migration in the economic dynamics of these countries. By now, in demographic terms, it is clear the need to be provided with a migrant labor force to fill the gaps that ageing leaves. On the other hand, it is not a question of a labor force purely and simply but of the most vulnerable, flexible and precarious workers, so that they can be inserted into occupations located in the lower strata of the socio-occupational scale that the same economic globalization generates, through labor market deregulation and flexibility.

Contrary to this structuralis approach, various authors have pointed out that labor immigration would be an unnecessary pressure on the labor market, causing a virtual native labor displacement from their jobs (Borjas, 2001;

Martin, 2002). In fact, the situation is much more complex since it combines economic conditions, resulting from globalization, with those resulting from the ageing population and the second demographic transition.

In the first place, the demographic change initiated in the last few decades, manifests itself increasingly in a persistent deficit of local labor. The population ageing along with the decrease of fertility in the second demographic transition framework, involves not only a slow and sometimes zero population growth, but above all, a substantial change in its ageing structure, increasing the adult age population and reducing that of young ages. This demographic change is already directly affecting the ability of advanced societies to internally supply the active population that they need to maintain the rates of economic growth and productive transformation. These are, in addition, economies that need to generate the necessary surplus to maintain not only their high living and sumptuous consumption standards patterns, but above all, they need to maintain and reproduce a daily wide leisure class (in the classical terms that Veblen suggested), especially in terms of a war industry and of an army that administers the economy and international policy which allow them to maintain their privileged and dominant hegemonic position in the world society.

Let's put it in simpler terms. The demographics in these societies shows a clear structural failure to generate the quotas of workers to fill the jobs that the dynamics and economic growth of these companies generate daily. To confront this structural imbalance between the internal demographic and economic dynamics, the solution has been to appeal to the mass immigration of workers, mostly from Third World countries, where they experience a different demographic regime.

In effect, and even in spite of the negative effects of the recent economic crisis in the generation and growth of employment, the last decade has already recorded a persistent and growing imbalance between the supply of jobs that economic growth generates that is consequently required by the capital reproduction, and the labor offer the local demography is able to generate.

In the case of Spain, for example, between 1999 and 2012, the economy managed to generate 3.8 million new jobs, despite the serious impact of the crisis in the past few years. However, the demographic dynamics of the Spanish population (without immigrants), managed to generate only 1.7 million new workers, thereby generating a labor shortage which reaches 2.1 million people. This is, the Spanish economy, even in a slow growth context derived from the past economic crisis, generates an employment offer, which is more than a 2.25 times superior to the population growth capacity of its active population. This labor deficit was on average higher than 12% of the local labor force each year between 1999 and 2012.

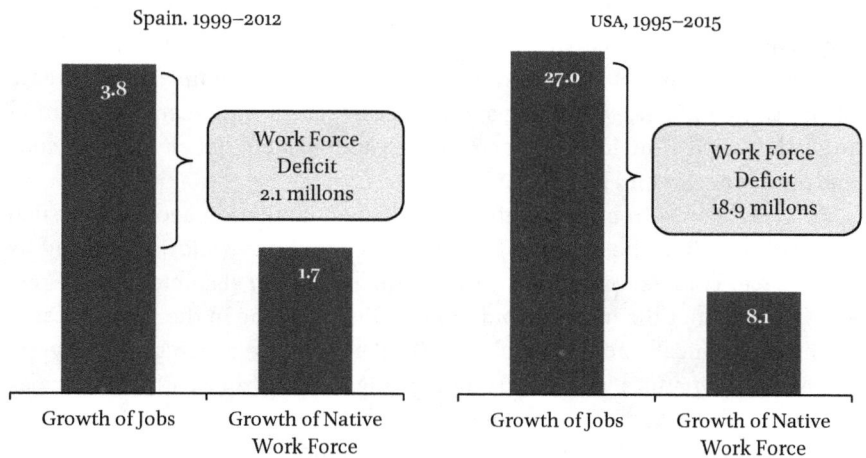

FIGURE 16   Spain and United States, labor force deficit
SOURCES: INE, ACTIVE POPULATION SURVEY, 1999 &2012; AND CURRENT POPULATION SURVEY, MARCH SUPPLEMENT, 1995 AND 2015

Into the United States, the situation is very similar. Between 1995 and 2015, the growth rate of its economy managed to generate 27.0 million new jobs. However, the demographic dynamics of its native population, scarcely could generate a labor force provision of 8.1 million people. In this case, the labor shortage is 3.3 times superior to the population capacity of its native population. This labor deficit was on average higher than 12% of the local labor force each year between 2003 and 2015.

Considering the above, our thesis is that in the advanced countries, immigration from peripheral countries helps to fill the demographic gap generated by the structural shortage of its current demographic reproduction patterns which manifests itself in all its magnitude in the persistent deficit of economically active population that we have previously shown, and that puts pressure on these societies to appeal to migrant labor to cover the occupations that the economic dynamics is generating each year. In this framework, we can understand not only the dynamics and volume of these countries labor immigration, but also its role to counteract the effects that the native population ageing would have on its economic dynamics.

In fact, if we consider the migration tendency of Latin American origin in both countries, we can see that it has made an important contribution to partially meet the labor deficit that we have already pointed out for both countries. In the case of Spain, for example, between 2000 and 2012, Latin American immigration has helped to fill a third of the labor force growth in that country, despite the negative effects of economic crisis, especially with regard to the jobs reduction and employment reduction in various economic sectors where immigrants are preferably inserted (construction, for example). In the case of the United States, something similar occurs. Latin American immigration would have contributed to cover 50% of the annual labor deficit between 2003 and 2015 (Canales and Meza, 2016).

In other words, in both countries, the native population ageing is of such a magnitude than the demographic dynamics no longer allows restoring its labor force. This also presents a clear ageing process in absolute terms. However, the gap that the native population ageing is leaving in the youngest ages of the economically active population (under 50 years) is being offset by the population dynamics growth of migrant origin, both from Latin America as well as in other Third World regions.

In the case of the United States, the data are eloquent and illustrate how the ageing process directly affects the age composition of the native population. Between 2000 and 2015, 55% of the growth in labor composed by Latin American immigrants corresponded to persons under 50 years. Also, in the case of Latino native workers more than 80% growth corresponds to less than 50 years. These data illustrate that Latinos, both immigrants and natives, are an essentially young population that is not yet exposed to the ageing process as is the case with the native population and labor force of both African and white origin.

Among non-Latin whites an extreme situation of the ageing process is noticed. On the one hand, the working population under 50 is reduced by more than 14 million people, while on the other hand, the working population over 50 years of age increases by 12 million workers. Meanwhile, the labor force of non-Latin black origin also undergoes an ageing process, which although does not imply a drastic reduction in the under 50 year old workforce, it does carry a large growth of elderly population.

These data illustrate the dynamics of the ageing of the economically active population of the United States and show a process of demographic replacement of an ethnic group (non-Latin white) with an emerging one (Latinos, immigrants and natives). Everything indicates that in the medium term (from two to three decades) the ethnic composition of the US labor force will be "Latinized"; The current weight of the white non-Latino population will be reduced, as it is expected to occur at the level of the general population (Canales, 2017).

In synthesis, rather than a native labor force *displacement* process by immigrant labor force, what is happening both in Spain and the United States, is a virtual population *replacement* of one ethnic group by another, product to a large extent of the own insufficiency in native population demographic growth

TABLE 2  United States, 2000–2015. Labor force growth by ethnic and migratory origin and age groups

|  |  | Total | 15 through 49 years | 50 years or more |
|---|---|---|---|---|
| **Total** | | 15,817,394 | -4,432,985 | 20,250,379 |
| **Immigrants** | Latin American | 5,157,116 | 2,816,597 | 2,340,519 |
|  | Other countries | 4,103,339 | 1,450,969 | 2,652,370 |
| **Natives** | Latinos | 4,557,532 | 3,826,548 | 730,984 |
|  | Black no Latinos | 1,692,391 | -172,961 | 1,865,352 |
|  | White no Latinos | -2,232,645 | -14,318,965 | 12,086,320 |
|  | Others no Latinos | 2,539,661 | 1,964,827 | 574,834 |

Sources: Current Population Survey, March Supplement 2000 and 2015

However, if in demographics terms, labor migration contributes to cover the labor shortage that the advanced society's demography is generating, in economic and productive terms, labor migration has a significant impact on maintaining and enhancing the economic dynamics, and in this way, promote the capital reproduction and accumulation. In this regard, the data are also informative, in terms of showing how immigration contributes increasingly to the gross domestic product generation and capital accumulation in advanced societies.

In the USA case, the Gross Domestic Product (GDP) growth has been almost 3.8 thousand of billions of dollars. However, only 41% of this growth was provided by white non-Latinos labor force, despite the fact that they represented more than 60% of total employment. In contrast Latinos (immigrants and natives) contributed with 30% of GDP growth, and other immigrants aggregated another 17%. In other words, in terms of them contribution to growth economy, migrant minorities are more important than white majority, in about 6 percentage points.

This contribution to economic growth, shows the dependence level in the advanced societies economies with regard to the necessary immigrant

TABLE 3  United States of America. Gross domestic product by ethnic origin of labor force

|  | GDP (billions dollars 2009 price) | | Growth 2000–2015 | |
| --- | --- | --- | --- | --- |
|  | 2000 | 2015 | Volume | % |
| PIB Total | 12,559.7 | 16,348.9 | 3,789.2 | 100% |
| Whites no Latinos | 8,980.9 | 10,528.3 | 1,547.4 | 41% |
| Others no Latinos | 1,591.8 | 2,060.3 | 468.5 | 12% |
| Native Latinos | 481.6 | 1,012.1 | 530.5 | 14% |
| Latin American immigrants | 653.0 | 1,265.8 | 612.8 | 16% |
| Other immigrants | 852.5 | 1,482.4 | 629.9 | 17% |

Sources: Estimations based on Bureau of the Census, Current Population Survey, March Supplement, 2000 and 2015; and Bureau of Economic Analysis, Real Value Added by Industry, http://www.bea.gov/industry/index.htm

labor provision, at a time when it is faced with demographic insufficiency already manifested in its native population. In this regard, a dependence on immigration is shown even more clearly when we see the distinct trends of gross domestic product generated by each ethnic–migratory group during the current times of economic crisis and post-crisis.

During the economic crisis, between 2007 and 2009, the GDP of the United States fell from 14.87 to 14.41 billion dollars. This represented a cumulative 3.1% drop for the entire crisis period. However, when we compare the trend according to the contribution of each ethnic group of the labor force, we see different behaviors. On the one hand, the GDP generated by non-Latin whites fell by more than 230 billion dollars, while the GDP of non-Latin black workers fell by another 100 billion. Instead, GDP contributed by workers of Latin origin (natives and immigrants) fell by only 68 billion dollars.

Meanwhile, in the post-crisis economic recovery from 2009 to 2015, US GDP grew by more than $ 1.9 billion, representing a cumulative 13.4% growth (2.2% annual average). However, it is the Latino minorities, along with immigrants from other regions, who support this growth. In the case of white non-Latino

TABLE 4   United States of America. GDP and economic growth by ethnic origin of labor force (billions dollars, 2009)

|  | Gross Domestic Product | | | GDP growth | |
|---|---|---|---|---|---|
|  | 2007 | 2009 | 2015 | 2007–2009 | 2009–2015 |
| Total | 14,873.7 | 14,418.7 | 16,348.9 | −455.0 | 1,930.2 |
| Whites no Latinos | 10,050.9 | 9,818.0 | 10,528.3 | −232.9 | 710.3 |
| Others no Latinos | 1,881.4 | 1,780.8 | 2,060.3 | −100.6 | 279.5 |
| Other immigrants | 1,192.2 | 1,138.4 | 1,482.4 | −53.8 | 343.9 |
| Native Latinos | 706.8 | 723.5 | 1,012.1 | 16.7 | 288.6 |
| Latin American immigrants | 1,042.4 | 957.9 | 1,265.8 | −84.4 | 307.8 |

Sources: Estimations based on Bureau of the Census, Current Population Survey, March Supplement, 2007, 2010 and 2015; and Bureau of Economic Analysis, Real Value Added by Industry, http://www.bea.gov/industry/index.htm

workers, although they are 67% of the employed labor force, they contributed only 37% of total GDP growth. By contrast, Latino minorities (natives and immigrants) but only account for 14% of the employed labor force, contributed 31% of GDP growth.

These data illustrate an unusual event. The economic recovery of the United States in post-crisis is increasingly based on the contribution of workers of Latin origin and other ethnic minorities, and not so much on the contribution generated by the white majority.

In summary, all of these data illustrate the level of importance that immigrant labor achieves to sustain economic dynamic (cover labor deficits, contributions to GDP growth, sustain strategic sectors of the economy, and others) and therefore, for the capital reproduction and global accumulation process in developed countries, especially in these years of economic crisis and post-crisis. We are clear that migration is not the only factor, but also there is no doubt that it does have an important role.

## 4 Transnationalism, Social Networks and Remittances: the Reproduction of the Labor Force

As we have seen, labor migration helps to alleviate the labor force shortage that the advanced countries demographic dynamics continuously generate. By this means, as a labor force provider, labor migration also contributes in an important way to sustain the economic growth in these countries, and thereby to the reproduction and accumulation of capital. However, the labor migration contribution is not just to provide a workforce purely and simply, but of cheap labor, that is, at a low wage cost, as well as in conditions of vulnerability and social differentiation, that make them susceptible to be inserted into jobs characterized by their high flexibility and instability and also by being low-skilled, precarious and poorly paid.

In this sense, as a way to maintain this social segregation and economic discrimination situation, the latter as expressed by the low wages that migrant labor forces perceives, much of the costs of labor force reproduction has been transferred towards migrant's economies and communities of origin. It is a relocation process of the labor force reproduction, in such a way that in the case of the migrant population, the reproduction cost as a salaried-worker is not necessarily determined by the terms and lifestyles conditions prevailing in the destination societies, but to a large extent depend on the living conditions prevailing in the places of origin.

In fact, in a capitalist society, the exchange value of labor power is determined, as in the case of every other commodity, by the labor time necessary for the production, and consequently the reproduction of this special article. In this case, the salary and wages are determined according to their reproduction cost, i.e., by the costs and resources that are intended to reproduce the worker and his family, both on a daily basis and across generations. The wage must cover the social reproduction needs of the worker and his family, both in their daily lives as well as for the long-term, that is, their consumption expenditures for daily food, health, education, clothing, footwear, shelter, transportation, etc.

However, the workers and their families reproduction costs (and of the general population), are quantitatively very different, depending on whether it is the migration origin or destination country. This is especially true in the current migratory wave that originates in the underdeveloped countries of the South, and is directed to the Northern advanced societies.[6] In relation

---

6 This condition, however, does not seem to have had the same weight in the case of the late nineteenth and early twentieth century migratory wave where the differences between the

to health expenditures, for example, we estimate that in the Latin American countries, the annual expenditure per capita on health, is 6 times lower than the one given in the European countries inscribed in the Euro area next to the United Kingdom, and more than 12 times lower than that of the United States. Also, the annual spending per capita on primary education in Latin American countries, is 8 times lower than the Euro countries and the United Kingdom area, and more than 10 times smaller than that of the United States.[7]

In this way, to try to deal with the daily and intergenerational migrant labor force reproduction according to the costs that may arise from the living conditions in advanced societies, could turn out to be too costly, and would imply a significant wage rise of this migrant labor. In such a situation, the capital profit margins would reduce and therefore challenge its reproduction and accumulation ability, draining its competitiveness power at a global level (Bustamante, 1973).

In this context, we support that migrants' social networks that are materialized in the formation of transnational communities, along with enabling the migration reproduction as a social process. This becomes a mechanism through which it has been possible to transfer a large part of the reproduction costs of migrant labor force, from the destination economies in host societies, to families and communities of migrants origin in the sending countries.

Migration as a social process gives rise to a complex system of social and family networks, which, based on solidarity and reciprocity principles, enables migrant reproduction, as well as their families and communities, in what has been termed as a process of cumulative causation (Massey, 1990). In this context, several authors have raised that international migration would constitute a transnational strategy of social reproduction of migrants and their families (De Haas, 2007). To this, we add the thesis that family networks and migrants social capital, along with being a migration reproduction strategy as a social process, are also, and through the same process, a social reproduction form of migrant labor force, i.e., a migrant reproduction form as transnational workers.

If the migrants networks and social capital are the mechanism through which migration develops and perpetuates (allowing migrants to reduce the costs and risks of displacement, to be inserted in the destination place, to get jobs, to participate and join a community of *paisanos*), it is through the same process, and based on these same social networks, that much of that labor power reproduction cost is transferred to migrants themselves as well as to their families and communities.

---

cost of living, and consumption patterns in the late nineteenth century Europe were not very different from those of the United States, Canada, Australia or Argentina.
7   System on-line consultation of the World Bank http://datos.bancomundial.org/indicador.

If, from one perspective, social networks are part of the family and migration reproduction as a social process, we understand that this same process is equally an important part of the migrant labor force reproduction. On the one hand, those social networks set in motion a labor force that is available to be hired by capitalists and businessmen in the host countries. On the other hand, these same social networks, give sustenance to the social reproduction (daily and generational) of that workforce, freeing the host countries capital and economies from part of the labor force reproduction cost.

In this way, the migration reproduction, and in particular, the migrant labor force reproduction, acquires a transnational path, to the extent that it articulates and links the migrants settlements in the destination places with the communities of origin. In fact, along with human displacement, migration triggers a series of other material and symbolic goods exchanges, which flow in both directions between the communities of origin and destination, shaping in this way, the mechanism through which is transferred part of the labor force reproduction cost, from the migrant settlement society, towards their families and communities of origin.

Nothing exemplifies better this situation than the flow of remittances sent by migrants to their families every day in the origin communities which are mostly used to finance their homes consumption. In effect, just like in this globalized world, migration constitutes a system of labor force transfer from the Third World to the economies of the developed world, remittances represent a wage transfer system not only in the reverse direction, but as a constituent element of this global process which, in turn, is a frame for international migration at present (Canales, 2008).

In recent decades remittances worldwide have increased more than sixfold, from less than 100 billion dollars in the first half of the nineties, to 610 billion in 2016 and an estimated 635 billion for 2017. Although they suffered a momentary break and reduction at the time of the most recent economic crisis, their long term tendency has been one of continual systematic growth, making them one of the most stable and predictable international money flows in global capitalism.

The largest amount of money sent in remittances goes from core countries to the periphery. According to figures from CONAPO (2015), in 2014 the proportion of remittances originating in developed countries amounted to 85%, and 75% of all remittances were sent to developing nations. However, the composition of remittances has not always been the same. It is worthy of note that up until the first half of the 1990s, the principal receivers of remittances were developed countries. With the great flow of migration that started at

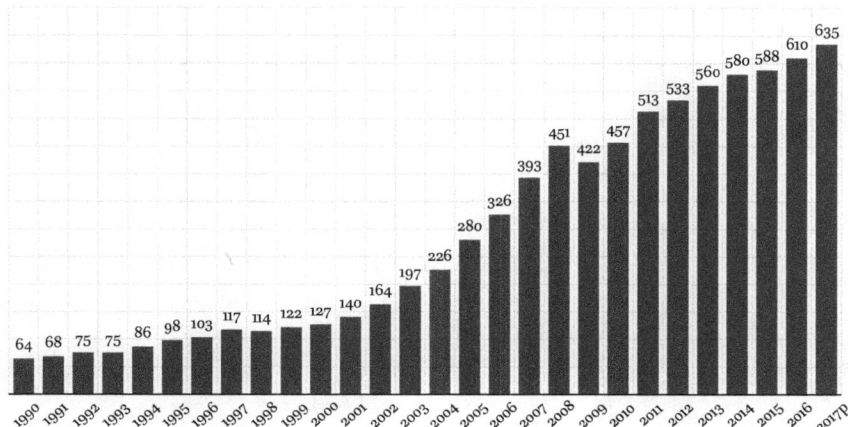

FIGURE 17    Global flow of remittances (billion US dollars)
SOURCE: CONAPO, YEARBOOK OF MIGRATION AND REMITTANCES, MEXICO 2016. TTP://WWW.MIGRACIONYREMESAS.ORG/TB/?A=93E0C5

that time, the relation was inverted, and now practically 75% of all remittances are to developing nations, and only 25% go to core countries.[8]

This redirection of the flow of remittances, in combination with their great stability, shows the importance they have for migrants and for the families receiving them. Even at times of economic crisis, loss of jobs, labor instability and deterioration of the living conditions of migrants in the country they immigrated to, the flow never dried up and was always kept at very stable levels that were even higher than those of other international flows of money received by developing nations.

The case of the Mexico-United States migration nexus allows us to illustrate these tendencies. According to figures from the *Banco de Mexico*[9] (BANXICO, 2017), the annual flow of remittances increased substantially, from under 6 billion dollars in the late 1990s to 26 billion in 2007. With the crisis in 2008, the flow of remittances stood still and then declined, though it was never at risk of stopping completely. The lowest level of remittances was reached in 2009 and 2010, with a figure of 21 billion for each year. Since then the flow has recovered as the US economic cycle has picked up steam, and in 2016 the sum of remittances was of 27 billion dollars, a figure higher than the previous record for 2007.

---

8   It should be pointed out that 85% of the remittances received by core countries are intra-regional, in other words they are sent from core countries to core countries (CONAPO, 2015).
9   Central Bank of Mexico.

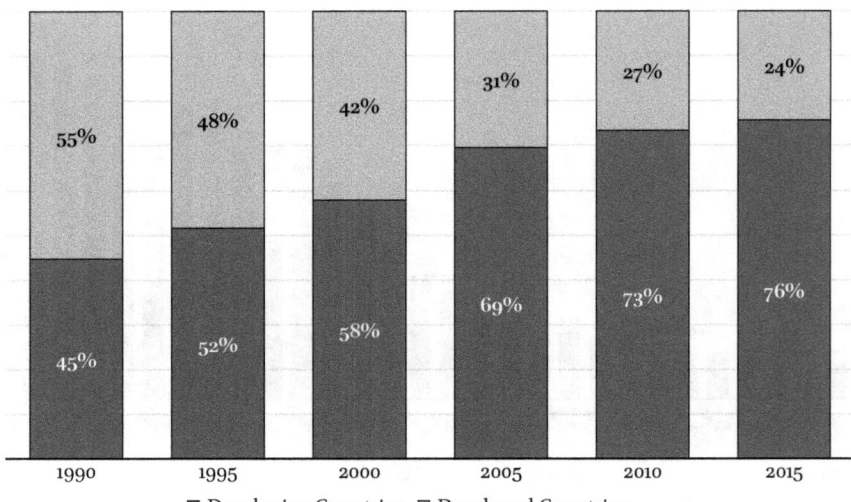

FIGURE 18  Remittances by receiving country (%)
SOURCE: CONAPO, YEARBOOK OF MIGRATION AND REMITTANCES, MEXICO 2016. WWW.MIGRACIONYREMESAS.ORG/TB/?A=00AAA2

With reference to the characteristics of those sending remittances from the USA, Mexicans show a greater propensity to sending remittances than other migrants and also send larger amounts. At USA, in 2008[10] over 35% of households with Mexican migrants sent remittances to their families in Mexico. Further, these households sent on average 8 thousand dollars that year, which amounts to approximately 18% of the income of households with Mexican migrants. Nevertheless these are generally households in a precarious situation socio-economically. According to income records in the USA, practically 46% of Mexican migrants are classified as being in a situation of poverty and/or social vulnerability, a situation that is distinct from that of other Latin American immigrants to the USA and that of migrants from other regions of the world.

In this sense, remittances are a fraction of salaries and fees that labor migrants perceive, which, in view of this, has the same economic function as any other salary: the workforce reproduction. What is peculiar in this case, is that the workforce reproduction occurs in transnational contexts and in globalized labor markets which are based on the transnational communities and families configuration. Remittances are the way in which a migrant salary fraction is transferred to their families and communities of origin to enable their social

---

10  Year for which there is statistical information at national level for the United States.

TABLE 5   USA, 2008. Characteristics of immigrant households sending remittances

| Region and Country of origin of immigrants | Households sending remittances | Average annual remittances (dollars) | Remittances / Income ratio | Poor and vulnerable population |
|---|---|---|---|---|
| Mexicans | 35.4% | $ 7,971 | 18.0% | 45.8% |
| Latino Americans | 30.5% | $ 5,899 | 10.0% | 30.5% |
| Others immigrants | 21.0% | $ 5,697 | 6.3% | 16.1% |

Sources: Current Population Survey, August 2008, Immigration/emigration

reproduction, as any other wage income does in these same communities. Remittances are, without a doubt, a wage-fund. That is its meaning and function as a macroeconomic variable.

However, remittances not only are part of the transnational reproduction process of migrant labor force, but also of socially exclusionary structural conditions and labor precariousness that these labor forces have to face. In other words, when analyzing the remittances in terms of their economic and social significance, we must not disregard this global context of social exclusion and segregation that characterize the migrants' labor insertion, because they (remittances) are a direct product of the global context. In the meanwhile, it is this structural framework of migrants social exclusion and segregation, which ultimately allows us to distinguish between the character and social meaning of remittances perceived by developing countries, from those perceived by the First World industrialized economies.

In other words, remittances also reflect a marked class character. They not only constitute purely and simply a wage-fund, but are workers wage income that combines a highly vulnerable and insecure labor insertion in the destination countries with a condition of poverty, marginalization and social vulnerability in their countries of origin. Thus, remittances make up a wage transfers system, flowing from fragile and vulnerable workers to their family members who live in conditions of poverty and social marginalization contexts. Consequently, it is not uncommon that, on the one hand, remittances are primarily oriented to finance the family consumption, helping to maintain a minimum standard of living, while on the other hand, does not flow in the necessary amounts and volumes to promote a genuine social mobility process (ECLAC, 2005).

These are, ultimately, a transfer of resources between families and low-income workers immersed in social vulnerability and economic insecurity situations which can help to alleviate this situation of poverty, but in no case to resolve it.

The Mexican case allows us to illustrate this thesis about the precarious socioeconomic situation of remittance-sending households from the United States, as well as Mexican migrants in general. In 2008 the annual income of Mexican households that sent remittances from the United States did not exceed 45 thousand dollars. Also 25% of Mexicans in the United States that year were below the poverty line, while another 21% was located in highly vulnerable households whose income did not exceed 15 thousand dollars a year.

Also, seen from the homes that receive them in Mexico, the situation of precariousness is not very different. The large annual volume of remittances is actually a statistical illusion. The 27 billion dollars that arrived in Mexico in 2016 are diluted between more than 91 million small daily transfers of money (BANXICO, 2017). In this way, each transfer is for very small amounts that do not exceed 300 dollars on average. This means that at the household level, remittances are made up of small daily transfers that only allows them to support the daily expenditure on consumption, food, and other basic necessities and services. Even with remittances, more than 44% of the receiving households are still living below the official poverty line in Mexico, which in urban areas does not exceed $ 200 per capita per month ($ 2.3 thousand per year), while in rural areas does not exceed $ 120 per month ($ 1,500 per year) (ENIGH, 2014).

However, remittances have great value for these homes, as they are an irreplaceable source of income that allows them to finance various basic and necessary expenses for their daily subsistence. In 2014 remittances they represented a flow of around 30% of money income of recipient households, a figure that allowed them to finance more than 54% of spending on basic goods and services (food, health, education, water, electricity, etc.) (ENIGH, 2014).

In summary, if with international migration, the communities of origin have become transnationalized, we can also affirm that the migrant labor force reproduction likewise becomes transnationalized. In this global era, the workforce reproduction has become deterritorialized, and adopts a translocal form, in this case, transnational, to the extent that it articulates fields and moments that are located in places separated by national boundaries. In this way, to the extent that the labor force social reproduction is based on international migration and on the transnational communities' formation, these same communities also start becoming part of an important contemporary society globalization process.

However, we must not confuse the transnational nature of migrant communities with their globalization. In the current globalization context, transnational communities and the "transmigration" acquire a special meaning. The social networks of reciprocity, trust and solidarity also operate as a way to deal with the social and political vulnerability problem which arises from the ethnic and migratory condition of the population, and that locates it in a social minority situation. Migrant workers, trapped in inequality and insecurity contexts generated by the process of globalization, are looking for articulating forms of responses, although not always an "exit" from this process, as actors within their own communities.

In this era of globalization, the spaces of negotiation and integration that were configured around the Welfare State and the process of modernization, become dismantled and fragmented, thereby strengthening the exclusion and social differentiation processes. In this context, you can understand the resurgence of basic and "primary" forms of solidarity, trust and reciprocity, as that which shapes and give substance to the transnational communities.

In this sense, its articulation through transnational communities create opportunities for action to confront their situation of social vulnerability through the communities themselves. The relocation risks, the settlement costs, the employment search, social inclusion within communities of destination, the everyday family reproduction in their home communities, among other things, tend to rest on the social relations and networks system that the transnational communities make up so as to facilitate both the movement and the migrant labor insertion.

Furthermore, the social capital of migrants enables them to face and set up responses to their precarious conditions of employment derived from the labor flexibility and contractual deregulation that characterizes labor markets in an age of globalization. In fact, the transnationalization of the labor force based on the communities' social networks can also be understood as a counterpart of the globalization of capital, though not necessarily as a globalization of the workers. In this sense, the dichotomy commonly raised in terms that capital is becoming globalized and work is becoming localized, in our opinion, is not correctly stated. On the one hand, it is important to distinguish between "labor" and "labor power". Labor, as concrete activity (utility-producing) or abstract process (value-producing), is as globalized as the capital itself. Labor power, on the other hand, is not. The globalization of the labor power would be the globalization of the individual workers, a process however that does not appear to assume the forms and content of labor and capital globalization.

On the other hand, it is necessary to distinguish the forms of globalization, that is, the entry/exit paths of globalization. While capital is globalized from above, and above this, it is the logic of capital that leads to the globalization process, the labor force enters in this process in a subordinated form, i.e., from below, with a limited scope to define its operation (Portes, Guarnizo and Landolt, 2003; Bauman, 2011). In this sense, we must not confuse the transnational nature of labor migration, with its possible and hypothetical globalization. Labor becomes global not because it is forming part of a transnational community, but because it is inserted into work processes that are part of the globalization. Conversely, the transnational communities are not the driveway to globalization for the migrant worker, but rather, they constitute a response strategy to which migrant workers may appeal, to deal with the costs of its access to labor markets that operate with a globalized logic.

The transnationalization is not the form that globalized labor assumes. On the contrary, it is a strategy developed by workers to deal with the conditions of globalized labor. In this way, the transnational communities define a field of action, a structure of options that the migrant workers can develop that allow him or her to assume and distribute the costs of their actions and reproduction in the globalized world. In this sense, social networks and the transnational communities have a dual role. As a response strategy, it serves to reproduce the conditions of social subordination generated by globalization. On the other hand, as a field of alternative action, the transnational communities can also configure social areas from which the reduced negotiating frameworks, imposed by globalization, can be transcended.[11]

Traditionally, these processes have been analyzed and conceptualized as a form of reproduction of the migrant community itself which, based on the interaction between two distant and geographically separated areas by national boundaries, acquires the name of transnational. In our case, we would like to give an additional turn to this same mechanism of community's social reproduction to focus on what we are interested in, which is the migrant labor force reproduction.

From our perspective, through the community and the family social reproduction, not only are people reproduced in abstract, but also and fundamentally, their social position in a particular context of economic and labor relations is reproduced. If from demography, anthropology or sociology, we

---

11   On this point, we would like to raise our distance with regard to certain authors that assume an optimistic and "celebratory" position concerning the ability of the migrant communities to deal with a hypothetical success, their social reproduction conditions. The opening of an alternative field of action, does not ensure that it is successful. Rather, it defines a field of confrontation, conflicts and contradictions that, more than determining a result, it defines the conditions under which it develops the collective and individual action.

can see the social networks, and its transnationality as a social reproduction strategy of population, families, and/or the community, as well as from the economy, and in particular, from the perspective of capital reproduction, we can see these same mechanisms as a social base for the labor power reproduction in the current context of economic globalization.[12]

Networks and the migrants' social capital are the migration reproduction mechanism as a social process. This is not a question of migration reproduction in general, but of labor migrants who are inserted into productive activities for capital in the destination countries, thus participating in the structure of social differentiation, i.e., of different social classes, within the context of a global society.

## 5  Conclusion

From the perspective of the functioning of economy, migration constitutes a demographic and social mechanism that contributes at least in two ways to the economic system reproduction, and by this means, to the capital accumulation at a global scale, namely:

– On the one hand, it contributes with the necessary volume of labor force to sustain the economic and productive activity in the destination countries, helping to make up for the demographic shortfall generated in these countries as a result of the combination of population ageing processes and the advance of the second demographic transition.
– On the other hand, it contributes with labor force which, while simultaneously presenting low costs of social reproduction, is inserted into the labor market in a context of high insecurity, instability and labor flexibility. It is a question of workers whose migrant condition (and most of the time undocumented) locate them in high social vulnerability situation.

Likewise, these economic and labor contributions of migrants are based on the formation of social networks that, from a system of solidarity, reciprocity and mutual support, allow that on the one hand, migrant workers move continually and recurrently from the origin communities towards the advanced

---

12  Consequently, it is not a question of different, new, or emerging processes, but of different interpretations of the same process. In fact, our interpretation intends precisely to integrate all these visions that have been developed from various disciplinary and research fields to carry out a broader and more comprehensive model of international migration. What's new in our proposal is not the fact of being aiming to emerging or new processes, but in how we read and interpret the same processes that have already been extensively documented by the most diverse authors.

societies' labor markets. Through networks, the displacement costs and risks are reduced, at the same time that it makes it possible to obtain jobs and to integrate to a host community. On the other hand, through these same social networks flow material, monetary, and symbolic resources, which enables families and migrants reproduction in their places of origin. In this case, the flow of remittances is highlighted, both because of the high amounts that they involve, and also because of its importance and social significance as a wage fund which support the social and economic reproduction of migrants and their families.

All of this, makes up a comprehensive system of the economy reproduction, where migration contributes in a double sense:
– On the one hand, as a labor power which is treated as a commodity that workers sell to the capitalist, they contribute through their labor (in concrete and abstract forms) to the reproduction and accumulation of the capital. It is a question of their contribution to the productive moment in the reproduction of the global economic system.
– On the other hand, through the networks and social capital that migrants put in motion when displacing, a reproduction form of that same migrant labor power is set up. It is in this case, the migration contribution to the reproductive moment of the global economic system.

The shared vision of both moments, allows us to understand that this is not purely and simply a matter of the labor force reproduction for the capital, but of vulnerable and unprotected migrant workers, susceptible to be inserted in highly flexible and unstable occupations along with high levels of job insecurity.

Likewise, migration contributes to reduce the labor force reproduction cost for the capital. In particular, the same social networks that, in one way sustain migration, in another contribute to transfer to the families and origin communities, part of the labor power reproduction cost.

In this way, the salary and remunerations paid to migrants in their destination places don't have to necessarily cover the whole cost of labor power reproduction, since part of it has been transferred to families in their origin places, and is covered with other family income and resources. In other words, both the daily and inter-generational labor power reproduction, rests largely on family and community resources, as well as in the expenses and subsidies that the origin countries' States make (education, health, transport, among others).

In this regard, we propose a paradoxical situation in relation to migration and globalization. As we have noted in previous chapters, although migrants almost never appear as one of the actors on which globalization concentrates the focus, their labor certainly constitutes a substantial part in a globalizing capital, to the extent that they constitute, as we have seen, a substantial element without which, the same economic dynamics of the developed countries would be seriously undermined. As labor (concrete and abstract), migrants participate directly in the globalization, and contribute to the capital reproduction and accumulation, at a global scale. Their concrete labor (utility-producing, use value labor) is embodied in all commodities that are produced around the world just as their abstract labor (value-producing, labor time) is objectified in the value of merchandise that is traded daily in diverse global markets around the world

However, as workers (labor power), migrants are continuously and permanently relegated to the confines of globalization, away from all the glamour that it holds, and always in the shadow of their labor. They are always merely supporting actors, only extras of a global production. As workers, their globalization is restricted to the deterritorialization of their reproduction spaces as labor force, that is, to the confined spaces of their communities that, although they adopt a translocal and transnational form, it is not necessarily a global form.

In this sense, migration sets up a mechanism that articulates two moments of economic globalization. On the one hand, as labor, it contributes to the globalization from above, i.e., to the globalization of capital along with their actors and representatives. On the other hand, as labor power, it is part of a globalization from below, i.e., to the globalization and deterritorialization of the workforce reproduction that global capital requires.

The problem for migrants is that the labor force is their only belonging, not their labor. Consequently, their labor is part of the big globalization of capital. In fact, for that to happen, they must previously alienate their labor force, selling it to the capital, which extracts the labor (value), and accumulates it in its global form, returning the worker (individuals) to their globalized forms of subordination.

While their labor, materialized in the most diverse products such as artifacts, goods and merchandise, circulate around the world, crossing borders, being part of the business of globalization; the workers who, from below, are the real architects of this process, remain consigned to a translocal displacement, to reproduction spaces which are restricted and locally placed or even exposed to various forms of territorial segregation. Their neighborhoods may be a characteristic of a global city, but they do not stop being local neighborhoods, ghettos of a globalization which excludes them in their process of reproduction. Here we have one of the great paradoxes of contemporary migration: the globalization of labor and production, i.e., of reproduction of capital, implies meanwhile that, the labor force reproduction is circumscribed and maintained in local areas. We arrived thus, to a new meaning for the concept of *Glocalization*, which is added to those of Bauman (1998) and Robertson (1992): The globalization of Capital and its accumulation, as the counterpart of labor force reproduction location, which sustains it and reproduces it.

In this sense, we can understand the double character of contemporary migration:
– On the one hand, as provision of labor power for capital, a capitalist strategy to obtain the necessary vital labor to sustain its extended reproduction in the framework of its own globalization.
– On the other hand, as a social process based on family networks and social capital, a strategy of workers (labor force) reproduction that, although it takes a transnational and translocal form, keeps being located and confined to local and foreign spaces, excluded from the show business of capital globalization and the new economy.

All of the above leads us to argue that in the context of globalization, the analysis of international migration must be necessarily sustained in the problematization of the inequality structures and social differentiation that arise from the globalization itself. Nevertheless, it is a question that has not always been recaptured in the debate Migration-Development. From the neoclassical approaches, for example, the inequality and migration problem, is faced as a transitory issue, to the extent that migration itself constitutes a mechanism for achieving the necessary balance, both in terms of wages and population living conditions, as into the asymmetries in the productivities and interregional levels of development.[13]

For its part, in the classic structuralist approaches, the analysis tended to consider the social inequality as a remnant or social backwardness. In the historical-structural approach, the stress was put on the social inequality, conceived in terms of social marginalization and exclusion to which certain sectors of the population are subjected (migrants, young people, women, peasants, informal sector, etc.). It dealt with supernumerary staff, who were constantly expelled from the labor market, forming an industrial reserve army, a constant workers oversupply. In this sense, the vulnerability and fragility framework of these temporary workers, rested precisely in their *exclusion* or labor market marginalization.

---

13  This is the case, for example, of the A. Lewis growth model with unlimited supply of labor force. According to this model, the social rural-urban inequality (traditional-modern) would tend to disappear to the extent that it starts an agrarian transformation process, in a horizon in which modernization was the strategy to be implemented in order to eliminate both the demographic imbalances, as the socio-economic inequalities.

From our perspective, however, we argue that with globalization new forms of social inequality are configured, which do not correspond with either the traditional forms of social exclusion, or even less, with the persistence of traditional social or pre-modern structures. In globalization, poverty and workers precariousness, in this case of migrants, is not the result of their labor market exclusion (unemployment, industrial reserve army, etc.), but on the contrary, it is a consequence of the manner in which they are included and integrated into the world of labor, precisely, as migrant workers. This is no longer an impoverishment due to social and economic marginalization, i.e. impoverishment as a result of being excluded or expelled from the labor market, the formal economy, etc., but on the contrary, it is a question of socially vulnerable workers, inserted in dynamic economic sectors.

In the current framework of economic deregulation and labor flexibility, it's the modernization and globalization processes themselves that create and reproduce its own forms of poverty and inequality, i.e. a modern and global poverty and social inequality.[14] As Beck (2000a) points out, in global society, capitalism has broken with the labor society and the welfare state bases, in a horizon in which economic growth no longer ensures neither the abolition of unemployment nor the improvement of population living and working conditions.

In this sense, in the case of migrants, they are not exposed to a situation of social exclusion in itself, at least not in its traditional sense. Rather, they are exposed to vulnerability and conditions of social inequality. In any case, if the concept of exclusion has to be used, this, has to refer to fragmented, vulnerable and precarious forms of inclusion rather than to an expulsion or marginalization of economy and society. In a strict sense, this is a contradictory process that is simultaneously of inclusion and social exclusion (De Souza Martins, 1998). It is a partial and contradictory inclusion from below, which is based on times and spaces of exclusion. In global society the social minority condition (migratory condition, in our case) ceases to be the risk of a possible economic exclusion, to become the necessary condition for its fragmented, partial and precarious inclusion (Canales, 2003).

In this way, in the global economic system reproduction of capital, accumulation and economic growth rests on the *ad infinitum* reproduction of this social inequality condition, which in this case, is also the basis for the migrant workers exploitation.

---

14  The corollary of this thesis is simple but radical: it is no longer possible to rely on a modernization or social development project to overcome poverty and social inequality, since these, far from constituting pre-modern societies remnants, are a constituent of globalization itself.

CHAPTER 7

# Migration and Social Reproduction

*Wherever I am*
*I never forget my roots*
*Countries where I have lived*
*They have joined nuances*[1]
    The Rose of the Winds
    MAKIZA / ANITA TIJOUX

∴

1   **Thesis**

Migration establishes a system of relations between social classes is set up which transcends and penetrates national borders, along with articulating in the similar process, the conditions and dynamics of origin and destination countries, social reproduction. As a social process, migration is a mechanism that contributes to the reproduction of class structure and social differentiation in the global world. It links the field and reproduction moments of the migrant labor force (based on the social networks system and the transnational communities), with the social reproduction moments and fields of the middle and upper classes into their destination societies through its increasing engagement in work and occupations inherent to social reproduction.

In the previous chapters, we saw how from demography, migration is a mechanism that links the population dynamics of origin places with that of host countries, setting up what we have termed a demographic reproduction regime at a global scale. We have also seen how from the economy, migration is also a mechanism that links the moment of labor power (migrants) reproduction with the moment of production itself, thus contributing to the reproduction of capital in this global age.

However although these approaches are important, we believe that they by themselves are insufficient to understand the complex meaning of migration

---

1   "Donde me halle, nunca olvido mis raíces. Los países donde he vivido, han unido sus matices". Original in Spanish.

in the global society. They provide an account of an initial level of structural analysis that explains the migration causes and its role in the economic reproduction of global capitalism, as well as the underlying demographic conditions. However, they do not go deeper into a second level of understanding migration that accounts for its role in the social reproduction in global society, how migration is part of a global configuration of class structures and social inequality at contemporary world.

## 2  Social Networks and SocialReproduction

International migration configures a survival and social reproduction strategy for the families in the migration communities of origin, mainly based on family networks and migrants social capital (de Haas, 2007). It is a question of family and community relations, such as kinship and *compadrazgo*, which are based on confidence, reciprocity and solidarity systems among members of the same community.

To the extent that this system of social relations networks adopts a transnational path, various authors note that the migrants social reproduction along with that of their families and communities also adopt this same transnational modality. The transnational nature of this social fabric, derives from the fact that it has been constructed based on practices, activities and exchanges that continuously cross political, geographical and cultural boundaries, which traditionally had framed and separated migrant's communities of origin and settlement. In this way, *transnationalism* is defined as the process by which migrants build these social areas which join their own communities and societies of origin with those of settlement (Goldring, 1997; Levitt and Glick Schiller, 2004).

In particular, this system of transnational social networks, once established, not only serves to sustain displacement of people, but also takes the form of a continuous flow of material and symbolic goods in both directions through which is formed a complex social system whose structures of material, social and symbolic relations transcend the communities national borders and territorial limits. What is relevant is that through this flow of goods, information, people, symbols, forms of power and authority, among others, is articulated the social reproduction of the origin communities with the social reproduction process in the migrants places of settlement in the destination countries (Canales and Montiel, 2010).

These social and family networks operate in the different levels and social fields that make up the communities. social reproduction. Through them, the community's members interact and develop their social, cultural, economic and political activities. Likewise, the practice of these actions and exchanges in transnational contexts strengthens the networks themselves, and allows the territorial expansion of the community reproduction areas.

Thus, for example, the labor insertion and the search for a job is extended not only to the community of origin territorial confines, but it also includes, in an important way, available work options in the migrants settlement locations. Through the social networks of each transnational community, information flows in both directions in terms of the needs and job options in each territorial scope. These networks facilitate the mobility of individuals from one place to another, minimizing the displacement risk, as well as the costs of settlement and integration into the labor market (Sassen, 1995). Frequently, migrants know, even before starting the trip, how they are going to cross, where they are going to arrive at each migration stage as well as where they are going to work and what would be their wages and working conditions in the destination places.

Similar processes correspond to the reproduction of the domestic unit and family life. In this case, even when a family, or household members may be territorially separated, their belonging to a transnational community allows the rebuilding of their home unit. Through social networks flows not only information but also ways of exercising intra-familiar power, domestic and daily decision-making, etc. (Delaunay and Lestage, 1998).

Such is the case, for example, with virtual transnationalization of care and maternity systems. Based on social and family networks, it is possible to articulate and complement the specific job that female migrants develop in the destination place in relation to the social reproduction process of their children in the origin communities (Herrera, 2005; Hondagneu-Sotelo, 2007; Ehrenteich and Hochschild, 2004). On the one hand, immigrant women find a labor niche in the care of the middle and upper class family's children as also in the care of the elderly and sick people in the destination places. On the other hand, to facilitate migration of these women, it is necessary a social and family network to ensure the care of their own children in their communities of origin (Parella, 2003).

In this way, immigrant women through their own labor migration, articulates the care of their children and, therefore their social reproduction, with the care and social reproduction of native middle and upper classes families in the destination places. The basis of this process is precisely the social network that extends from the communities of origin into the destination cities. In other words, through migration transnational networks, motherhood, care, and in general, social reproduction, both in the places of origin and destination, are no longer confined to the local spaces but rather obtain a transnational character (Hondagneu-Sotelo and Avila, 1999).

For its part, the relations and community structures reproduction also adopts a transnationalized form. The forms of power, social differences, and in general, social, cultural and political structures that each community constitute are also remitted from the origin country, to the places of settlement (Smith, 2006; Rivera, 2004). However, and this is important, *transnationalism* not only involves to transfer this system of relations and social structures, but also, a modification of them.

Thus, as an example, we can cite the expansion of women's roles in households in which the household head has emigrated. In these cases, the woman must expand their traditional responsibilities, including part of the tasks and responsibilities that have traditionally been assigned to the male, both as a provider subject of material resources to assure family reproduction, and subject on which a big part of the power structure within the family rests. The long period of absence of this male figure involves changes in the women's roles, later becoming evident in family conflicts at the time of reunification, either by the return of the household head, or by the rest of the family migration and its reunification in the destination places.

For its part, the increasing share of female and family migration has allowed women to have access to social contexts in which the gender distinction is constructed based on different principles and social relations than those prevailing in the communities of origin. This has allowed, in general terms, a positive alteration for the benefit of women concerning power relations within the family and the community, but this does not imply, however, an absence of conflict and daily tensions (Hondagneu-Sotelo, 1994 and 2007). Something similar can arise in connection with the intergenerational relations, that is, a change in the roles and relative positions of the young, adults and the elderly people.

Also, community and social networks not only allow the reproduction and changes in the relationships and community structures, but on this basis, there is also a reproduction of the prevailing forms of social inequality (Tilly, 1990). Just as the networks contribute to reproduce and perpetuate processes and social relationships, they also contribute to reproduce the forms and character of these processes and social relationships.

In the case of social inequality, for example, this is created and reproduced to the extent that at the same time that they configure networks of social inclusion and belonging to a transnational community, it also shapes ways of exclusion and non-membership to national communities. Each form of inclusion is also a form of exclusion. This is, the social network allows access to certain flows of information, exchanges, and social positions. But it is also an exclusion form in a double sense. On the one hand, it excludes from the migrant community other individuals who do not belong to the social network. On the other hand, it also prevents members of the transnational community from accessing other social networking of information exchanging.

In this way, social networks at the same time that they extend and modify, recreate different forms of inequality.[2] Thus, for example, in the search for a job through social networks, the migrant does not obtain the *optimal* employment for him/her, according to the "objective" market conditions and their own capabilities. He/she only gets the *possible* job, that is, the one that is accessible to the social networks of which he/she participates (Requena, 1991). In the search for a job they don't have all the theoretically available options but only those that are accessible through family contacts and *paisanos*. In this way, gaining employment and therefore the labor insertion form is based on the network extension and the social and cultural capital.

A typical example is the articulation of the migrants' social networks with the subcontractor's field of labor, which allows migrants to gain access to an employment quickly and safely, but in a high flexibility context, and where the social network itself may serve as a labor control mechanism. In no few instances, the contractor has family (or *compadrazgo*) ties with their employees, which generates tensions and conflicts between the two social roles (Zlolnisky, 2006).

In this way, social and family networks, not only give sustenance to the migration and migrants reproduction purely and simply, but through this, they contribute to the reproduction of their position within the social structure, both in the places of origin and destination. In this case, they are migrant workers inserted in precarious work conditions, high flexibility, without benefits, and in many occasions, with high social and political vulnerability derived from undocumented status. Social networks, as well as transnational communities, fail to solve this situation simply because they are not solution strategies that put an end to insecurity and economic subordination. Rather, they form a mechanism that at the same time that the migration social process is reproduced, it also reproduces the migrants' social situation, i.e., its relative position compared to the other strata and social classes.

Thus, for example, through social networks, migrants access to jobs, occupations, houses, social life spaces, etc., but it is a question of social fields where the same socio-economic situation is reproduced. In other words, social networks are a capital of great value, and of great power to confront and achieve

---

2   However, it should be noted that the network reproduction reproduces the inequality, though it does not perpetuates their forms. As well as the relationships and social interchange, by means of networking, involves the reproduction, extension and transformation of the same networks, in the same way, they would allow the forms of inequality transformation.

the survival and reproduction in adverse social situations of high vulnerability. But this does not add up to a strategy of solution and overcoming these structural conditions which, in many cases, define and determine the relative position of the subjects, particularly in relation to their subordinate status, along with the lack of social and political bargaining power.

Without doubt, specific cases may be documented where migration and social networks have provided for a social mobility of the migrant and their families. However, beyond their testimonial value, these are many times an exception to the rule and move completely away from the regularity that migration statistics shows. It can operate as an option within the migrant imaginary, the illusion of eventually achieving the famous American dream, but in no case does it constitute a real and effective option for the whole of the migrant population and their families.

Ultimately, social networks are an essential component of social capital that allows the configuration and reproduction of transnational communities. Such social networks form the basis of both solidarity relations and mutual assistance among its members, as well as the generation and reproduction of class, gender and generational social inequalities, which are often ignored by the most romantic and celebratory versions of the transnational migration model.

## 3      Migration and Social Reproduction in Host Societies

Just as demographic reproduction nor the reproduction of the capital (economy) in a globalized world are no longer confined to the boundaries of the existing States and national societies, the social reproduction (social stratification) of those countries cannot be circumscribed to the narrow confines of the national societies. In this regard, we have shown elsewhere how in the case of advanced societies such as Spain and the United States, the social reproduction of its middle and upper classes has also had to adapt to these times of globalization through opening spaces to incorporate social subjects (immigrants) and social fields (their families and communities) that are clearly beyond the society limits and Spanish and American state (Canales, 2015b and 2013). It is a question of the creation of intersection spaces between social processes that previously were held not only as distant, but also independent and autonomous.

This set of changes in the social reproduction dynamics is not separated from the social and cultural transformations that for some decades experience advanced societies in the framework of what Bauman (2000) has named as the advent of liquid and postmodern societies. On the one hand, the same economic development promotes new consumption and lifestyle patterns, favoring the commercialization of many activities linked to social and daily reproduction, which earlier occurred in the private and family life spaces. The individuation processes and changes in the role of the home and family, for example, along with the increasing incorporation of women into public life and labor, involve a certain liberation and emancipation of the ancient chains that tied them to household tasks.

These social changes also open up a space for the increasing incorporation of immigrant workers, men and women, in these various activities related to native population social reproduction. From this perspective, international migration also helps to sustain the social, cultural and demographic changes that characterize contemporary advanced societies. Thus, for example, both the children and the elderly care, as domestic service itself ceases to be an inherent task of native women and becomes a commercialized labor made by immigrants but under conditions dictated by the labor flexibility and contractual deregulation of post-industrial societies. In this way, we can state that one of the international migration roles is to provide the necessary workforce to sustain social reproduction of the native population in the destination country.[3]

The following is an analysis that seeks to illustrate this model that enhances the understanding of the importance of migration in advanced societies. We begin with an analysis of the changes in the occupational structure in core economies which under globalization, have involved an increasing job polarization and labor markets segmentation. At this level, we want to emphasize the importance of immigration to fill both, the demographic deficit of labor force, and

---

3  Another way that this native population social reproduction delocalization takes on in the core countries, is the provision of goods and services. Globalization itself has relocated its production in the Third World countries, taking advantage of lower wage costs. An example of this, is the growth of the in bond industry in Mexico, Central American and Asian countries. They are factories for assembling final products, many of high tech such as plasma televisions, personal computers, cellular phones, tablets, and an endless number of modern electronic products which are not intended for local consumption, but to that of the core countries population, thereby contributing to reduce the economic costs of its social reproduction. In this case, even if the worker remains tied to its local spaces, their work, reflected in the goods and merchandise he/she produces, goes through various paths of globalization. What is relevant in this case, is how, once again, the social reproduction of the core countries population, is articulated and directly dependent upon the labor power reproduction in the peripheral countries. This is how a life style reproduction, with its privileges, conveniences and comfort, is based on a labor force reproduction in conditions of high labor insecurity and social vulnerability, totally removed from those globalization privileges and comfort. For more details, see Castillo, 2016, Cypher and Delgado, 2010, and Cypher, 2009.

the needs of workers who are in low-skilled and highly flexible occupations with high degrees of labor precariousness and flexibility.

### 3.1 Globalization and Employment Polarization

Migration's contribution to social reproduction in host societies is part of the economic and labor dynamics resulting from the globalization of economy in those societies. This is no time to review and discuss this process, as we are only interested in taking up the changes in labor market dynamics and occupations structure that are derived from it and make up the structural framework to facilitate the insertion of migrant workers into the labor market.

In this regard, various authors point out that in terms of the work organization, globalization has meant the passing from the already classic Fordism mass production industrial model, to a *just in time* flexible production, based on the post-Fordism principles of industrial organization (Lipietz, 1997). If in the first, a national productive base was articulated with a global marketing, in the second one, globalization has also reached the same work process (Hobsbawm, 2000) Also, if the first one gave rise to a social and state order, identified with Keynesianism and the Welfare State as regulatory frameworks of the economy, the second one gave rise to a new world economic and social order, based on neo-liberalism and the market as a mechanism for (de)regulation of the economy functioning.

This context of flexible production and markets deregulation, raises numerous changes in the economic structure and dynamics of today's societies. Among them are the changes that affect the employment and occupations structure, and in general, the capital-labor relations which are the basis for the emergence of a new class structure and social stratification.

If the new productive matrix is the basis of the new form adopted by the process of capitalist accumulation in globalized economies, the polarization of occupations is the basis for the emergence of a new class structure and social stratification in advanced societies.

In particular, the new class structure is settled up a new polarization and social differentiation pattern, based on two different and complementary processes:
- On the one hand, the restructuring of the labor regime based on the new flexibility structures and labor deregulation, resulting in what Beck (2000b) termed a labor risk regime, which replaces the labor regime and social institutions that have emerged through the Welfare State.[4]

---

[4] As the author points out, in the information society the Fordism regime of work organization tends to be replaced by a risk regime which, through labor flexibility, tends to "blur the

– On the other hand, the transformation of the occupation system based on their increasing segmentation along with the differentiation and social and labor inequality that they entail (Sassen, 2007; Pioré, 1979). The advent of an economy of information leads to the occupational structure polarization in the informational societies with the consequent increase of occupations and activities located at the ends of the socio-occupational stratification (Castells, 1996).

In this labor risk regime, the positions and growing occupations are not only the "richest" in information or built-in knowledge, but also there is a sustained increase in the services occupations and low-skilled jobs. It is about the quantitative boom of *non-informational* jobs, but as its counterpart, they are part of the new social structure that characterizes the informational society (Bauman, 2011; Kumar, 1995).

This is not about residual occupations nor remnants of pre-informational societies. Nor does it correspond to marginalized jobs or those "excluded" from the production and reproduction of the informational society. On the contrary, they correspond to jobs and occupations that arise with the informational modernity itself, but that are exposed to extreme forms of wage flexibility and contractual deregulation, which has involved its social and economic devaluation. They correspond to occupations that are important pieces in the reproduction process of the informational society (Sassen, 2007).

In quantitative terms, this polarization is perceptible in a significant change concerning the relative weight of each activity and occupation that has to be understood in the light of two complementary processes.
– On the one hand, the development of jobs with high informational content, which require high levels of human capital training and development, and consequently, are well-paid, highly valued, and inserted in flexibility logics that allow its continuous adaptation to market changes, without loss of employment quality.
– On the other hand, the quantitative increase in jobs of low-paid, precarious, unskilled and with low levels of human capital, whose performance does not necessarily incorporates informational processes. They correspond to highly unregulated and flexible jobs, but in a completely opposite direction to the previous ones.

Figures for the United States and European Union illustrate the process of polarization of occupations. Between 2000 and 2016, employment increased from

---

boundaries between work and not work both in the temporal dimension As in the spatial and contractual; Paid work and unemployment are extended and have increasingly invisible contours socially speaking" (Beck, 2000: 86).

# MIGRATION AND SOCIAL REPRODUCTION

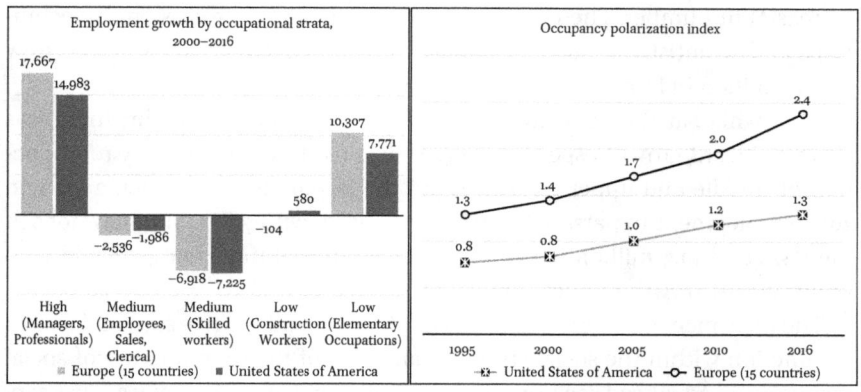

FIGURE 19   USA and Europe (15 countries). Employment growth and occupational polarization
SOURCES: US CENSUS BUREAU, CURRENT POPULATION SURVEY, MARCH SUPPLEMENT 1995, 2000, 2005, 2010 AND 2016; AND EUROSTAT, EMPLOYEES BY SEX, AGE AND OCCUPATION, HTTP://APPSSO.EUROSTAT.EC.EUROPA.EU/NUI/SHOW.DO?DATASET=LFSA_EEGAIS&LANG=EN

a rate of 14.5 to 18.1 million new jobs a year, figures that show an increase of 10% in the United States and 13% in Europe. However, this rate of growth was not reflected equally in all occupations.

While jobs at the very top and at the very bottom of the occupations hierarchy are the most dynamic and have the highest rates of growth, those in the middle ranges are stagnating and depressed, and even show an absolute decrease in the rate of employment. This unequal tendency is directly linked to the processes of de-industrialization and tertiarization characteristic of the new productive matrix of the core economies.

On the one hand, de-industrialization and the relocation of capitals and productive processes from the core to peripheral economies has provoked a substantial loss of productive posts both in the European Union and the USA. In the case of Europe, de-industrialization meant the loss of 7 million jobs between 2000 and 2016, equivalent to 20% of the productive jobs in 2000. In the case of the United States, although the loss of jobs was much the same in absolute terms, it represents a larger proportion as it implies a reduction of 25% in directly productive activities.

On the other hand, the tertiarizing of the economy turned out to be the basis for new forms of polarization and differentiation of occupations in advanced societies. Middle range jobs were reduced in number (hired staff, office workers, and other services in support of management and production), while the number of jobs at the pinnacle and the base of the pyramid of occupations increased in number. The number of jobs for qualified professionals, technicians and scientists,[5] as also for managers and business administrators, grew by 17.7 million in Europe and nearly 15 million in the US.

Meanwhile, at the opposite end of the occupational hierarchy, there was also significant growth especially in jobs devoted to the day-to-day reproduction of middle and upper class strata of the population.[6] Between 2000 and 2016, employment in personal services increased, with 7.8 million new jobs in the USA, and 10.3 million in Europe, figures representing over 40% and 33% accumulated growth respectively.

The relevance of this growth lies in its absolute and relative size, and also in its function within the social structure and that of the reproduction of social inequality in advanced societies. These are jobs that are essentially a necessary counterpart complementing the increase in jobs on the opposite side of the structure of occupations. The increase in the number of people in employment with high levels of income, resources and purchasing power (professionals, managers, CEOs and others) has resulted in a greater demand for personal services, whether highly qualified (interior designers, psychiatrists, exclusive boutiques, etc.) or less qualified (domestic help, cleaning and maintenance services, food preparation, household and house services, personal caring, and many others).

Both the one type and the other are counterparts of the same process of tertiarization although their linkage is no longer in spaces of production, where manual, ethnical and professional workers were joined in the space of the factory. Their linkage is now external and is mediated by the commercializing of these personal and care services, and of construction. The relation of this emerging upper middle class to this new lower class is through the market, and it is contractual instead of being an economic-productive relation. For this reason it is much more exposed to various forms of deregulation of contracts and labor flexibility, factors that form a context of high labor precariousness that translates into precarious working conditions for those employed. So it is not strange that those employed in such jobs tend to be mostly immigrants and other subjects in conditions of social vulnerability.

---

5  These are two distinct types of jobs. There are professionals and technicians who lend their services to companies in the processes of research and development, innovation and the application of new technologies, and to company development and business management. But there are also professionals in social services, education, health and various public services offered by both the State and the private sector that are directed to the general population.

6  This covers a wide variety of personal services, like maids and housekeeping cleaners, food preparation, concierges and the cleaning and maintenance of houses and buildings, gardeners, chauffeurs, services for repairing goods, personal care services, and others.

Of equal interest is the observation that this process of job polarization has been taking place in an uninterrupted systemic fashion from the 1990s to date, both in the United States and in European Union. We can see this in the polarization index, which measures the relation between jobs at the lowest and highest ends with regard to the number of jobs in the middle range. As in the United States, so in Europe a continual systematic growth is observed in the polarization of occupations. In Europe polarization increased by more than 80%, passing from 1.3 in 1995 to 2.4 in 2016. And in the United States, the figure for polarization grew by 62%, from 0.8 in 1995 to 1.3 in 2016. The latter is a most illustrative case. The change is from a situation in the 1990s, where jobs in the middle range of the employment structure predominated, to the current situation in which the roles of different types of job are reversed, showing the polarization of employments and the segmentation of labor markets, phenomena that are a simple reflection of the differentiation of society into strata and social classes ever more distant from each other and segmented by the dynamics of labor markets.

In effect, in the Fordist regime of production and industrialization, in the context of a Welfare State, the structure of employment should be sustained by a greater volume of middle range workers. Such an arrangement was also part of a system of social and political stability, in which the middle classes played a central role in the cohesion of society. In the present period of neoliberal globalization, the Work Society is becoming Risk Society (Beck, 2000b). Flexibility, deregulation, individualization and other processes of Postmodern Society become a Labor Risk Regime. The previous occupational and social structure based on the predominance of the middle classes is disarticulated, the effect of which is principally on people belonging to the middle range strata, who find themselves under pressure to rise through the development of professional skills or else sink into more precarious living and working conditions.

What this analysis of figures shows us that the process of socio-occupational polarization forms the basis of the new shape assumed by the structure of social classes and social inequality in advanced societies. We can see that work has been losing its role as a mechanism of social cohesion and integration, to become a device by which classes are differentiated, with the social segregation of demographic groups. As distinct from the case in previous times, when work functioned as a way of incorporating individuals into the structure of society, forming part of the processes of social integration and mobility, today work has lost this binding role to become, in fact, its opposite, a mechanism that sanctifies inequality, segregation and the separation of classes from each other, making social mobility, and the integration of classes in a single social, political and economic fabric, harder to achieve. Segmentation of labor markets amounts to the segmentation of society into strata and social classes without further economic or productive relations between them.

### 3.2  Racializing Social Inequality and Class Structure in the United States

If we analyze these processes of occupational polarization through the lens of the ethnic and migratory condition of workers, we can see how socio-occupational differentiation is dressed in the ethnic and racial clothing upon which processes of social segregation and political and economic discrimination are based (Maldonado, 2009; Hondagneu-Sotelo, 2007). It follows that statistical data for the case of the United States, presented below, will allow us to illustrate how and to what extent the occupational polarization described above acquires a form of *racialized* social and labor inequality.

The combined effect of demographic change (which implies a higher rate of growth of ethnic minorities in comparison with the white majority) on the one hand, and the different patterns of insertion into the labor market by each ethnic and migratory group on the other, have resulted in a transformation of the ethnic and racial composition of occupations, and in this way in a reconfiguration of the structure of classes and social inequality.

Up until the year 2000, white workers in the United States were the absolute majority at all levels of employment, which reflected their demographic majority in the country. However, their majority was more obvious in the higher social strata, and less pronounced in the lower ranks. At higher levels of employment, whites had 82% of all management positions and 80% of professional jobs, in spite of the fact that whites represented 74% of people in employment. While in the case of jobs devoted to social reproduction of the population, whites occupied only 62% of positions at that level.

In the case of Latinos, the situation is the reverse. In the same year, they represented 10% of the employed population, a figure that increased to 18% in construction work and 15% in social reproduction. But at the top of the hierarchy of jobs, Latinos occupied only 5% of the management and professional positions.

Currently this ethnic-migratory differentiation in the structure of employment has been accentuated and deepened. In 2016, non-Latino whites accounted for 64% of the employed population, but in the higher ranks they had a large majority of the jobs, holding 75% of management posts and 71% of professional jobs. This proportion is systematically reduced as you go down the structure of employment, and in services of social reproduction the figure for non-Latino whites is reduced to only 50% of the workers employed in social reproduction services.

# MIGRATION AND SOCIAL REPRODUCTION

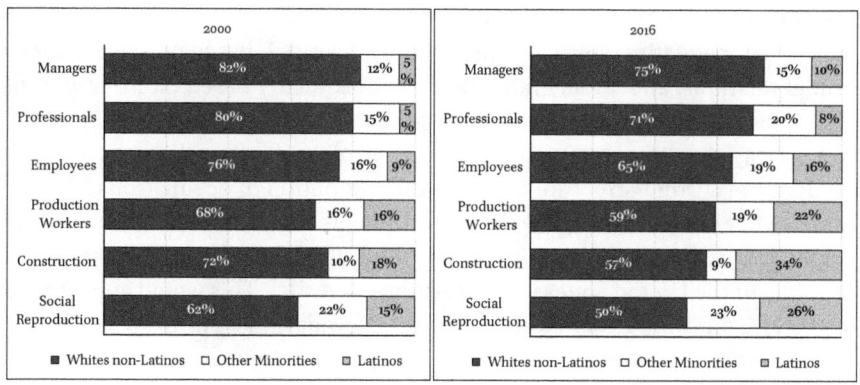

FIGURE 20   United States of America. Ethnic composition of occupational strata
SOURCES: CURRENT POPULATION SURVEY, MARCH SUPPLEMENT 2000 AND 2016

Latinos, on the other hand, show a change in the opposite direction, specializing more and more in jobs at the base of the occupational pyramid. Currently they provide 26% of the people employed in social reproduction services and 34% of those in construction, even though they only represent 16% of all those in employment. While at the top of the occupation pyramid they still have a low presence with just 8% of the professional and 10% of management jobs.

These figures illustrate our thesis about a *racializing* of the structure of occupations and that of social inequality in the United States. Further, the demographic growth of Latinos has not been accompanied by a process of social mobility that would allow them equal access to the middle and upper ranks of the social pyramid, and they have tended to stay relegated to lower and middle range jobs that are less appreciated socially and have lower incomes (Fritz and Stone, 2009).

Although ethnic stratification has always been a feature of the matrix of occupations in the United States, the current situation differs from that of other times in that the great majority of citizens used to be white, representing 80% of the population and the work force, with small ethnic and migratory minorities. Whereas now, as mentioned in previous chapters, we are a step away from a different phenomenon, where the demographic predominance of the white majority is being seriously challenged by two complementary dynamics. First by the demographic growth of the minority with Latino origins, and secondly by the ageing and demographic decline of the white population.

In this context of demographic change, the processes and tendencies of an ethnic stratification of occupations and the racializing of social inequality have reached quite unexpected dimensions never seen before in modern

Western societies, that are only comparable to the structures of differentiation and social inequality typical of pre-modern societies – based on slave labor or feudal relations, and: at any rate openly and explicitly based on principles of ethnic and racial discrimination and segmentation.

One way of getting closer to an appreciation of the depth of this situation is to analyze the current structure of ethnic differentiation of occupations in those States where there is a larger presence of people of Latino origin who are actually prefiguring the change in demographics that is on its way to the whole republic of the United States in the next three decades. This would apply to the states of California, Texas, Florida, Arizona, Nevada and New Mexico.

Currently, the ethnic composition of the population in these 6 states shows that the whites have ceased to form a demographic majority, with only 45% of the total population falling into that category. While the second largest racial group is that of the Latinos, with 35% of the total population. The ethnic and migratory origins of the rest are found in the 10% who are Afro-American, the 8% who are of Asian origin, and the 2% who are Native American Indians.

However, this composition of the population is not reproduced equally at all levels of the occupational pyramid. As seen in the next Figure, there is a clear ethnic differentiation, with whites tending to predominate at the top levels of occupation, while at the lower levels the population of Latino origins tends to predominate. In the first case, whites have 61% of the management and 58% of the professional jobs, areas in which Latinos have only 20% on average. By contrast, at the lower end of the occupational pyramid, whites have only 33% of the jobs in tasks of social reproduction and 34% in construction jobs, while Latinos have 47% of the first and 59% of the second.

The *racializing* of the structure of employment is evident. The relevance of this situation in 6 states is that it prefigures the structure of ethnic and occupational differentiation that the matrix of employment in the United States is heading towards. This is not just a process of labor segregation against a demographic minority, which has been the case in the United States up until now, first with respect to the Afro-descendant population and now with regard to the Latino population (Massey, 2007). This is a social phenomenon that goes deeper and has to do with the prevailing system of social differentiation sustained by racial and ethnic factors that directly affects over a third of the population.

It consists of the formation of a social structure sustained principally by two social classes which might be the same size demographically but are found at opposite ends of the occupational structure. Affiliation or belonging to those occupational strata is not a function of economic, meritocratic or strictly occupational factors, but a direct function of belonging to an ethnic and

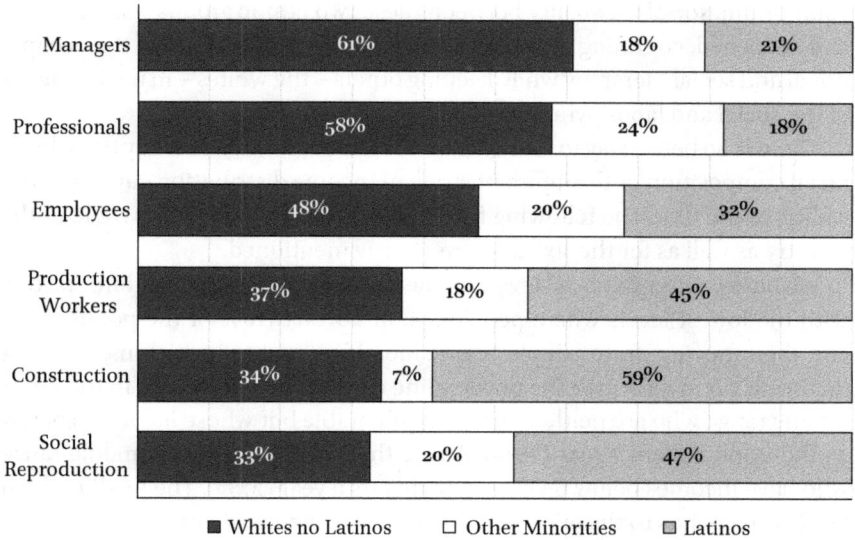

FIGURE 21  California, Texas, Florida, Arizona, Nevada and New Mexico, 2016. Ethnic composition of occupational strata
SOURCE: CURRENT POPULATION SURVEY, ASEC, 2016

demographic community. This is the full expression of racism, where ethnic discrimination acts as the structuring factor of social and occupational differentiation. In this context, social mobility between classes becomes an almost impossible prospect for both groups. The whites hardly face a serious risk of going down in the occupational pyramid and the Latinos do not have a better option for rising in the labor hierarchy. For the first group, the color of their skin will always work for them as an underlying capital that will allow them to keep their privileges. For the second group, their ethnic origins form a barrier that is almost impossible to get over in order to improve their position in society and have access to the benefits and privileges that are reserved for others. Such rigidity in the structure of society indicates the reassertion of old oligarchic structures that are more like a caste structure than a modern democratic stratification of social classes.

These statements might be considered somewhat outrageous. However, the data that we have examined fully supports them. In these 6 states, where 31% of the population of the USA reside, the virtual equilibrium between the population with white origins and that of Latin origins has not translated into a similar balance in terms of gaining access to different posts and occupations in the occupational pyramid. To the contrary, in spite of the demographic equilibrium, social inequality between these two ethnic groups is maintained and deepened, confining some – the Latinos – to inferior strata of the occupational and social hierarchy while keeping others – the whites – in the top layers of the social and labor pyramid.

There is no better way to illustrate these statements than to study the ethnic-racial composition of the different strata of income distribution currently prevailing in the USA. The following figure gives information for the whole of the country as well as for the six states previously mentioned.

We have chosen six social levels on the basis of income distribution. Starting with the lowest levels where people live in poverty (16% of the population), and then moving on to people in a vulnerable situation, which means their income is up to 50% over the poverty line (10%). Next are people in the lower middle range who are neither poor nor vulnerable but whose income is below 25 thousand dollars a year (28%). Above them are those in the middle range who have incomes below 60 thousand dollars a year (27%). The medium high level corresponds to those earning less than 100 thousand dollars a year (11%), and those in the top range receive incomes above that figure (7%). The figure below shows the ethnic-racial composition of each of these 6 income brackets, both at the national level and in the six states we had chosen, where the presence of the Latino population has modified the demographic balances between the two principal ethnic groups: whites and Latinos.

It may be observed that at the national level, while there is a large absolute majority of white people in the top ranks, whites account for less than half of those in the lower ranks. And the population of Latino origin shows the

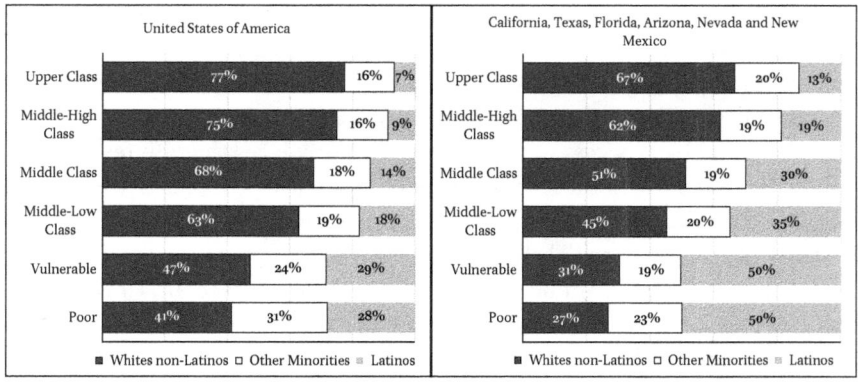

FIGURE 22　United States of America and selected states. Ethnic composition of population by income strata, 2016
SOURCE: CURRENT POPULATION SURVEY, ASEC, 2016

opposite situation. There are almost no Latino people in the top ranks (7 and 9%), and their share of the lower ranks is much above the national average. This indicates that while the higher ranks are composed essentially of members of the white population, in the lower ranks, ethnic minorities predominate, with the Latinos standing out.

The situation in the six states we selected separately reveals this phenomenon even more clearly. In the highest ranks the predominance of the white population is evident, accounting for between 62% and 66% of the people in these social classes. To the contrary, in the lowest ranks their share is reduced to 31% and 27%, a long way below their average demographic weight (45%). In the case of the Latino population we observe the opposite. Although they account for 35% of the population, they only represent between 13% and 19% of those in the highest ranks. Whereas in the lowest ranks (the poor and the vulnerable) they account for 50% of the population, a figure much higher than their relative weight overall.

The figures from the six states tell us we are in a situation where new demographic balances do not appear as new social and economic balances. To the contrary, upon this new ethnic-demographic composition of the population, a structure of social differentiation has arose based on the ethnic condition of the population. In these states the distribution of income does not reflect the new ethnic and demographic balances of the population, but is sustained by processes of *racializing* social inequality and class structure more profoundly than these appear at a national level.[7]

### 3.3 Migration, Work and Social Reproduction in Advanced Societies

This polarizing trend in occupations offers us the structural context from which to analyze and understand the role of migration in the reproduction of native population, and in particular, their styles of life, patterns of behavior and consumption, derived from the advent of a postmodern society, and from the consolidation of individuation processes.

In this regard, recent studies on the labor migrants insertion have documented its growing role in various economic activities directed towards the social and daily reproduction of the native population in the host countries, especially that of the medium and high socioeconomic strata (Vershuur, 2007; Sorensen, 2004). We are referring to works such as domestic services, the boom of care and attention industry for vulnerable groups (adults, children, the sick,

---

[7] In the following chapters we shall explain in greater depth the social and political implications of this racialized structure of class inequality, in the context of demographic change as already described.

among others), maintenance and cleaning work, as well as many other personal services (food preparation, restaurants, gardening, among many others). In this regard, in a recent study, we have estimated that between 2000 and 2012, in the United States and Spain, Latin American immigrants represented respectively 40% and 50% of the new workers employed in this type of activities associated to reproduction (Canales, 2013).

In general, it is a question of various occupations in what has been termed proximity services, or services that ensure the reproduction of daily living that correspond to those remunerated activities that are designed to meet directly the needs of individuals and their families in their domestic environment or that lead to their reproduction as individuals and families (Parella, 2003). Undoubtedly, the most typical case is the one related to domestic service, but it is not the only one (Hondageneu-Sotelo, 2007). Along with them, many other activities and occupations oriented to the care of sick people, children and older adults have proliferated, as have those related to food preparation, cleaning, maintenance and many others.[8]

The commercialization through the market of domestic service and other personal services and similar activities is not something new in capitalist society. The novelty of the present situation is that in developed countries, the massive demand for this type of workers is given in the context of social and demographic changes that we have already pointed out. We refer to the second demographic transition and the individuation processes that sustain it. In this way, the aging of the population along with the massive entry of women into the labor market, the changes in formation and household structure, the fertility reduction, among others, are driving an increasing demand for workers who engage in such jobs. However, these same processes of social transformation have implied that native workers who previously were engaged to these same tasks (women in domestic service and people care, men in maintenance tasks, food preparation and construction, for example), are reducing in volume, since they are increasingly opting for other less precarious and better valued jobs which have greater social prestige, wages and more decent working conditions (Parella, 2003).

This situation is manifested in a structural imbalance between supply and demand in the labor market, which opens space for immigrant men and women from peripheral countries to be incorporated into these markets in

---

8    According to Gregson and Lowe (1994), as early as the beginning of the nineties in the United Kingdom, more than 75% of middle-class families, where both spouses were working, a third person was hired for household tasks. Also, 40 percent of families with pre-school children hired a nursemaid to care for their children.

MIGRATION AND SOCIAL REPRODUCTION                                                      187

the central European countries (Escrivá, 2000). In effect, the native middle and upper class women address the incompatibility between maintaining a paid employment and returning to the field of domestic work (along with facing the fact of an increasing shortage of local labor to take on these jobs) by hiring immigrant women to do the most arduous housework for them, such as cleaning, maintenance and people care, among others. Nothing could illustrate better this situation than the role of migration in occupations aimed to sustain the social reproduction of the native population as well as to their lifestyles and consumption patterns.

In this regard, the data for the United States are eloquent. In 2016, almost 25% of Latin American workers were concentrated in only 6 types of occupations, all of them crucial for social and daily life reproduction of active population. Latin American immigrants contributed with 49% of employment in maids and housekeeping cleaners, 32% of cooks (not chefs), 31% of people who works in car wash, parking, service station, and similar cars services, 30% of janitors and building cleaners, 28% of workers dedicated to the food preparation and 20% of workers in the care industries.[9]

These data illustrate the high degree of dependency that such activities and occupations have in regard to the Latin American labor market insertion

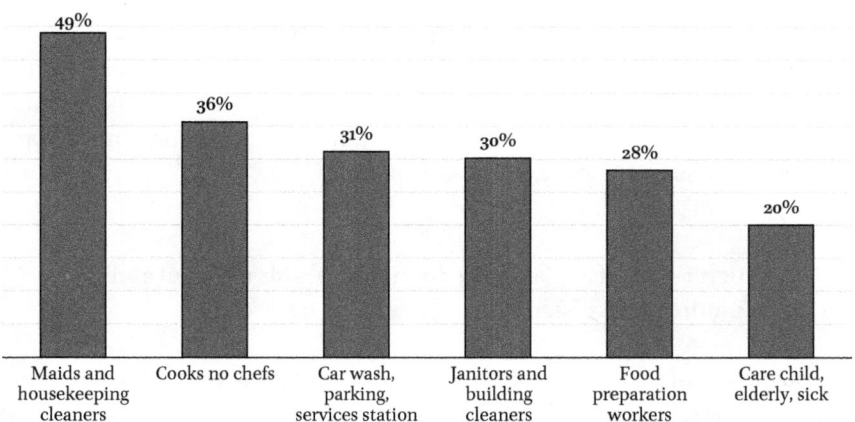

FIGURE 23    United States of America, 2016. Employment of Latinos (migrants and natives) in selected personal services (%)
SOURCES: CURRENT POPULATION SURVEY, ASEC, MARCH, 2016. US BUREAU OF THE CENSUS.

---

9   In addition, Latinos employed as construction laborers provide 41% occupancy, and Latinos employed as agriculture laborers providing 50% of the workforce.

and how dependent is the social and daily life reproduction of the native population upon Latin American immigration.

In this context, the polarization of occupations that arises with the process of economic globalization, does nothing but contribute to the configuration of various labor niches in which are usually inserted mainly migrant workers. However, these are not only low-skilled labor, but also of a very low social value, resulting in low wages, contexts of precariousness, absence of formal regulatory frameworks all of which involve an important degree of social disrepute. In this context, it is not surprising then that there arise a process of *ethnostratification* (Catarino and Oso, 2000) or of reproductive services *racialization* (Hondagneu-Sotelo, 2007), i.e. a socio-labor differentiation based on ethnic-migrant factors, rather than each individual's labor credentials.

In this regard, within a labor market like this, a process of occupational segregation operates that directly affects immigrant women, which regardless of their job qualifications, tends to be relegated to these jobs upon which would operate what Parella (2003) calls a triple discrimination since they are woman, immigrant and worker.[10]

Considering the above, there is no doubt that the analysis and understanding of migration and its contributions to the host societies should not only consider their strictly economic and labor aspects, but also be framed in the depth of the social and demographic transformations of these societies which arise with the globalization and advent of a postmodern society. We refer to the individuation processes which are revealed among other things, in the emancipation of women, in the advance towards the second demographic transition and in the ageing of developed countries populations, among many others (Herrera, 2007; Beck and Beck, 2002).

## 4   Migration and Social Reproduction: Towards a Global and Comprehensive Vision

Through migration, a global system (translocal and transnational) of social reproduction is taking shape. In effect, migration allows for the articulation of the social reproduction process of native population in the destination place with the social reproduction of population in the places and communities of origin. The migrant contributions in the occupations and social reproduction activities

---

10   This situation pointed out by S. Parella is evidenced by the fact that 93% of Latinos employed in domestic service are women, as well as in the care of children, elderly and sick, where 90% are women.

of the native population confirms the first part of this thesis. The social and family networks role as well as remittances, both put into operation from migration itself, give an account of the second part of this thesis.

But we can give an additional twist to this analysis. Migration not only articulates the native population social reproduction with those of the origin communities, but it also deals with the articulation of mechanisms and reproduction processes from different social classes, and by this means, the reproduction of a global and transnationalized class system.

Social networks and remittances not only reproduce migrants, in abstract, but a specific economic and social subject. Namely, they reproduce a worker whose job is to give sustenance to the middle and upper classes via their role in social reproduction in the host country.[11] Conversely, the social reproduction of these high and middle social classes (in the case of the United States, non-Latino white population, mainly) does not occur in abstract but, through migration, reproduction is based, at least in part on the social reproduction of migrant workers and their families in the origin places.

In this way, migration sets up a workforce transfer that contributes to the middle and upper classes families reproduction in the destination places, while the wages that these same families pay the migrant, sent as remittances to their families, constitute a transfer in the reverse direction that contributes to the migrants and their families reproduction. By this means, their labor force reproduction is a basis for the circuit of transfers, flows of people, remittances, and symbolic and material goods, and may be renewed over and over again.

In this way, individuals and populations that apparently have no link or direct contact (migrants families in the origin communities, and the middle and upper classes population in host societies), are linked by labor migration, which, like a hinge, is a mechanism that articulates the reproduction of different and distant populations from the social and territorial point of view. Nothing exemplifies better this situation than the migration role in a system of transnational motherhood configuration, and that can also be extended to the care industry transnationalization (Herrera, 2005; Hondagneu-Sotelo, 2007; Ehrenteich and Hochschild, 2004). In the first case, it is the work of migrant women in the child care for middle and upper classes families in Europe and the United States. In order to develop these jobs, these same

---

11  We refer to workers inserted in occupations such as domestic service, people caring, food preparation, waiters, cleaning and buildings maintenance, janitors, gardeners, and in general, activities oriented to the population social reproduction, especially in areas of daily life.

migrant women have had to rely on the social and family networks they have in their home communities, upon which rests the care of their own children that they have left behind. This is a clear example of how social reproduction in the destination is not only linked but based on the migrant social networks that allow them to perform tasks of caring other people's children. Thus, transnational motherhood becomes a transnational mechanism of class society reproduction.

The comfort and privileges that characterize the life style and quality of a child who, in many cases is the son of a professional woman in the core countries and who could also work as an executive at places such as Wall Street is sustained on the precariousness, poverty and vulnerability that characterizes another son's daily life that migrant women have left in the origin community and whose care has been turned over to his grandmother, aunts or older siblings. The wealth and comfort of one, is based on the poverty and vulnerability of the other. But also, the subsistence of the latter, the migrant son, becomes materially possible by the remittances his mother sends, which form part of the salary she receives for her work by taking care of foreign children.[12]

In effect, the growing demand in the core countries for migrant women, preferably coming from Third World countries, to perform this type of domestic service tasks, the so-called reproductive and personal services, entails an evolving form of the social division of labor which adopts a transnational character that is based on a form of "transferring ethnic and social inequalities" (Parella, 2003:15), which goes from the women in the core countries, that become emancipated and released from the old chains that tied them up to the household tasks, towards the immigrant women who require those incomes for their own social reproduction but are forced to neglect their own reproductive responsibilities within their families who have remained in the countries of origin.

---

12   If this situation could be defined as a link from below, from the lower spaces of globalization, from its inner courtyards, they also allow us to identify those links that are given from above, from the globalization itself. It is likely that this same professional woman, executive from Wall Street, or from any transnational corporation, participates in the economic or financial decision making that directly affects the country economies where the female migrant comes from and which is hired for domestic service for her son caring. And if you want to further complicate the issue, we don't have to forget that it is very probably that the brothers, cousins, or older children of the same migrant, has remained in their community of origin and are inserted in any manufacturing company, assembling products for re-export which are demanded and consumed in the home of that same professional woman, thus contributing to reproduce its standard and quality of life.

Even though, at the moment we are not interested in entering into the debate, we cannot ignore the paradox that this emancipation process of women implies in the core countries. In this regard, the least we can say, is that it is a fragmented emancipation which reproduces social and gender inequality. Undoubtedly, it favors, in some aspects, the women of core countries, but it does not necessarily break with the gender inequity in those same countries. This inequality only would have been transferred from the native women towards immigrant women. In essence, the liberation of some (native women), although partial and incomplete, rests in a certain way, on the oppression of others (immigrant women) (Gregson and Lowe, 1994).

In effect, the liberation of women in the central European countries has not freed them of the tasks and reproductive services of the stigma that characterizes them since immemorial times. It is a question of liberating women in particular, i.e. the freeing of persons with first name and last name, not a general emancipation. While women have been released from the domestic work, or at least from their hardest and worst stigmatized tasks, it has not involved a transformation of the character and lack of social and symbolic value of those tasks. At the end of the day, men are still the most favored with this situation, as it allows them to continue avoiding its responsibilities in the domestic area (Parella, 2003).

In other words, and as always happens, the social reproduction of some (middle and upper classes, native, etc.) is based on the social reproduction of others (working classes, migrants, poor, etc.), and *vice versa*. What is specific to all this in the era of globalization is that this process takes a translocated and transnational form, i.e., it has also been globalized.

In these times of globalization, the social reproduction processes that were previously confined to local spaces (nationals), are now part of global spaces (transnationals). Precisely, these global fields are configured through international migration through the intersection between local processes of social reproduction, which means, spaces that interconnect the social reproduction of some and others. Figure 24 illustrates this thesis on the global interconnection of these local spaces of social reproduction.

Commonly, studies on the migrant labor insertion has focused on the operational conditions of labor markets in the destination places, and in particular, on how, through migration, it articulates a demand for labor force in the place of destination, with a work force supply generated in the places of origin (Bustamante, 1973). In this first area of analysis, the important thing is the dynamics of these labor markets, and in particular, the determinants of demand and supply.

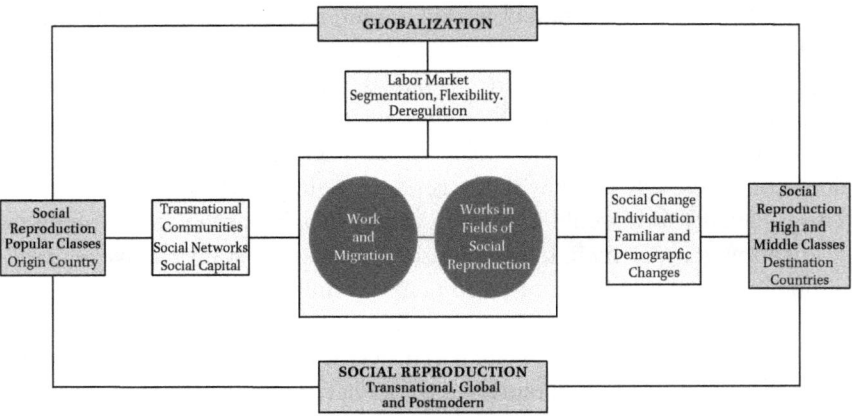

FIGURE 24   International migration and social reproduction in global society

In both cases, we can appeal to the globalization approaches in the sense that it helps us to explain the transformations in the labor markets functioning. We refer to the changes in the structure of occupations, to the specific dynamics of each sector of activity, to the processes of contractual deregulation and labor flexibility among many others (that is what is represented in the central and high part of the figure).

In a second moment, we can extend this analysis by incorporating other dimensions and social processes. In one case, we can take, for example, social and demographic changes in the host societies which arise with globalization and the advent of a postmodern society. Here we refer, for instance, to the increasing incorporation of native born women to labor markets, to the cultural changes along with transformations related to demographic and social behavior linked to post-modernity, as well as to the demographic change, expressed both in the advent of a second demographic transition that distorts principles and values of the family, the offspring and the roles within the home, as well as in the populations ageing in developed countries (Herrera, 2007). In this sense, labor immigration, simultaneously of supplying the deficit that population demographic change leaves, also contributes to reproduce these social and cultural changes of society which are reflected in the consumption and lifestyles patterns of the native population, especially of middle and upper classes, which are the ones that have made the most progress in these processes (that is what we have represented in the center-right of the figure).

On the other hand, and from the perspective of migration as a social process, we are able to incorporate the role of social and family networks in the transnational community's formation, through which this cumulative causation mechanism is generated and that allows social reproduction of migrants and their families through the perpetuation of international migration itself. In this sense, we can say that the gaze of migration partly moves away from their structural and contextual aspects, to penetrate into the migration social process which are the spaces of everyday life and its role as material, symbolic and cultural support of the migration process (represented in the central-left part of the figure).

In these first ones, we can include theoretical models of transnationalism as well as the transnational motherhood and care industry, to the extent that these models are based on the combination of different and distant spaces. On the one hand, changes in the dynamics of families, ageing, and other social and demographic processes that characterize contemporary developed societies. On the other hand, the system of social and family networks that support international migration in the current times. Similarly, not even in these conceptual models is set aside the structural conditions analysis of labor markets operation in the framework of economic and productive transformations arising from the globalization of the contemporary world.

However, we can add to this a third level of analysis involves the integration of all of the above from the approach of a global society reproduction (that is what we have represented in the left and right ends of the figure).

On the one hand, the immigrant's work helps to sustain not only the general quality of life in the destination countries, but also and primarily the reproduction, in a framework of social, economic and demographic transformations in this global and postmodern age. Likewise, it is not only a question of the population's reproduction in the abstract, but of certain groups, social classes and strata, i.e., it is not social reproduction in the abstract, but that of certain social groups, and therefore, the perpetuation and reproduction of their social position in a social and class structure at a global level.

On the other hand, social and family networks, not only contribute to the reproduction and perpetuation of migration, as pointed out by Massey, Durand and Malone (2002), but through this, contribute to the social reproduction of communities. Also, it is not a question of its reproduction in the abstract but of the reproduction and perpetuation of their social status as communities and migrant families, i.e., the reproduction of their position in a social and class structure at a global level.

Combining these two aspects, we can say then that they are but two sides of the same overall process: the reproduction, at a global level, of a social structure in which we can identify various strata, social groups and classes, different and distant, but articulated and integrated into their social reproduction. In other words, through migration, social reproduction of middle and lower classes in the countries of origin is to some extent, articulated with the social reproduction of the middle and high-strata population in the countries of destination. This integration, or rather, these intersection fields of local processes of social reproduction is what we want to highlight in terms of setting up a global process of reproduction.

It is interesting in this light to consider the proposal by Bauman (1998), who uses the concept of *glocalization*, to refer to a new form of social stratification at a world level. For him *glocalization* is a neologism that makes it possible to refer to globalization and localization as simultaneous complementary processes.

According to Bauman, globalization and localization make up the forces pushing for a new polarization and stratification of the world's population, all as manifested in the opposition between the global rich and the local poor. One group is free to choose its fate and for the other its fate is implacable destiny. Some inhabit the global village, but the others are pariahs of globalization. *Glocalization* is, then, a structure of inequality that creates payouts and an accumulation of privileges for some and a lack of rights for others, producing in its wake both wealth and poverty, power and impotence. *Glocalization* is definitely the spatial form assumed by social stratification at a world level, where "the new frontiers of inequality increasingly separate those who are able to connect to supra-national networks from those who are cornered in their local hideouts" (García Canclini, 2014: 31).[13]

This differentiation between the globalized rich and the localized poor is constructed and reconstructed in the same geography, reshaping the spaces and territories of communities. One example of this is the new class structure that has emerged in advanced societies, seen in the racialization of social inequality. This concerns not only the classic division of rich and poor, but how this opposition between classes and social strata, which is reconstructed within advanced societies, also forms transnational spaces, that is, dynamics of social reproduction that transcend national boundaries. Natives and immigrants, wealth and poverty, center and periphery, the included and the excluded, are not broken up into separate or discontinuous spaces any more, as in the recent past, but intermingle here and there, in nations as in a single community, in societies migrated to as well as in those emigrated from. The global and the local

---

13   "las nuevas fronteras de la desigualdad separan cada vez más a quienes son capaces de conectarse a redes supranacionales de quienes quedan arrinconados en sus reductos locales". Original in Spanish.

are, therefore, just two dimensions of the same process, the two faces that the historical contradiction of capitalism is currently seen in.[14]

The social reproduction of the middle and upper classes in advanced societies is as linked to the social reproduction of the communities of migrants in their countries of origin, as the accumulation of capital in the core economies is linked to the extraction of value and riches from under-developed nations. If the world economy has become a single globalized system through the integration of markets and the flow of the capitals and commodities of the world, the class structures and the social reproduction of these classes have also been globalized through migrations. Social inequality has been globalized, and racializing is just one form adopted by ethno-stratification and socio-economic differentiation of the one from the other, of the origin from the destination and of migrants from natives.

---

14  In this social differentiation scheme, migrants play a particular role, as a central component of this new class of local workers. Through their work they are part of globalization, but their social reproduction (living conditions, incomes, etc.), are always relegated to the local spaces.

CHAPTER 8

# The Central Place of Migration in the Reproduction of Advanced Societies

> *And the world is so big*
> *And one so small*
> *I only go for the Rose of the Winds*
> *We are children of the Rose of the Winds*[1]
> The Rose of the Winds
> MAKIZA/ANITA TIJOUX

∴

1      Thesis

International migration occupies a central place in the reproduction of advanced societies. On the one hand, as a demographic component, they contribute to cover the population gaps left by ageing and declining birth rates, and thus, support the demographic reproduction of the population. On the other hand, as a labor force contributes to cover deficits labor and sustaining capital accumulation and reproduction of the economy. Finally, as workers, they preferentially insert themselves into tasks of the daily reproduction of the middle and upper classes, contributing to their postmodern lifestyles and patterns of consumption in a globalized world.

2      International Migrations: the Theoretical-methodological Debate Revisited

International migration has grown from a simple matter of academic interest to become one of the main themes of the political debate at a global level. Along with issues such as global warming, globalization, regional inequalities

---

1   "Y es que el mundo es tan grande, y uno tan pequeño. Sólo me dirijo por la Rosa de los Vientos. Somos hijos de la Rosa de los Vientos". Original in Spanish.

and demographic change, it constitutes a topic that is already present not only in the big global forums, but also in the parishioners talks in bars and cafes of each neighborhood corner. As in the debate of other topics, this one on migration does nothing but to recreate, in this field, the positions and debate on our present and future society. As well as in those other big issues, there is a profuse and broad discussion, which involves polar opposite positions as those who advocate the total closing of borders, mass deportations of undocumented immigrants, the criminalization of undocumented status, building more walls; to those who are in opposite and conflicting positions who promote the total abolition of national borders and the free movement of people and workers, and even the possibility of establishing a formula of a global supranational citizenship.

Despite this wide range of positions, the academic debate, and above all, the political debate, has been finally heavily dominated by conservative visions of society that frequently question the migration role in the changes taking place in society. A clear example of this is the minimal and barely significant progress that has been made in the different Global Forums on Migration and development. In them, the vision of developed countries is what often predominates. These countries are the main destination areas of contemporary migration, and not only impose their interests, but in addition, restrict the possibilities of a global consensus on this issue, and have been reluctant to sign and/or ratify various international conventions on human, social, labor and political migrants' rights.

Beyond questioning the political and ideological positions represented by them, our critique focuses on the theoretical and methodological shortcomings that underlie these dominant discourses about migration, particularly in relation to their failure to account for the changes that contemporary society has experienced in the last few decades, and of the role that international migration has played in them. In this regard, three axes allow us to synthesize our critique of these theoretical and methodological approaches.[2]

– In the first place, it is worth mentioning the so-called methodological nationalism that permeates and underlies almost all the discourses on the causes, conditions and consequences of international migration. As we have pointed out in various sections of this book, it is a legacy from modernity,

---

[2] In addition, at least two other large methodological legacies of social science may be added, whose critique allows us to undress the nature and uses that the social research has had in the era of Modernity. I refer to the ethnocentrism, on the one hand, and the androcentric on the other. In both cases it is the imposition of one social vision of society coming from dominant positions, according to which, the European (or the developed world) in a case, and the masculine, in the other, become the *natural* forms of social issues.

which basically consists in the form in which the analytical categories and frameworks for understanding modern society are delimited and built. According to this principle, modern social theory and the thought of modernity is based on the correspondence between State, Nation and Territory. The national state, is restricted to its territorial confines, and it shapes an analysis, observation and theorizing entity in itself, independent of the other nation states. From this, any social process becoming object of study for any of the social sciences, is built based on this principle. National societies, which are seen as a whole in themselves, make up a context for the analysis of any social process, and become the unit of analysis for the study of global processes, which are conceptualized as processes and international relations, i.e. *between*-nations.

- Secondly, it should be noted the persistence of a methodological dualism. At the time of analyzing the causes and consequences of migration, a fundamental dividing line is usually established as to how to address and problematize migration in and for the countries of origin, versus how it is done in and for the destination countries. In the sending countries, migration is seen as an opportunity for development, both by the financial support that remittances can represent, as for the contributions that returning migrants can make, in terms of human capital, technological innovation, entrepreneurship, etc. In the host countries, on the contrary, migrations are seen as a social and political problem, derived from the large volume that they represent, and the low level of assimilation and difficult adoption of the new societies ways of life, favoring instead both the reproduction of cultural patterns and senses of identity and belonging with regard to their communities of origin. A hope of development for some (origin), a source of problems and multicultural conflicts to others (destination). Undoubtedly, this is an ideological and biased construction of an issue that is much more complex and diverse than often assumed.

- Thirdly, we cannot fail to mention the absence of a conceptualization and analysis of changes experienced by society over the last few decades, changes which are underlying the structural, social and political conditions that give origin and have triggered the current migratory flows at a global level. The continuous reference to neoclassical economic models (with their different derivations like the new home economics in particular), reinforce this ahistoricism present in the main discourses on the causes and consequences of contemporary migration. In general, these discourses do not make many references to the impacts that could take place on contemporary migration, processes such as the increasing globalization of world economy, the rise of new productive models which are based on new principles of work organization and production ("toyotism", labor flexibility, contract deregulation), as well as the so-called "structural adjustment" policies, an euphemism to refer to the imposition of the neoliberal model as the guiding principle of the world economy, among many others.

In contrast to these dominant approaches, and in seeking to give answers to these theoretical and methodological shortcomings, there arise various proposals to analyze and understand migration. Without wishing to give an exhaustive view, we will mention only three of them, which are precisely, those who have served us for the development of our proposal for an analytical model based on the role of migration in the reproduction of contemporary society. I am referring to the globalization approach, the perspective of transnationalism and the analysis model based on the social and family networks system.

- Globalization and migration. According to various authors, globalization corresponds to the transition from an industrial society to an *informational society*, where the latter reconfigures the foundations of the industrial economy through the incorporation of knowledge and information into the material processes of production and distribution. In terms of its political economy, globalization refers to the new world-economy schemes of territorial organization where the rules of the oligopolistic competition and the international division of labor are substantially redefined. In this context, the globalization and flexibility of the production system configures the pillars of capitalist restructuring, simultaneously defining the new system of rules on the basis of which would be operating the capital/labor relations in the current world.

Without going into details concerning the debate on globalization, we are interested in focusing attention on the new patterns of immigrant labor insertion and their links with the changes that globalization has introduced in organizational forms and labor relations. The flexibility and labor deregulation strategy, which directly affects the working and hiring conditions, seem, however, to be the basis of a new kind of job offer for the migrant population. Thus, for example, there is a significant increase of migrant workers in jobs such as cleaning and buildings maintenance, janitors, gardeners, dishwasher, employees in restaurants, house cleaning, maids, and other similar occupations of low qualification and poor working conditions. In this way, migrant workers, make up a population base for the configuration of the new proletarian workers in the framework of post-industrial society.

- Transnationalism. At present, migration is a complex and diverse process, which can no longer be reduced to the mere movement of people. Migration not only involves a flow of people changing the habitual place of residence from one place to another, but this massive displacement of people, is accompanied by a no less important and significant flow and exchange of materials and symbolic goods between the places of origin and destination. Through migration, a complex system of social, family and community networks is configured, through which a process of movement and exchange of people, money, goods, services and information in both directions is activated. Based on this system of circulation and exchange, there is an articulation of the everyday life of immigrants in the places of destinations, on the one hand, with their communities of origin, and on the other hand, forming one large translocal community whose spatial forms transcend traditional national territorial borders.

This is a configuration of transnational communities, a concept that seeks to apprehend the spatial form that the expansion and deterritorialization of communities adopt: their growing multi–localities (*pluri-locality*). In this framework, the migrant condition is transformed, it ceases to be the person who leaves a community, to be the demographic support of its community development and expansion. As we have previously said, to emigrate is no longer synonymous with *leaving behind*, but of *bringing with* themselves. Migrants do not leave behind their community but carry it with them wherever they go.

– Social networks. To think about migration in terms of its transnationality, cannot be dissociated from the social networking and community system on which the construction and configuration of these transnationalized spaces is sustained. It is a question of the formation and accumulation of the migrants social capital, which has been shaped based on relationships of trust, reciprocity and solidarity that are present in all family and community relationships that, in the particular case of migrant communities, through the movement of its members, these social networks and social capital become transnational networks.

Now, this social networks system serves to recreate, although in a transformed way, the sending community in the places of settlement, and in this way to reproduce the community in the context of its transnationalization. In fact, through the social network structure of each transnational community, information flows in both directions, in terms of the needs, work, education and health options along with the most diverse tasks and activities of the economic, social and cultural life of communities and families, in each territorial scope.

Supported by these networks, the mobility of individuals from one place to another is facilitated, in the sense that these family, friends and *paisanos* networks allow them to minimize relocation risks as well as settlement and job seeking costs in destination communities and the costs of family reproduction which have been left behind in the country of origin.

In this context, the thesis being presented here is that based on this social networks system, a process of *cumulative causation* would be activated and sustained, that enables the reproduction of migration, migrants and their communities, regardless of the structural factors that at the beginning could have triggered the migration process. Family and community networks become social resources (social capital) on the basis of which migrants, their families and communities can deploy various strategies to deal with their own survival. The success of these social reproduction strategies is based on the strength of these family and community networks, which contribute to the survival, maintenance and reproduction of migrant, family and community.

## 3  Migration and the Reproduction Approach

Returning to these approaches, we now propose to go a step beyond, picking up and framing their particular contributions in a more comprehensive and global approach which integrates and articulates these dynamics in a single conceptual and methodological formulation. In this sense, the Reproduction model has enabled us to move forward in such a direction. With this, we have given a shift towards the question about migration, by expanding the analytical horizon beyond the demographic phenomenon that migration involves in itself, beyond social networks that it involves and reproduces, beyond the transnational communities that creates and recreates, and beyond the globalization processes that triggers it.

We should concern ourselves about the forms that contemporary social reproduction is assuming, and about the role or function that international migration has in it. Before moving forward in this, we would like to make some reflections on the scope of this concept, as well as its contributions in terms of the varied viewpoints from which it may be approached.

The Reproduction model allows us to integrate in a single theoretical statement a wide range of processes that had traditionally been dealt with in isolation, in this case, the different approaches and dimensions from which international migration has been addressed. But what does the term Reproduction allude to in particular? From where does its explanatory force derive?

In the natural sciences, Reproduction represents the continuity in time and space of certain structures, this is, the permanence of the material conditions associated with the form of existence of such structures. In this regard, Maturana (2002) and Maturana and Varela (1987) raised precisely that, it is the concept of *autopoiesis,* which means self-organization of their own reproduction that defines the living systems.

In the social sciences, this concept acquires a greater complexity connotation, at least in a double sense:
- On the one hand, we can raise Maturana's thesis again, in terms of considering society as a self-reproductive system, or in other words, what is essential to refer to society as a system, is its capacity to organize its own reproduction, incorporating the dynamics, rationalities and functionalities of the most diverse processes, agents and structures that allow and enable its self-reproduction, this is, that give life to its own movement as a social system.
- On the other hand, reproduction cannot be confused or reduced to what would be a renewal process purely and simply. Rather, reproduction refers to a dual process of change and continuity of the material and symbolic structures. That is, at the same time that it refers to the social structure's permanence it also refers to the conditions for its change, with which it opens up to an analysis of the formation, dissolution and transformation of certain social structures.

This double aspect of permanence and change, indicates in turn two basic features of the reproduction concept that we cannot overlook, namely:
- Its multidimensional nature. The concept of reproduction refers to the articulation of different social dimensions and analytical levels, thereby exceeding the traditional dualisms and dichotomies that set individuals against society, action and structure, micro and macro, symbolic representations and material conditions, among many others. In this sense, the very concept of reproduction makes up a field of *mediations* (Zemelman, 1992) of these different dimensions of social processes.
- The change is not "exogenous" or "independent" of the social structures. Rather, this three-fold social process of formation, dissolution and transformation is the product of certain contradictions and internal conflicts that the reproduction process works to set in motion.

In this sense, the Reproduction model requires a careful attention to be paid to the societal movement, its development and constant evolution. This allows us to identify the various factors that impel it, simultaneously to identify the contradictions and tensions that are generated between them. Meanwhile, nothing indicates that the societal movement may be soft and smooth and free from conflicts and tensions. On the contrary, all societal processes are set up from the way in which tensions are resolved among the different processes, structures, fields, ambiences and social subjects. Similarly, in the reproduction of society, mechanical determinism has no place. A series of options and possible futures among which the possibility of crisis and collapse is always present, as well as historical regressions or its antithesis, revolutions and radical changes which could imply historical leaps.

Considering the above, the analytical model we have proposed in this book contemplates the ways in which international migration contributes and participates in the societal reproduction of our times. With this model, we want to make progress in improving the understanding not only of migration but also and through it, in a better understanding of contemporary society. This approach is sustained by the articulation and integration of the three theoretical and methodological approaches that we have already defined in a same model: the globalization approach, the prospect of transnationalism, and the analysis of social networks. This integrative proposal offers options to try to solve some of the major theoretical-methodological weaknesses which we have identified and pointed out in the case of traditional approaches.

On the one hand, the globalization approach allows us to locate the analysis concerning migration and reproduction of society in the current historical context. That is to say, through this approach, we are interested in going back to the historical and structural conditions that are in the material foundation that both trigger and cause international migration are based, as well as the forms that the process of reproduction takes in today's society. In this regard, the globalization of society is also the globalization of its reproduction, a process in which migration, becomes both a consequence and one of the modes that the society reproduction process adopts on a global scale.

Also, the transnationalism approach offers us the possibility of breaking up with methodological nationalism, which is very present in almost all of the formulations of social-political analysis today. From this point of view, it is imperative that migration and other analysis categories configure a spatiality that disrupts from its roots the classic territorial formulations that take as a unit of analysis the nation state. Precisely, the transnational gaze requires taking as the unit of analysis the fields of translocal relations, which in this case, involve supranational fields.

Thirdly, the social networks approach associated to the social capital of migrants, allow us the recovery of the actor in the whole analysis. This is, if with globalization we recover the historical-structural context, the networks approach offers the gaze and direct participation of the actor in the migration process and in the process of social reproduction of contemporary society. In this regard, the vision coming from social networks, and its most direct expression, transnational communities, configures a favorable field for the analysis of what various authors have referred to a globalization from below, this is, from the actors, and especially from those disadvantaged actors who are in situation of social, political and economic vulnerability in front of a globalization which is imposed on them from the capital, the state, and the ruling classes.

Finally, the model for analysis that we propose starts from the basic premise that migration would have a double status in relation to the reproduction of the social issue.

– On the one hand, it is a structuring factor of the social process that contributes to the structuring of certain social fields in which the reproduction of society develops.
– On the other hand, it is a process that is also structured by both the force of the historical and structural conditions that determines it, as by the practice and action of subjects, individuals and social institutions immersed in these structural conditions.

## 4  The Central Place of Migrations in Advanced Societies

This double vision or theoretical-methodological migration status, is what enables us to reformulate its field of problematization as an object of study. If migration is a process that is not only structured by historical conditions but in addition, is a structuring factor of the social matter, then it is not only relevant and pertinent, but absolutely necessary and essential to analyze and conceptualize migration from its contribution to societal dynamics and movement, i.e., its ability to influence the forms the process of reproduction takes at this historical conjuncture, in a global and postmodern society.

Nothing could illustrate this thesis better than the analysis of the current centrality of immigration in the reproduction of advanced societies which is the main destination of contemporary immigration. In effect, and considering the ongoing structural transformations in our societies, we can consider at least three areas from which to analyze and understand the central role of migration in its reproduction.

– On the one hand, the demographic transformations, derived from both the ageing of native population and the advent of the so-called second demographic transition, which is expressed mainly in the family dynamics and reproductive changes of the population which is based on the individuation processes proper of postmodern and globalized societies of the current world.
– On the other hand, we cannot fail to mention transformations of the economy, especially the ones in the world of work and the labor market derived from the globalization processes of the economy and world production.

- Finally, we must also consider the equally profound transformations in social and cultural life which are the same ones expressed in the advent of liquid societies as well as the individuation of social life, all of which are typical processes of the postmodern world in advanced societies.

For each of these processes it is possible to quote a wide literature that debates the scope and various forms they have taken as well as their possible variants and consequences in the most diverse fields. What we are interested in here, is to make visible immigration as a field of articulation and integration of these phenomena, while helping to address various problems and tensions that the very dynamics of these advanced societies processes generate. The following diagram enables us to illustrate this thesis on the centrality that international migration begins to assume in the structuring of advanced societies.

In the first place, the demographic change initiated in the last few decades, manifests itself increasingly in a persistent deficit of local labor. The population ageing along with the decrease of fertility in the framework of the second demographic transition, involve not only a slow and sometimes zero demographic growth, but above all, a substantial change in the age structure increasing the adult age population while lowering the proportion of those at a younger age. This demographic shift is already directly affecting the capacity

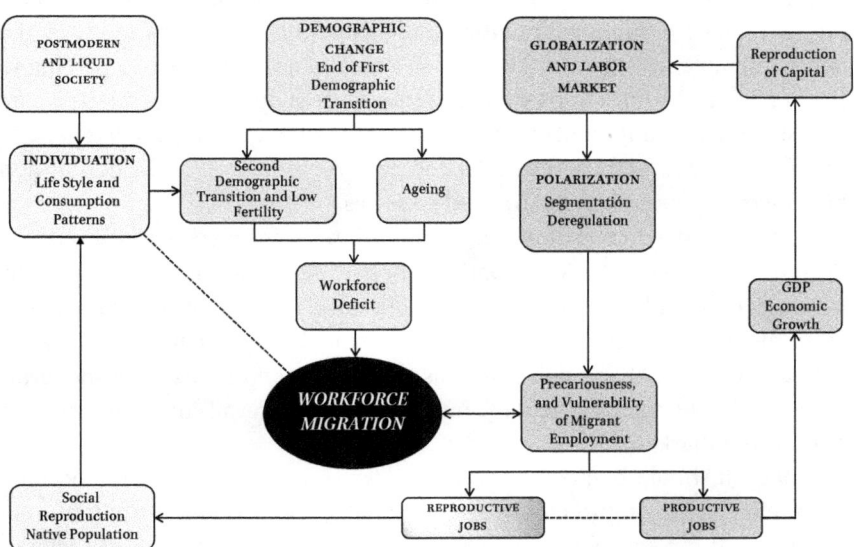

FIGURE 25  The centrality of international migration in advanced societies

of advanced societies to provide the necessary active population to maintain the rates of economic growth and productive transformation. Besides, these are economies that need to generate the necessary surplus to maintain not only their high living standards and sumptuous consumption patterns, but above all, they need to maintain and reproduce every day an expansive leisure class (as originally contemplated by T. Veblen), especially in terms of a war industry and an army of economy administration and international politics, allowing them to maintain their privileged and dominant hegemonic position in the world.

Demography in these societies shows a clear structural failure to generate the contingent of workers to fill the jobs that the dynamic and economic growth of these same societies need on a daily basis. Faced with the structural imbalance between the internal demographic dynamics and the economic one, the solution has been to appeal to the massive immigration of workers, mostly from Third World countries, where they inhabit a different demographic regime.

Parallel to these demographic changes, the developed economies are experiencing a series of economic and productive transformations in a context of globalization. For our discussion, the most important thing about these processes refer to the changes in the dynamics of labor markets in these societies. In particular, we wish to focus attention on the increasing polarization of the occupational structure which indicates that along with the boom in jobs and workplaces directly inserted in the economy of information, on one hand, various low-skilled productive activities and occupations which are highly fragile and vulnerable emerge and expand, on other hand, but that run parallel to the first ones. We refer in particular to jobs such as domestic service, the care industry, maintenance and cleaning, food preparation, among many others, all of them linked directly to the social and daily reproduction of the middle and high income population of advanced societies.

In this polarized context of occupations derived from economic globalization in the advanced societies, various market niches would be taking place, in which preferably immigrant workers are often inserted, who, as a result of their migratory condition and on many occasions undocumented, do not have the necessary social and political tools to confront and renegotiate the terms of insecurity, vulnerability and job instability which prevails in these segments of the labor market.

Finally, it should be noted that this polarization and boom of the occupations related to the reproductive and personal services, is familiar with the social and cultural transformations that, for some decades, advanced societies have been experiencing in the framework of what Bauman has called as liquid societies. On the one hand, the economic development itself promotes new consumption and lifestyle patterns, favoring the commodification of many activities linked to social and daily reproduction which used to be performed in the various fields of private and family life. The individuation and changing processes affecting household roles and family, alongside the increased incorporation of women into public and labor life, involve a certain liberation and emancipation of the ancient chains that tied them to housework.

These social changes, also open up a space for the increasing incorporation of immigrant workers, men and women, in these various activities related to the social reproduction of the native population. From this perspective, the international migration also helps to sustain the social, cultural and demographic changes that characterize contemporary advanced societies. Thus, for example, both child and elderly care, as domestic service itself, stops being a native women's task, and become commodified labor made by immigrants, but under the conditions dictated by the labor flexibility and contractual deregulation of post-industrial societies.

## 5    The Contradictions of the Model: Demographic Replacement

Although our focus is to identify the functions and forms that migration adopts as a structuring process of society reproduction, this does not invalidate or imply leaving aside the possible contradictions, tensions or dilemmas that these forms and functions involve. On the contrary, our interest is precisely to identify those tensions, characterize them and to measure their importance and significance.

This is particularly true in the case of demography. In particular, in the case of the United States and Europe migration addresses the demographic gap generated by both ageing and the decline in the fertility resulted from the Second Demographic Transition in these countries. In this case we note that, for several of these countries, immigration has become a central part of its population reproduction system. With this, we are referring not only to the population increases that immigration directly generate, but also to the indirect one that subsequently immigrants produce in the natural population growth through child bearing.

In this way, the ageing and declining population of developed countries signifies a growing reliance upon migrants as the social reproduction of its population depends directly on the demographic contributions that immigration makes, particularly those coming from the Third World countries. However, the ageing and decline of population themselves propitiate that immigration results in a deep transformation of the ethnic composition in the core countries.

In other words, the same benefits that this demographic regime generates for the developed countries, demographic sustainability to their social and economic reproduction, have their own contradictions which are manifested in the magnitude of change in the population composition that this regime of demographic reproduction generates in those same societies. If, on the one hand, immigration makes it possible to compensate for the demographic and labor gaps that the population ageing leaves, it is also, on the other hand, the basis for demographic transformation of these societies. Immigration not only helps to support the population reproduction of the core countries, but it also entails the fate of transformation and change in the ethnic composition of that same population.

In the case of the United States, for example, recent Health Department reports indicate that currently 25% of births correspond to mothers of Latino origin, that is, one out of every four new Americans by birth, corresponds to a baby of Latino origin. This number prefigures the dimension and magnitude of the change in the population composition of that country according to their ethnic and migratory background. If to this, we add that the fertility levels of the Latino population far outweigh that of the native population (which is even slightly below the levels of demographic reproduction), the future demographic changes will acquire levels of great importance that will question the current political and social balances based on a demographic structure which is being transformed rapidly.

This is the contradiction raised in the core countries in the face of this global demographic reproduction scheme. On the one hand, given the ageing that those countries are facing, immigration allows for demographic sustainability to the economic and social reproduction of their populations. But simultaneously, the combination of both processes, ageing and immigration, is giving rise to the ethnic and demographic transformation of the first world populations. In other words, the current dilemma in the core countries, is that, to reproduce economically and socially, they need to transform demographically. The problem is that this is not just any demographic transformation, but one that carries the questioning and erosion of the foundations that sustain the current demographic hegemonies to be reproduced (class, ethnic, generational, among others).

In this framework, we can understand the depth and historical significance of the dilemma that the First World countries are currently facing, namely:

- The social and economic reproduction process is guaranteed based on the adoption of a policy of openness and tolerance to immigration, but that carries a deep ethnic and cultural transformation of its population.
- A radical policy of control and disparagement of mass immigration is implemented, but at the risk of entering into a process of demographic unsustainability that would put at risk not only the population stability, but also the economic and social stability of these countries.

It is a dilemma of a demographic type but that has crucial economic, social and political implications. Its importance lies in the impacts that an active population reduction would have on the development of core countries productive and economic forces. In other words, if this immigration and ethnic transformation is not maintained, the economy itself, along with the demography of those countries, would be seriously compromised.

CHAPTER 9

# Latinos in the USA: the New American Dilemma

*And if I was born outside,*
*I'm proud of it.*
*And if I have indigenous blood,*
*So much the better, because it is beautiful*[1]
    The Rose of the Winds
    MAKIZA / ANITA TIJOUX

∴

1      Thesis

The ageing and decline of the population in advanced societies have made the dynamics of their economy, and the social reproduction of their inhabitants, directly dependent on the contributions made to the country by immigration. However, the same demographic processes propitiate an ethnic change of the current social and demographic balances. The political dilemma facing advanced societies is that to ensure their reproduction they must open themselves up to immigration, but this involves the possibility of becoming multicultural societies where the political hegemony of the present ethnic and demographic majorities would be radically altered. This is the basis for political conflict, of which there are signs in the current migration crisis of Europe, and for the rebirth of racism and xenophobia in the United States.

"Race remains a potent and often divisive force in our society" (*The New York Times*, 2017, January 10). With these words former President Barack Obama referred in his departing speech to the problem of racism and xenophobia in the United States, and he saw it as one of the big subjects still to be addressed that will define the social and political agenda of his country. In the same speech he drew attention to the role that immigrants have always played in the construction of Democracy in the USA.

---

1   "Y si yo he nacido afuera estoy orgullosa. Y si tengo sangre indígena, mejor, porque es hermosa". La rosa de los vientos. Original in Spanish.

Racism and ethnic differentiation have always been part of the social and cultural structure of the United States. Several authors have studied its historical formation, as well as the mechanisms used by it over time for its reproduction and transformation (Bonilla-Silva, 2002; Omi and Winant, 2015). Further, a an interesting discussion began a few years back about the new forms that ethnic discrimination in contemporary US society might be taking. Some said that the country would be living in a post-racial period, an idea based on the fact that a representative of the Afro-American community had risen to the top of the government of the USA (Love and Tosolt, 2010; Ono, 2010).

It does not cease to be revealing that it was Obama himself who pointed out that even if intentions were good, such visions of a post-racial society were never realistic. It is historically revealing that it should have been precisely the first president of Afro-American origin who took up the question of racism and immigration, and that did so precisely in the context of the subsequent emergence of a character like Donald Trump who has reinstalled racism and xenophobia as an essential question in US politics and society.[2]

The exposition set out in this book gives us a frame of analysis for understanding and comprehending the political and demographic juncture that the United States is passing through at present, which is not essentially different from the situation that a number of European countries are currently going through with the rebirth of supremacist and extreme right wing groups. To begin with, it never ceases to amaze how easily all these groups can raise the flag against immigration and go on from there to build a whole policy against the rights of the various minorities. It is not just a question of migrants, but also of women, youth, Moslem, religion, gender identities, and many other targets. It would seem that the immigrant is the catalyst,[3] the point of encounter from which extreme conservatism re-arises, and once in place, begins its attack on all social and political minorities.

Yet the irony of fate is curious. The risk does not originate in the others but in themselves. It is the demographic dynamics of the natives, that is, of the whites, the Europeans or Arians, that has created the great demographic

---

2  Nothing exemplifies it better than the demonstrations of white supremacists, the Ku Klux Klan, and other racist groups in Charlottesville, Virginia, in August 2017, and the suspicious silence that the White House kept for several days regarding acts of violence and terrorism driven by those groups in those demonstrations.
3  Whether the migrant is there for work, or to join the family, or is a political refugee or displaced from his home by social violence, or escaping from natural disasters, no matter, each is treated with the same suspicion and are regarded as a risk to maintaining and perpetuating the status quodisorders

disorders the deficit of workers, the need for immigration and immigrants to keep up standards of living in postmodern liquid societies, the patterns of consumption and work in the age of information and a global economy, the profit rates and the accumulation of capital in a post-Fordism age of global factories, with the deregulation of labor markets and making employment and labor ever more "flexible".

The ideas and reflections expounded in this book allow us to create a frame of analysis and understanding for current political situations in the face of immigration in advanced societies, and at the same time, to comprehend the bases and the circumstances of the emergence of a character like Donald Trump in the United States, as well as its limits and scope, and the emergence of a discourse of hate against all social, ethnic, sexual and gender minorities.

To start with, it makes it possible for us to identify the structural processes underlying the current contingency, and these allow us to understand the scope, the transcendence and the viability of the different political positions adopted in response to the present historical juncture. In our case we take the United States as an example to analyze the question of racism, and social class inequality, from the perspective of the goals and challenges presented by the change of demographics experienced by that country. We take as our starting point impacts on the ethnic composition of the United States population that are seen in a process of replacing the demography of the current white, native, majority with people of Latino origin and from other immigrant minorities. However, the same model for understanding the problem can be applied to analysis of the situation in Europe today where an identical contradiction is reproduced, albeit with different aspects and adopting other forms of expression, between the demographic structures of the local population and the needs and urgencies of the economic and class structures of European societies.

## 2       Demographic Change and Ethnic Replacement

For roughly the past thirty years, the United States has been undergoing a process of transition leading it away from the traditional demographic structure based on an undisputed predominance of a white majority, to a more evenly balanced structure in which whites cease to be an absolute majority and share their position at the top with the Latino population (Canales, 2015). This is a process of demographic replacement sustained by two strong tendencies, i) the decline of the white population, as the result of its ageing and low birth rate, and ii) the surge and expansion of the Latino population, as a product of immigration and a higher birth rate.

i) The low birth rate of the white population is explained by the coming of the Second Demographic Transition, a model that shows a continual decline of the fertility rate even to levels below that of simple replacement (Van de Kaa, 1987). This decline would be based on processes of individuation in social and family life, contributing to a weakening of the family as an institution and a strengthening of the individual, and of rights and self-realization in various areas of social, economic, political and cultural life, that transcend narrow family circles (Beck and Beck-Gernshmein, 2002). For the United States, the figures are eloquent: the total fertility rate of white women has come down from 3.5 children for women of reproductive age in 1960, to 2.0 in 1990, and is now at 1.7 (Heuser, 1976; Martin et al., 2017).

Demographic ageing, in turn, corresponds to the last phase of the First Demographic Transition and is expressed in the composition of the population by age group, where the senior adult population has acquired an ever greater absolute and relative weight as a result of two simultaneous processes. Firstly, a decrease in the number of births and in the number of children and young people, and secondly an increase in the numbers of adults as a consequence of increased rates of longevity and life expectations. More people all the time are living longer (Anderson and Hussey, 2000; Coleman, 1993). In the case of the white population of the United States, the index for ageing illustrates the scale of this process. If in 1980 there were 60 senior adults for every 100 children under 15, today this relation is more than twice as large, with 150 senior adults for every 100 children.[4]

ii) With regard to the population of Latino origins, its growth is explained both by the surge in immigration during the 1980s and its greater birth rate and fertility. Immigration explains the increase from 4.0 million Latin American immigrants in 1980 to 11.5 million in the year 2000 and 21.4 million in 2016. The increase through new births is seen in the figures from 2005 to 2015, when the gross birth rate among Latinos was approximately 20 for every thousand Latino residents in the USA, far higher than the average for the white population and the national average which came in at 11.2 and 13.5 thousand births per thousand inhabitants, respectively (Martin et al., 2017).

The higher birth rate is explained by two factors. First, the greater fertility of the Latino population, and secondly the larger proportion of women of child bearing age (from 15 to 49). In the first case, the total fertility rate of Latino women was 2.12 children per woman, higher than the figure for white women, who had just 1.7 children per woman (Martin et al., 2017). And with regard to the second reason, in 2015 Latino women of a childbearing age accounted for

---

[4] The author's own estimates based on the US Population Census of 1980 and 2000, and the CPS for 2016.

53% of all Latino women, while in the case of the white population, women of a childbearing age only represented 42% of all white women (CPS, 2015).

A higher birth rate combined with a high rate of immigration, form the demographic basis of the large increase in the population of Latino origin in the United States. It is relevant to the present study to estimate and differentiate the contribution of each of these two components to the demographic growth of the Latino population. Between 1980 and 2016, the population of people with Latino origins increased by 48.1 million, with 64% of the increase explained by the net growth of the Latino population born in the United States, while the net increase in the number of Latin American immigrants arriving accounts for the remaining 36%.[5] More recently, the proportion of Latinos born in the USA has become even greater. This shows that although immigration is not an unimportant factor, the greater weight of an increase in the number of Latinos is the result of their greater fertility and higher birth rates, that is to say, of an increase in the number of Latinos born in the USA. So whatever walls and restrictions are imposed on immigration, these will certainly not stop the demographic growth of the Latino population.

The combination of these processes, a decline in the white population and an increase in the Latino population, forms the basis of changes in ethnic composition that the United States is currently experiencing, and is set to lead eventually to a process of ethnic and demographic substitution, making the USA move on from being a country of whites as it was historically to being a society of demographic minorities.

It can be seen in Table 6 that from the time when it became an independent country at the end of the 18th century until the end of the 1970s, the United States was always a country with a white majority, an ethnic group that accounted for over 80% of the population, reaching its maximum in the 1920s, when whites accounted for nearly 90% of the population.

However, the white population of the United States has been in a demographic decline to such a point that whites currently account for only 61% of the population, a tendency meaning that in the year 2044 for the first time in the history of the country, whites will cease to be an absolute majority and will represent only 49.9% of the population, going down again to 44% in the year 2060, a proportion that will continue to grow smaller as the decades pass.

As for the ethnic minorities, they have always been demographic minorities, in most cases representing no more than 20% of the population. However, a process of change started in 1980 that has led to their currently accounting for 39% of the population, which would mean their share increasing to 56% in

---

5  The author's own estimates based on the US Population Census, 1980 and 2000 and CPS 2016.

2060. In other words, in just a few decades, *the minorities will be in the majority*. Among these minorities the Latinos stand out, having come from forming less than 5% of the total population in 1970, to representing 17% today, and, it is estimated, 30% in 2060, as their share increases every decade of the new century.

This situation might be thought of as something out of a science fiction movie, except that it is already happening in several states of the American Union. In California, for example, until the middle of the twentieth century the white population held its position as a large demographic majority accounting for 87% of the population, while Latinos and other minorities scarcely accounted for 7% and 6% respectively. But by 1970 an incipient change was to be seen, with the whites keeping their place as a majority, but one reduced to 76%, while the Latino share of the population had risen to 14%, beginning a process of sustained growth uninterrupted to date. According to the figures of ACS (2015), whites have not only ceased to be the demographic majority

TABLE 6    USA. 1780–2060. Population by main ethnic groups

| Year | Population volume (thousands) | | | | | |
|---|---|---|---|---|---|---|
| | Total | Whites non-Latinos | Blacks non-Latinos | Latinos | Asian | Other minorities |
| 1780 | 2,780 | 2,205 | 575 | nd | nd | nd |
| 1800 | 5,308 | 4,306 | 1,002 | nd | nd | nd |
| 1820 | 9,638 | 7,867 | 1,772 | nd | nd | nd |
| 1840 | 17,063 | 14,190 | 2,874 | nd | nd | nd |
| 1860 | 31,443 | 26,923 | 4,442 | nd | 35 | 44 |
| 1880 | 50,150 | 43,207 | 6,581 | 190 | 106 | 66 |
| 1900 | 75,240 | 65,763 | 8,834 | 291 | 114 | 237 |
| 1920 | 105,730 | 94,624 | 10,463 | 216 | 182 | 244 |
| 1940 | 131,811 | 116,479 | 12,866 | 1,878 | 255 | 334 |
| 1960 | 179,469 | 153,533 | 18,860 | 5,456 | 980 | 639 |
| 1980 | 226,281 | 180,256 | 26,760 | 14,609 | 3,500 | 1,155 |
| 2000 | 281,422 | 194,433 | 35,292 | 35,241 | 11,549 | 4,906 |
| 2015 | 321,419 | 197,554 | 39,650 | 56,477 | 17,097 | 10,640 |
| 2040 | 380,219 | 195,197 | 48,162 | 91,626 | 33,872 | 11,362 |
| 2060 | 4,16,795 | 1,81,930 | 54,028 | 119,044 | 45,822 | 15,970 |

Sources: US Census Bureau (1975 and 2014), US Population Census from 1880 to 2000, and ACS (2015).

but with 37.8% of the population they have been overtaken by the population of Latino origins, who represent 38.8% of the total. So in less than 50 years, the ethnic composition of the population of California has reversed, prefiguring the social and demographic future that is foreseen for the whole of the United States in the upcoming decades. This is not a question of speculations and demographic conjectures, but a situation that is an undisputable reality in California, as in other states of the American Union, such as Texas, New Mexico, Arizona, Nevada, and Florida.

The process of *ethnic replacement* that we have documented here is already a structural part of the demographic dynamics of the population of the United States. A way of demonstrating this idea is to analyze the changes in the ethnic composition of births currently occurring in the country every year. From 1970 to 2015, the number of children born in the United States has been stuck between 3.7 and 4 million live births every year. However, the composition of these clearly shows the process of ethnic and demographic replacement that the country is already experiencing.

In 1970 the number of births to white mothers amounted to 77% of those born, while babies with Latino mothers accounted for only 7%, and the remaining 16% corresponded to the birth of babies to other ethnic minorities (Afro-Americans, Asians, Native American Indians, and others). So in 1970 the demographic primacy of the white population held and was reproduced through its lead in the number of births.

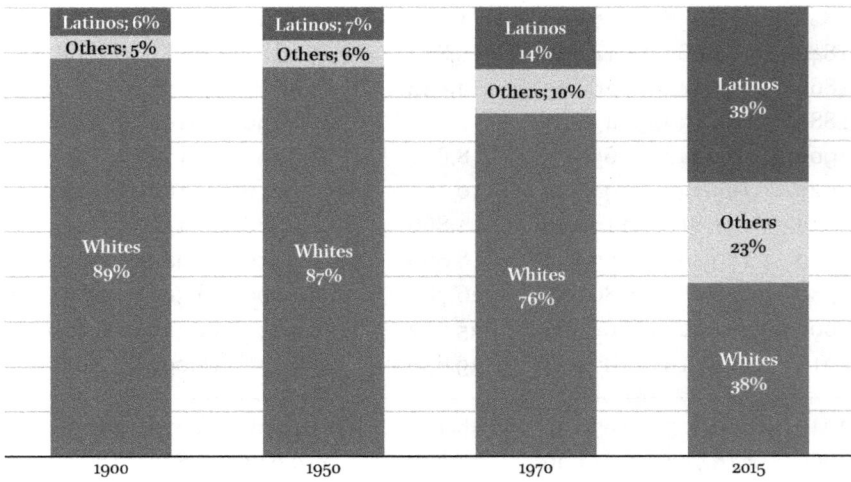

FIGURE 26   California, 1900–2015. Population by major ethnic group
SOURCES: GIBSON & YOUNG, 2002; AND ACS 2015.

However, this situation started to change considerably in the 1980s. By 1985, though whites formed 80% of the population, they contributed only 68% of all births. Whereas the Latinos, who accounted for only 7% of the population, produced 13% of all births (see Table 7). This difference between whites and Latinos is one of the origins of the change of demographics and the ethnic replacement currently seen and will determine the dynamics of the population for the next few decades.

Currently, the white population contributes only 53.5% of all births and it is expected that this figure will be reduced to just 33.4% in the year 2060; in other words, only one of every three new Americans by birth will be a white person. By contrast, although Latinos accounted for only 17% of the population in 2015, they contributed nearly a quarter of all births, and they are expected to produce 28.8% in 2030 and 34.6% in 2060, exceeding by then the number of births to the white population. The other ethnic minorities in turn show a tendency very similar to that of the Latinos.

These figures provide a clear example for how a change of demographics and a process of ethnic replacement are a social phenomenon that is already being lived and experienced in the United States. Newly born American citizens today are prefiguring the ethnic composition that the Census Bureau has estimated for the whole population in the next few decades. This shows that however great the desire to close the country's borders to immigration may be,

TABLE 7   USA 1970–2050. Births by ethnic origin of mother

| Year | Births | | | |
|---|---|---|---|---|
| | Total | Whites non-Latinos | Latinos | Others minorities |
| 1970 | 3,689,490 | 2,835,996 | 255,268 | 598,226 |
| 1985 | 3,760,561 | 2,556,855 | 481,058 | 722,648 |
| 2000 | 4,058,814 | 2,362,968 | 858,820 | 837,026 |
| 2015 | 3,978,497 | 2,130,279 | 956,498 | 891,720 |
| 2030 | 4,198,020 | 1,846,306 | 1,210,207 | 1,141,507 |
| 2045 | 4,331,771 | 1,669,062 | 1,385,657 | 1,277,052 |
| 2060 | 4,518,941 | 1,509,742 | 1,563,125 | 1,446,074 |

Sources: Martin et al., (2017), and US Census Bureau (2014)

to do so would not be enough to stop and contain a demographic change that the US population is already experiencing, and this is for two reasons.
- First, these tendencies in the ethnic composition of births illustrate how the process of demographic replacement is not only due to the effects of immigration, but is principally the result of the declining demographics of the white population seen today in its declining birth rate and fertility.
- Secondly, these changes in the ethnic composition of births tell us that ethnic and demographic replacement is a process that started over 30 years ago, in the 1970s and 1980s, and is therefore already part of the demographic structure of the United States.

This change in the composition of births has a direct impact on the age structure of the population. In this sense the ethnic composition of age pyramids helps us to illustrate the basic features of this process: i) the scale of demographic change and ethnic replacement going on, and ii) the irreversibility of the process, at least in the medium term, that comprises the next five or six decades of the century.

Age pyramids show us how this process has already changed the ethnic composition of the youth and infant population, and how over the years this process will expand to cover the rest of the age groups, thus affecting the whole demographic pyramid of the United States.

As indeed expected, the white population was the demographic majority in nearly all age groups in 1980, with 72% of those under 10 years old, and 91% of the over 80 years of age group (see Figure 27). It was not until 2015 that relevant changes began to be seen, prefiguring the scale of the changes to come in the next few decades. Although whites have kept an undisputed majority among the over 60s, with over 80% of the population of that age, things are not the same in the younger cohorts.

In the case of youth (young people aged 15 to 29) although the predominance of whites still holds, it is a significantly smaller majority. In 1980, the proportion of inhabitants of that age who were white, was 78%. But by 2015, only 55% of young people were of white origin, bringing the relation between the young white population and that of ethnic minorities into a closer balance.

In the case of children and adolescents under 15, this reduction is even more significant. In 1980, 75% of those under 15 were of white origin, but by 2015 the relation has become almost equal, with the whites accounting for just 51% of all the infant and adolescent population.

In both cases the phenomenon is one of great importance, because beyond the common idea that children and young people are the future of any society, is the obvious fact that the ethnic composition prevailing among the infant and juvenile populations today is the same as the one that will predominate in

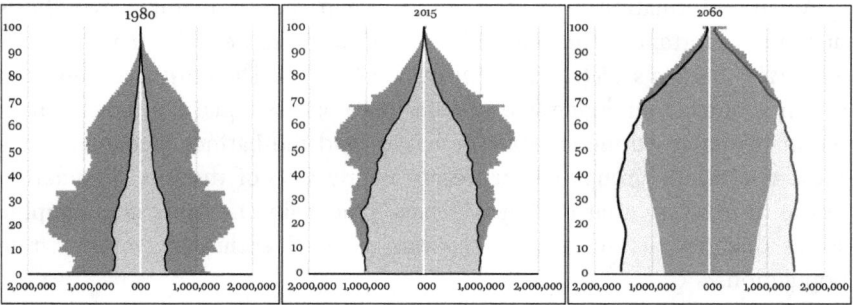

FIGURE 27   USA, 1980–2060. Population pyramid, white non-Latino and Latinos.
SOURCES: US CENSUS BUREAU (1980 AND 2014); AND ACS (2015).

the next few decades among the population as a whole. So it is that the change of ethnic composition already being experienced by the infant and juvenile population today, prefigures the scale and the size of the demographic change and ethnic replacement that the whole population of the United Sates will experience in the next few decades.

In effect, as the demographic projections of the Census Bureau of the United States illustrate, it is estimated that the current white predominance will be restricted by 2060 to the senior adult population (those over 65), and will be seriously reduced even in this age group. Only 55% of the elder people will be of white origin, while the remaining 45% will belong to the various minorities.

In the other age groups, the whites will be in a definite minority, with only 43% of young adults (aged between 30 and 64), and only 38% of the young population (aged 15 to 29) being white, and less than 36% of the children and adolescents under 15 still that category. These figures tell us that the ethnic replacement will continue and become even faster after 2060, when the number of whites in the last groups in the age pyramid of the population in which they still have a majority gets smaller.

To sum up, the demographic change we are talking about is not a bet on a possible future, but a real fact, a social and demographic process that has started and which will unfold in the next few decades, irreversibly. For this reason it is not enough to impose policies restricting immigration, because the demographic changes are already baked in the cake and are actually occurring among the population currently residing in the USA who are part of the country. No walls can stop this demographic change or contain it as one of its principle actors is precisely the same white population who have been experiencing a demographic decline for some decades as a result of their low birth rate and progressive ageing.

All the information presented here so far points to a simple hypothesis of great importance. *The United States will cease to be a country of whites and will become a society of demographic minorities.* The ethnic composition which is already emerging is based on more or less equal numbers of people in two large ethnic groups: the whites and the Latinos. Between them, these two ethnic groups will represent nearly 75% of the total population in the near future, that is, they will have practically the same demographic status that just a few decades ago was reserved exclusively to the white population.

## 3   The Racialization of Inequality and the New American Dilemma

During the most recent elections in the United States, Jorge Ramos pointed put on several occasions that "without Latinos there is no government". By which he meant to emphasize the political importance the Latino vote has been gaining since the demographic changes we have mentioned. We would go a little further, and say that *without Latinos there is no future* in the United States.

This is the fear of the white supremacists, of Trump and others who project the object of their fear onto Mexico and Mexicans. They are beginning to realize that Latinos are more and more becoming the demographic force that will transform the United States, taking over from the white population and replacing it in that role, as it enters into a long period of decline and ageing which will prevail during the whole of the twenty-first century (Ortman, Velkoff and Hogan, 2014). In opposition to Trump's discourse, it is Latinos and immigrants who will make America great again, as some placards declared in recent demonstrations in Texas: *Immigrants make America great.*

Figures again provide an eloquent illustration of the scope of this point. If the United States did not have its Latinos and immigrants, it would enter into a chronic deficit of labor that would have a direct effect on its hegemonic position as the top political, military and economic power in the world.

We define this labor deficit as the difference between the number of jobs that the economy creates in a year and the size of the native economically active population (labor force) that creates the demographic dynamics, that is, the employed and unemployed natives of the country without including immigrants (Canales and Meza, 2016). On the basis of this definition we estimate that the labor deficit has developed in three stages in recent years.

- To begin with, before the economic crisis around 2008, the labor deficit shows a steady rise, from under 13 million workers in 2003 to nearly 18 million in 2007.

- Secondly, and as expected, as an effect of the economic crisis the deficit was reduced to 9.6 million in 2010. However, it remains true that even at times of crisis, the deficit of labor was still a structural factor, and even at the worst time it represented 7% of those in employment.
- Finally, since, 2010 a recovery in the economy has re-encouraged growth in employment, making the deficit of labor reassume its tendency to rise, with a shortfall of 9.6 million workers in 2010 increasing to 18.9 million in 2015, a figure that represents nearly 13% of jobs in the economy today.

The structural deficit of labor is a condition that favors and encourages immigration, in which Latin American immigrants assume a role of great importance that becomes even more so at times of economic crisis. Even before the crisis, Latin American immigration covered 74% of the structural deficit in the labor market. This amount increases to 84% during the crisis years (2007–2011) and stays above 78% in recent years of recovery in employment and economic activity in the USA.

These figures show the great weight of Latin American immigration in the dynamics of labor markets in the United States, through its contribution to supplying the structural deficit of labor created by the imbalance between the economic-productive and the demographic dynamics of the native population. It should also be noted how important this situation is for restarting the United States economy after the crisis of 2008.

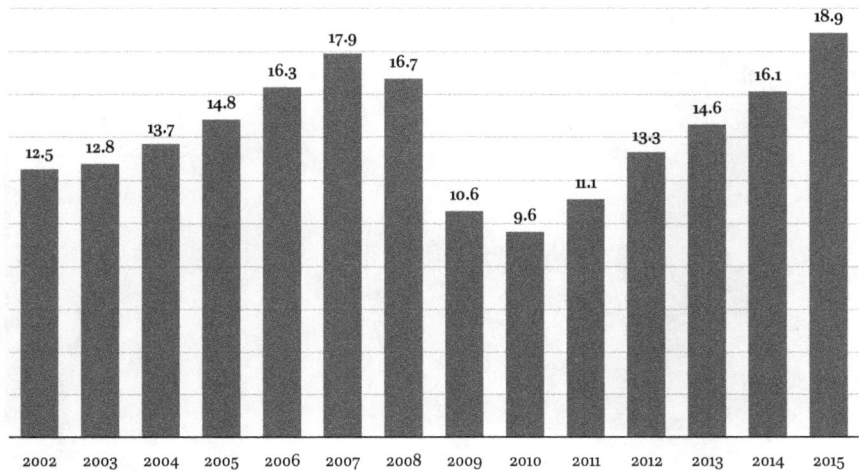

FIGURE 28   USA, 2002–2015. Labor force deficit (millions of people)
SOURCES: CURRENT POPULATION SURVEY, MARCH SUPPLEMENT, 2002 TO 2015. US CENSUS BUREAU.

The contribution of Latinos and other ethnic minorities to covering the labor deficit is also reflected in their input to the growth of the economy and the Gross Domestic Product (GDP) of the United States. Between 2000 and 2015, the GDP of the United States grew by approximately 30%. However, although white workers accounted for 67% of the labor force, they only contributed 41% of the growth of the economy. The remaining 59.2% came from ethnic and demographic minorities taken as a whole. Once again, the Latinos stand out, as they alone contributed 30.2% of the growth of GDP, spread between Latino immigrants (16.2%) and their descendants born in the United States (14%). The rest of the growth in GDP came from immigrants from other countries (16.6%) and the other ethnic minorities (12.4%).

These figures show us the degree to which the economic dynamics of the United States have become dependent on the labor participation of ethnic minorities and in particular that of the population with Latino origins. Or to put it another way, the scale of the risk and vulnerability that the US economy is exposed to as the demographics of the white population decline. For the moment we can state that on the basis of this composition of GDP growth, the growth of the economy in the United States is sustained more and more by the input of the ethnic minorities, in comparison with that of the white majority. In this sense, the demographic growth of the Latinos is an important, fundamental, resource at the disposal of the United States economy to keep genon-erating the economic surpluses that are necessary for it to maintain

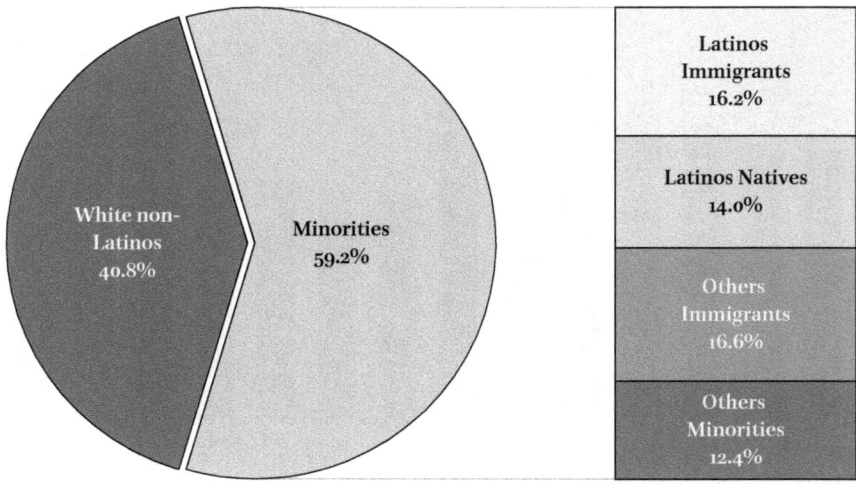

FIGURE 29    USA, 2000–2015. Growth of GDP by ethnic origin of labor force
SOURCES: CURRENT POPULATION SURVEY, MARCH SUPPLEMENT, 2002 & 2015.

its hegemonic position as a political, military and economic power in global terms.

With regard to the contribution to economic growth in this situation, it does not have a correlation in the distribution of the benefits of development and well-being that this economic growth creates in the United States. To the contrary, we are faced by a situation in which social inequality is racialized, that is to say, a structural situation in which one's ethnic condition turns out to be a key factor in the configuration of differences in standards of living for the population, in the inequality of the distribution of income and economic resources, in the precariousness of employment and the segmentation of labor markets, in occupational segregation, and in various forms of economic and salary discrimination.

3.1 *Occupational Segregation and the Racializing of Social Inequality*

Even though Latinos, migrants and other ethnic minorities are the engine of demographic and economic growth in the United States, the prevailing structure of occupational segregation and social inequality marginalizes them and excludes them from the benefits of development (Caicedo, 2010). It can be seen immediately that the minorities tend to be relegated to the lowest positions in the occupational pyramid, and to the lowest levels of the social pyramid and that of income. Social inequality acquires a racialized form in which the position occupied by any individual on the social scale is directly determined by his ethnic and migratory origin (Canales, 2017).

Figures show that in 2016, 45% of white employees were in jobs at the top of the labor pyramid (CEOs, company directors and professionals) and only 17% were at the base (day laborers, building workers and those providing personal services requiring little in the way of qualifications, including personal care, maids, cleaning and maintenance). While the distribution of Latinos is the opposite, with 36% employed in occupations at the base of the occupational pyramid and only 22% employed in positions at the top of the labor hierarchy.

What is relevant, at any rate, is that these figures show that while whites are experiencing an upward polarization of occupations, with those at the top of the pyramid almost three times the number at the base, in the case of Latinos the situation is reversed, with the majority in the most precarious and vulnerable posts, accounting for more than 65% more than those employed at the opposite end of the labor hierarchy.

This differentiation in the way labor is inserted in the market is also reflected in social and income inequality. While in the case of whites there is a relatively more balanced composition of the various levels of income, with the middle income population predominating, in the case of Latinos there is

TABLE 8   USA. 2016. Population occupied and total population by major ethnic groups and occupational and income strata

| Strata[a] | Population occupied by occupational strata | | | Population by income strata | | |
|---|---|---|---|---|---|---|
| | Whites non-Latinos | Other minorities | Latinos | Whites non-Latinos | Other minorities | Latinos |
| Total | 100% | 100% | 100% | 100% | 100% | 100% |
| Low strata | 17.0% | 22.7% | 36.0% | 27.4% | 45.4% | 52.3% |
| Middle strata | 37.7% | 39.1% | 42.2% | 43.0% | 35.5% | 35.5% |
| Upper middle and high strata | 45.3% | 38.3% | 21.8% | 29.5% | 19.0% | 12.1% |

a   The upper middle and high occupational strata correspond to managers, CEOs and professionals; Middle strata are employees and skilled workers; And the lower strata are unskilled workers, construction workers, and low-skilled personal services workers (domestic service, care, and the like).
   The low-income strata correspond to people with annual incomes no higher than 1.5 times the poverty line; Middle strata are persons with incomes above 1.5 times the poverty line and less than 50 thousand dollars annually; And upper middle and high strata to people with annual incomes over 50 thousand dollars.
Sources: Current Population Survey, ASEC, 2016.

a clear concentration of employees at the lowest levels. In effect, 52% of the Latinos belong to poor or vulnerable strata (under the poverty line or with incomes not much above that level), and only 12% are in the upper middle or highest levels of income (with an income of over 50 thousand dollars a year). The other minorities reproduce the same pattern as the Latinos, though to a lesser extent.

Now it might be thought that as the white majority gets smaller in number and is replaced by Latinos and other minorities, ethnic inequality in the way labor is inserted in the market would be reduced. In other words, it might be expected that the demographic replacement of whites by Latinos would take place with small variations at all occupational levels and in all social classes. This is certainly not the case. To begin with, we can illustrate the point with the current situation in states like California, where the demographic replacement of whites by Latinos has not substantially changed the racialization of social and occupational inequality. As we pointed out before, in California although whites and Latinos share the top place as demographic minorities, with 37.8% and 38.8% of the population respectively, they are a long way from sharing the same social and class structure, and to the contrary, the racialization of social and occupational inequality we have mentioned at national level is reproduced there.

Both with regard to insertion into the labor market and insertion into socioeconomic structures, California practically reproduces the same structures we have seen at national level. In the first case, white employees in positions of management and professional jobs are almost five times as many as those working as day laborers in construction or in low skill personal services. Also,

TABLE 9  California, 2016. Population occupied and total population by major ethnic groups and occupational and income strata

| Strata[a] | Population occupied by occupational strata | | | Population by income strata | | |
|---|---|---|---|---|---|---|
| | Whites non-Latinos | Other minorities | Latinos | Whites non-Latinos | Other minorities | Latinos |
| Total | 100% | 100% | 100% | 100% | 100% | 100% |
| Low strata | 14.8% | 17.0% | 34.6% | 26.9% | 36.5% | 52.2% |
| Middle strata | 31.3% | 34.1% | 44.1% | 37.9% | 36.6% | 36.2% |
| Upper middle and high strata | 53.9% | 48.9% | 21.3% | 35.2% | 26.9% | 11.6% |

a  The upper middle and high occupational strata correspond to managers, CEOs and professionals; Middle strata are employees and skilled workers; And the lower strata are unskilled workers, construction workers, and low-skilled personal services workers (domestic service, care, and the like).

The low-income strata correspond to people with annual incomes no higher than 1.5 times the poverty line; Middle strata are persons with incomes above 1.5 times the poverty line and less than 50 thousand dollars annually; And upper middle and high strata to people with annual incomes over 50 thousand dollars.

Sources: Current Population Survey, ASEC, 2016.

whites earning over 50 thousand dollars a year, who at the national level outnumber those who are at levels of poverty or vulnerability by only 7%, are 30% more numerous in California.

It is impressive how virtually the same distribution by occupational category and level of income as the one we observed at national level, is reproduced. This is of great relevance because it tells us that even in the context of losing its demographic predominance, the white population has been allowed by the political and social structure to keep its economic privileges and even to increase them. Whereas in the case of the Latinos, their demographic growth and the fact that they have now become the largest ethnic group in California has not brought them any socio-economic benefit, or any process of upward social mobility, whether seen from the point of view of occupations or incomes. In other words, they continue to suffer the same unmet needs and violations of their social and labor rights as at the national level.

### 3.2   *Productivity, Wages and Economic Discrimination*

According to economic theory, the wage or salary each employee receives is directly determined on the basis of the value of their productivity (Reisman, 1990; Krugman and Wells, 2006). The explanation of this idea is relatively simple, and is based on the fundamental principles of neo-classical economic theory.[6]

This economic theory says that the value of labor, in other words the salary that needs to be paid to a worker, is directly determined by his productivity. In situations of equilibrium, and when there is no wage discrimination, the remuneration for paid work should be equal to the value of the marginal product of the work (Becker, 1971). The value of the marginal product is established as the market value of what the marginal worker produces; in other words, the price of goods multiplied by the amount of goods produced.

On the basis of this principle for establishing the amount the labor force is paid, one would expect that differences in pay that can be observed between one social group and another would be a function of their different

---

6   According to other approaches and economic theories, wages are determined on the basis of other principles. So, for example, from a Marxist perspective, wages are said to be determined on the basis of the value of the goods and services needed for the reproduction of the labor force, and not on the basis of the value of the goods produced by that labor force. Variations of this theory build on the approaches of institutionalists, Neo-Ricardian, Weberian and Structuralists, among others. Something similar has been proposed from the approaches based on imperfect competition. Our own interest in referring to the neo-classical principle is to illustrate that the situation of vulnerability and discrimination affecting Latin American immigrants can be demonstrated even from more conservative and orthodox perspectives.

productivity. According to the same principle of proportionality we would have a situation of economic and wage equity, meaning that every worker would be getting an income in wages that depended on how much he contributed to production, and this would be expressed in the value of his productivity.[7]

In the opposite case, however, where the level of remuneration is proportionally lower than the rates of productivity corresponding to a particular stratum of the work force, we would have a situation of wage discrimination, that is to say, one in which the wages received did not correspond to the amount that economic theory says would be due to the worker (Cain, 1986). In which case, the negative discrimination suffered by that particular group of workers could also be seen as positive discrimination enjoyed by some other group of workers.

It should be noted that in all cases we are referring to a strictly economic discrimination. Indeed the measure of the discrimination (positive or negative as it might be) is made by comparing data observed on the amount of remuneration received for paid work (wages and salaries), with the value that would be due to this ethnic of workers group, according to their corresponding rates of productivity. In such a case the situation would be one of economic equity, where differences in wages and salaries were proportional to corresponding differences in the mean rates of productivity. This idea calls for two comments.

– Following this principle, differences in wages and remuneration received by workers would be legitimate if they corresponded to differences in the contributions made by each group to the economy. In other words, it is economically just and fair for whoever creates a greater economic benefit to also receive a higher economic benefit (wage, remuneration or income).

– This is a principle of economic equity that is radically different to principles of social equity and justice. Which is not to minimize the value of such principles of social equity. In fact, we wish to show that Latin American immigrants not only face a panorama of social and political discrimination, but in addition to that, have to deal with a situation of economic discrimination: they are not paid according to their contribution to the economy, their rate of productivity.

In order to estimate and calculate the scale of wage discrimination, we shall use a base method for estimating GDP and productivity rates that we

---

[7] According to John B. Clark (1899), this principle not only fulfils the criteria for economic efficiency but is also a principle of economic justice for the distribution of wealth. It should be noted that John B. Clark was the first economist to formulate this principle according to which the salary of the labor force is determined in terms of the value of its marginal productivity.

developed for use on other occasions (Canales, 2011) along with information on the amounts paid in remuneration to workers reported by the US Census Bureau through its Current Population Survey. In concrete terms, we can measure wage discrimination as the distance (difference) between the pay received on average by Latin American immigrant workers, and the value of their contribution to the economy, measured through the value of the mean rates of their productivity.

Following the principle for determining pay proposed by neo-classical economic theory, one would expect that on average Latin American immigrant workers would receive an amount in remuneration corresponding to the value of their mean productivity rate. However, the figures available for 2003–2015 tell us that while the productivity of Latin Americans is only 16% less than that of other workers, the average pay received by them is nearly 35% less than the amount received by other workers in the United States.

In monetary terms, this discrimination translates into a net transfer of the value that is generated by Latin American immigrants and other ethnic minorities, and is appropriated by workers of white origin. In concrete terms, in the period 2003–2015, for example, Latin American workers received on average wages of 27.6 thousand dollars a year, while workers from other minority groups received on average a wage of 39.5 thousand dollars a year, and workers of white origin received a wage of 46.4 thousand dollars. But on the basis of the principle of mean productivity, the remuneration the workers received should have reached 37.2 thousand dollars a year for Latin American immigrants, and 43.5 thousand dollars for the other ethnic minorities, a figure very close to the amount earned by workers of white origin.

In the case of the Latin American workers, this represented an annual net loss of value of 9.5 thousand dollars, and the loss for the other ethnic minorities was just 4 thousand dollars a year. To the contrary, workers of white origin received a net transfer in their favor of 2.7 thousand dollars a year each.[8]

In relative terms, these figures mean that on average over the whole period of 2003 to 2015, Latin American immigrants kept only 74% of all the wages and salaries that were due to them according to their productivity, and the remaining 26% was transferred to other social groups, which provides us with a measure of the level of wage discrimination that directly affects Latin American workers in the United States.

In other words, if the principle of equity and economic proportionality in the determination of wages proposed by neo-classical economic theory to

---

8  The amounts do not tally because they are averages per worker, so the differences would need to be contemplated by the number of workers in each ethnic group.

TABLE 10   USA, 2003–2015. Annual net transferences of earnings between major ethnic groups of workers (dollars 2009)

| Year | Latino American immigrants | Other minorities | White non Latinos |
|---|---|---|---|
| 2003 | −9,747 | −4,401 | 2,518 |
| 2004 | −9,943 | −4,029 | 2,497 |
| 2005 | −10,585 | −3,680 | 2,513 |
| 2006 | −9,472 | −4,176 | 2,636 |
| 2007 | −8,851 | −4,315 | 2,707 |
| 2008 | −8,821 | −4,145 | 2,620 |
| 2009 | −8,813 | −3,375 | 2,318 |
| 2010 | −9,049 | −3,906 | 2,593 |
| 2011 | −8,994 | −5,033 | 3,037 |
| 2012 | −9,498 | −4,567 | 3,141 |
| 2013 | −11,344 | −4,130 | 3,244 |
| 2014 | −9,280 | −2,589 | 2,351 |
| 2015 | −8,867 | −3,026 | 2,595 |
| 2003–2015 Average | −9,537 | −4,009 | 2,713 |

Sources: Current Population Survey, March Supplement, 2003 to 2015.

be respected, the pay received by Latin American workers should be nearly 33% higher, a situation that would certainly have beneficial effects in terms of the standard of living and well-being of the Latin American population residing in the United States.

Now it should be noted that this form of wage discrimination against Latin American workers, goes beyond the conditions that determine their labor situation, in other words their level of qualifications or their undocumented status, and similar aspects. Independently of all of that, Latin American migrants receive a level of pay for their work that is significantly lower than what they should be getting on the basis of their level of productivity.

We know that because of their level of qualifications, or because they are in an irregular situation as migrants, or for other reasons, Latin American migrants find they are segregated into jobs with lower productivity. To which a new level of discrimination should be added: one that corresponds to being

paid less than the amonnt required byetheir economic productivity. Latin Americans are faced by a double process of discrimination.
- Social discrimination (of the first order), on the basis of which they cannot attain positions of employment with greater productivity that would be better paid and involve more dynamic activities.
- Economic discrimination (of the second order) making pay even in these lower productivity jobs less than it should be in order to match their contribution to production, a rate of pay that itself would be significantly lower than the national average.

We are used to hearing the argument that the low wages of migrant workers in the United States are due to their lack of qualifications (years at school, work training, human capital, etc.) and their being without papers. The figures and estimates we have presented show that that explanation is insufficient. Their shorter schooling, lack of proper papers, etc. only allow us to explain why Latin American workers take employment in precarious positions and in low productivity economic activities. This is certainly a first level of discrimination that does explain low income and wages received by immigrants.

But on top of this discrimination of the first order, there is a second type of strictly economic discrimination. Wages and salaries received are even lower than what economic justice requires them to earn according to their productivity rate. So the discrimination is twofold. Not only are they segregated into low productivity low wage jobs, but once there, they are not paid a wage proportional to the value of their productivity. Due to extra-economic factors, they fail to receive (i.e. they transfer to others) more than a quarter of the value of the pay that corresponds to them according to economic theory as a just measure.

To sum up, a second level of discrimination, of an economic type, is built on the basis of a situation of segregation and social and ethnic discrimination. Latin American immigrants are not only segregated into jobs with less productivity and requiring less qualifications, with low wages, and highly precarious and vulnerable conditions of employment, but even in these jobs, the wages received are lower than what the principle of economic equity says they should earn, that is to they get paid less than the amount required by their contributions to the economy measured by their productivity. It is occupational segregation that makes them take up precarious, vulnerable, low wage jobs. It is economic discrimination that makes it impossible for them once they are there to assert their right to earn a wage appropriate to the value of their productivity.

Analysis of the figures for occupational segregation and economic discrimination allow us to understand the racialized form currently adopted by the structure of classes in contemporary US capitalism. Racism and the racializing of inequality have always been features defining American society. The big difference with the ethnic segregation experienced now which is expected to become more acute in succeeding decades, is the demographic context and the process of demographic replacement which frames these processes of social inequality.

In earlier times, characterized by the large demographic predominance of the white majority, racial and ethnic segregation affected a minority of the population. Until quite recently, the class structure maintained and reproduced this situation of white predominance at all levels of society. Social classes, though differentiated and unequal, were not equally differentiated by skin color or ethnic-migratory origin. To put it more simply: social inequality, labor vulnerability and precariousness and poor living conditions included whites as well, who were also the demographic majority in the lowest ranks of the social pyramid and the occupational hierarchy.

With demographic changes, however, social inequality assumes a double character. First, like all class structures, it reflects a form of socio-economic inequality, deriving from the occupational differentiation generated by the productive matrix. The inequality is of an eminently economic-productive nature, which takes shape in the occupational pyramid. In the case of the United States and European countries, this socio-economic inequality is expressed in the polarization of the structure of occupations we described above, and brings with it a surge in economic activities and employment positions located at the extremes of the occupational pyramid, to the detriment of those located in the middle strata.

Further, this economic-productive differentiation also assumes an extra-economical form, a form of social inequality that is built and shaped on the basis of non-economic factors, of a social and cultural type, where ethnic-racial distinctions and one's migratory condition acquire a fundamental role. This is the *racialization* of social inequality, where one's insertion into different occupational and social class ranks is no longer directly determined by one's position in the labor and economic-productive matrix, but is mediated by the color of one's skin, and by one's migratory origin. One's ethnic-migratory condition thus becomes a factor for social inclusion or exclusion. Inclusion, because it is what determines the way you are inserted into the socio-economic structure. Minorities are not excluded from the system; they are not relegated or segregated to marginalized ethnic ghettos of the economy and of society. But it is a matter of differentiated insertion, unequal in terms of the position of each individual in the ethnic-racial matrix of society (Canales, 2007).

Such is the case of the Latinos in the United States. Their ethnic-migratory status is so much a factor of exclusion from society, that Latinos are segregated into jobs with low wages, low productivity, precarious conditions of employment, flexible hours and short contracts, etc. But these jobs are most necessary for sustaining the social reproduction of the middle and upper classes of society, that is, for keeping up the social reproduction of the dominant culturally hegemonic groups, who in the present case are the population with white origins. Latinos are excluded from the benefits of contemporary ultra-modernity, but are included as unqualified labor. As individual persons and as workers, they are excluded from globalization, relegated to local impoverished spaces of life and reproduction, but they are transnational, i.e., transnational based on the locality and the poverty, never on globalization. And yet their work, the fruit of their economic activity, is an expression of globalization. It might materialize in the various items of merchandise that have become icons of globalization (in the production of smart TVs, smartphones, digital notebooks, cars, or in the cleaning and maintenance of shopping malls, amongst other things), or else their work materializes in the private spaces of social reproduction by the others, the whites of the middle and upper classes, who are central actors in the globalization of consumption and social life, subjects of the first order of postmodernity in liquid societies.

This is racism at its maximum expression, with no demographic measurements to conceal it. Classes are seen to be differentiated by color, gender, ethnic and migratory origins. Therefore, the reproduction of society as a whole and of its class structure is racialized, taking color and form according to the ethnic-racial matrix.

However, with the demographic changes already being felt in advanced societies, this form of contemporary racism marks an explosive situation. It is not possible to keep the privileged positions of some and the segregation of others, the hegemonic positions of some and discrimination against others, when the demographic equilibrium between one group and the other is broken, when the demographic relation between a majority of one kind and minorities of another has split open and been inverted, when the first are no longer necessarily more numerous than the rest, when one group dominating the demographic composition of the population pyramid has as large a share as another. In other words, it is not possible to maintain a situation of power when the demographic balances no longer correspond to the political balances, when the asymmetries of power are moving in the opposite direction to the asymmetries of demographics.

## 4 Final Reflections: Latinos and the New American Dilemma

In the context of the ethnic and demographic replacement that we have described in this work, one wonders how long the current racialization of social inequality can go on? What will happen when the new demographic balances that are on their way are not reflected in new socio-economical balances? Will it be possible to keep Latinos down at the lowest levels of the social and occupational structure, even when they come to comprise over 30% of the population, and the whites account for only 45%?

The case of California demonstrates that a change in the ethnic composition of the population is not necessarily accompanied by a similar change in the ethnic composition of the socio-economical structure. Quite the contrary, as figures speak volumes and illustrate the opposite thesis, that demographic replacement is more likely to reproduce and accentuate racial inequality, and consolidate the present system of ethno-stratification of society.

In this sense the questions mentioned refer us to a highly unstable social and political scenario exposed to the possibility of social and ethnic eruptions, which, unlike the movements in the sixties focusing on the struggle for civil rights would this time mean a confrontation between two ethnic groups in a demographic situation where neither of them can claim a position of demographic predominance.

The new demographic balances that are approaching do not seem to be compatible with the maintenance and reproduction of racialized forms of social inequality and the class structure. For as long as these forms of social and ethnic segregation affected only a small demographic minority, their contradictions could be taken up and absorbed by the social system. However, when this racial segregation affects a significant proportion of the population while simultaneously maintaining and benefiting an equally small demographic minority, the situation becomes potentially explosive.

In the present context it is possible to foresee that the mechanisms of social and cultural cohesion that prevailed in the past, will lose their efficiency and effectiveness for controlling the new tensions and contradictions that racial segregation implies in a democratic society. It is clearly obvious that when demographic balances begin to change, as currently happening, this racializing of social inequality will upset the current political balances between the different ethnic and demographic groups that make up the population of the United States. This would mean an unstable situation requiring either an authoritarian imposition of the current state of affairs and present situation, or else its transformation through more egalitarian and democratic forms after a profound renegotiation and reformulation of the ethnic-social pact on which the American Union is built. In which case racism, as a de facto social power, will have to cede to other forms of relations and structuring of the social classes and of the distribution of power and the privileges and benefits of development.

To paraphrase Gunnar Myrdal (1944), we can say this is definitely the *New American Dilemma* which is already making its appearance and assuming various shapes, and will define the political and social evolution of the United States in the present and the near future, that is, it will form the base of one of the columns supporting class struggle in the United States in the course of the 21st century (Camarillo and Bonilla, 2001).

For white supremacists, the question presents itself in terms of how to deal with this process of ethnic replacement that is bearing down upon them, that they have virtually no tools or resources for turning back. How are they to keep their privileged position in the current racialized structure of social inequality, and the benefits they derive from the current form of ethno stratification of society, in the context of demographic changes so profound that they will lead to an ethnic replacement of the white population by current minorities. Not a small question, as they are seeing a weakening of both the material and the symbolic bases of their supremacist discourse, and of the benefits and privileges they enjoy as the result of their hegemonic position in society.

At this juncture, the option of controlling and reversing the process of ethnic replacement has become unlikely, for at least three fundamental reasons.

– In the first place, the economic and political risks are too great. To reduce the growth of Latinos by restricting immigration, instituting massive deportations or even just failing to grant citizenship to the children of immigrants, would be a direct attack on the necessary provision of labor and would consequently threaten the development of the productive forces of capital. Economic growth would be directly affected, hence the creation of the surpluses necessary for maintaining the current standards of living of the white population, and to still be the top economic power in the world and not lose the country's political and military hegemony in the world.
– Secondly, the social risks are also too great. The social reproduction of the middle and upper classes, who are mostly made up of white populations, their patterns of consumption, and their styles of life would be directly affected. Processes of individuation, female emancipation, and in general all the advances made in a liquid postmodern society are supported in the main by the work done by migrants in various areas of daily life. The care industry, maids and domestic service, the cleaning and maintenance industry,

personal services in restaurants, private transport (taxis) and many other jobs all depend to a large extent on migrant labor. Migrants are a new class of poor who sustain the postmodern lifestyles and the globalized patterns of consumption of the new middle and upper classes.
- Thirdly there is something that the white supremacists tend to ignore. One of the central components of ethnic replacement is the demographic decline that the white population is already experiencing, a process that started with their lower birth rate and progressive ageing, and is expected to last for at least several decades more as the new century matures. In other words, the main enemy of the white supremacists is, paradoxically, not only and exclusively the demographic dynamics of the "others", that is, of the Latinos, but that of their own fellows, that of the white population. They have their enemy at home with them, and the tendency that is presented to them demographically as their new manifest destiny is quite unavoidable.

The question for white supremacists is therefore how to take up the defense of their interests as a class and as a political faction, of their privileged positions and the benefits awarded to them by this system of racializing social inequality, that they see threatened by the imminent approach of demographic changes. This is the background that can help us to understand how a character like Trump can burst onto the stage and why the white supremacists in the United States who support him have reappeared on the scene, but it also explains the eruption of extreme right wing groups and political forces in Europe under the same banners of xenophobia, discrimination and racism.

From our perspective, what we are seeing in the United States and Europe is the white supremacists taking up positions to deal with a social and political dispute that has started, and cannot be stopped by walls. Trump, Le Pen, Wilders and others like them are the public figures that the white supremacists are trying to rally around to gather forces for the approaching class struggle. They are not trying to stop the demographic changes from happening (something that has been quite impossible for several decades) but to reconfigure the balance of forces and to reposition themselves in the new political scene that is being prepared so they will be able to keep the privileged positions they currently hold in the racialized structure of social inequality and the class structure of their countries.

Their whole strategy, which includes a vociferous, extremist and arrogant tirade against immigration, in one case against Latinos and in the other against Moslems, against the equality and the rights of ethnic, religious, gender and class minorities, is an attempt to weaken the "other", the Latino, the immigrant, the black, the Muslim, women, and so many others. A last, desperate attempt to hold them in the same conditions of social and political vulnerability, in isolation and in subordinate positions, with the conditions for their survival and permanence in Europe or the United States continually at risk. However, the bad news for them is that their societies are not as they were in the past and never will be.

In the case of the United States, for example, we are witnessing a very special conjuncture in its three hundred year history. As a Nation, as a Community and as a Population, the United States is facing a unique moment in modern times: the birth of a new ethno-demographic matrix that will transform its structure and organization as a society. In this new matrix, the Latinos have a transcendental part to play. They are the fourth root to be integrated into American Culture. They are a fourth vector of this matrix of identity, and as such they are helping to forge a new identity for the American Union.

In this context the tensions, contradictions, conflicts and political struggles that are arising again today are no more than an expression of the historical transition of a social system with white majorities to a society of demographic minorities, where demographic change comes as much from the decline of some (whites) as from the rise of others (ethnic minorities and Latinos).

These are the bases of *The New American Dilemma* that will permeate and characterize the class struggle of the present 21st century in the United States. In this context, we can see how racism has come back to the center of social conflict and as in the 1960s, those who seek to keep their privileges will be opposed to those seeking to break with the racialization of social inequality.

However, as distinct from what happened in the sixties, the present struggle against racism and racists will take place in the framework of a breaking up of the demographic balances that sustained the predominance of the white majority and the subordination of the ethnic minorities. This struggle between classes will occur in a country of demographic minorities, no small consideration given that it will redefine the current correlation of forces and the accumulation of social and political resources by each of the actors in the fight, weakening the power of the white majority and repositioning the different ethnic minorities politically.

At any rate, the future is not yet written, although there are possibilities on the horizon which will be realized in one way or another, depending on the way in which each actor faces this historical juncture on the resources and support each is able to obtain, on their strategies, and above all, on the force that is built up to make them political and social subjects facing this class and ethnic struggle which has already started, and will continue during the next decades of the century.

# References

Acosta, Pablo; Cesar Calderón; Pablo Fajnzylber and Humberto López. 2006. "Remittances and Development in Latin America". *The World Economy*, 29(7), 957–987.
ACS. 2015. *American Community Survey, 2015*. U.S. Department of Commerce, US Census Bureau.
Adams H., Richard Jr., & Page, J. 2005. "Do international migration and remittances reduce poverty in developing countries?" *World Development*, 33(10), 1645–1669.
Adelman, Irma and J. Edward Taylor. 1990. "Is Structural Adjustment with a Human Face Possible? The Case of Mexico". *Journal of Development Studies* 26 (3):387–407.
Alarcón, Rafael. 1992. "*Norteñización*: Self-Perpetuating Migration from a Mexican Town". In J. Bustamante, C. Reynolds and R. Hinojosa (eds.) *US-Mexico Relations. Labor Market Interdependence*. Stanford University Press. Stanford, California. United States.
Al-Ali, Nadje, Black, Richard and Koser, Khalid. 2001. "The limits of transnationalism: Bosnian and Eritrean refugees in Europe as emerging transnational communities". *Ethnic and Racial Studies* 24 (4): 578–600.
Alleyne, Dillon; Claremont D. Kirton and Mark Figueroa. 2008. "Macroeconomic Determinants of Migrant Remittances to Caribbean Countries: Panel Unit Roots and Co-integration". *Journal of Economic Literature*, Classifications: D,E60,C23. 137–153.
Amin, Ash. 2000. *Post- Fordism, a reader*. Blacwell Publisher Ltd- Oxford, UK.
Amin, Samir. 1996. *Les défis de la mondialisation*. Paris, France, L'Harmattan.
Anderson, G.F. and P.S. Hussey. 2000. *Population aging: a comparison among industrialized countries*. Health Affairs, 19, no.3 (2000):191–203. DOI: 10.1377/hlthaff.19.3.191
Appadurai, Arjun. 1990. "Disjuncture and Difference in the Global Cultural Economy". *Theory, Culture and Society*. Vol. 7. pp. 295–310.
Ariès, Philippe. 1980. Two successive motivations for the declining birth rate in the West. *Population and Development Review*. 6(4), pp. 645–650.
Banco Mundial, 2006. *Global Economic Prospects 2006. Economic Implications of Remittances and Migration*. Washington DC, The World Bank.
Banco Mundial. 2004. *Poverty in Mexico: An Assessment of Conditions, Trends, and Government Strategy*. The World Bank.
BANXICO, 2017. *Sistema de información económica. Balanza de pagos*. México, Banco de México. http://www.banxico.org.mx/estadisticas/index.html.
Basch, Linda; Glick Shiller, Nina; Szanton Blanc, Cristina. 1994. *Nations unbound. Transnational projects, postcolonial predicaments and deterritorialized nation-states*. Pensilvania: Gordon and Breach Science Publishers, 1994.
Bauman, Zygmunt. 2011. *Collateral Damage. Social Inequalities in a Global Age*. Polity Press, Cambridge, UK.
Bauman, Zygmunt, 2000. *Liquid Modernity*. Polity Press, Cambridge, UK.

Bauman, Zygmunt. 1998. "On Glocalization: or Globalization for Some, Localization for Some Others". *Thesis Eleven*, Number 54. SAGE Publications.
Beck, Ulrich. 2000a. *What is Globalization?*, Oxford Polity Press, Cambridge, UK.
Beck, Ulrich. 2000b. *The Brave New World of Work*. Oxford, Polity Press. UK.
Beck, Ulrich and Elisabeth Beck-Gernshmein, 2002. *Individualization*. London, SAGE Publications.
Becker, Gary. 1971. *The Economics of Discrimination*. Chicago: University of Chicago Press.
Becker, Gary S. 1960. "An economic analysis of fertility". In Ansley Coale, *Demographic and economic change in developed countries*, Princeton, Columbia University Press.
Becker, Gary S. 1981. *A treatise on the family*, Cambridge and London, Harvard University Press.
Becker, Gary. S. 1966. *Human Capital. A Theorical and Empirical Analysis, with Special Reference to Education*. United States, Columbia University Press.
Bell, Daniel. 1973. *The Coming of Post-Industrial Society. A Venture in Social Forecasting*. New York, Basic Books.
Benítez, Raúl. 1994. "Visión latinoamericana de la Transición Demográfica. Dinámica de la población y práctica política". In *La Transición Demográfica en América Latina y El Caribe*. Acts of IV Latin American Population Conference. Vol. 1, First Part, Mexico. ABEP, CELADE, IUSSP, PROLAP, SOMEDE.
Binford, Leigh. 2003. "Migrant Remittances and (Under) Development in Mexico". *Critique of Anthropology*, September, 23: 305–336.
Böhm-Bawerk, Eugen von. 1959 (1890). *Capital and Interest: A Critical History of Economic Theory*. South Holland, Ill. The Libertarian Press.
Bongaarts, J. (2001). "Fertility and reproductive preferences in post-transitional societies". Pp. 260–282 in: R.A. Bulatao and J.B. Casterline (eds), *Global Fertility Transition, Supplement to Population and Development Review*, Vol. 27, New York, Population Council.
Bonilla-Silva, Eduardo. 2002. "We are all Americans!: The Latin Americanization of Racial Stratification in the USA", *Race and Society, vol. 5*, p. 3–16.
Borjas, George J. 2001. *Heaven's Door: Immigration Policy and the American Economy*. Princeton, Princeton University Press. United States.
Borjas, George. 1990. *Friends or Strangers. The Impacts of Immigrants on the U.S. Economy*. New York, Basic Books.
Borja, Jordi & Manuel Castells. 1997. *Local y global. La gestión de las ciudades en la era de la información*. Madrid: Taurus.
Bourdieu, Pierre, 2011. *Las estrategias de la reproducción social*. Buenos Aires, Siglo XXI Editores.
Bourdieu, Pierre. 2005. *The social structures of the economy*. Cambridge, UK; Malden, MA. Polity.
Bourdieu, Pierre. 1980. *Le sens Practique*. Paris, Francia. Les Éditions de Minuit.

Bourdieu, Pierre. 1976. "Marriage strategies as strategies of social reproduction". In: Forster, R. and Ranum, O. (eds.). *Family and society. Selections from the Annales, Économies, Sociétés, Civilisations*. Baltimore: The Johns Hopkins University Press.

Bourdeiu, Pierre and Jean Claude Passeron. 1977. *Reproduction in Education, Society and Culture*. Sage Publications London – Thousand Oaks, CA – New Delhi.

Brenes Camacho, Gilbert, 2009. "The pace of convergence of population aging in Latin America: opportunities and challenges". In *Demographic transformations and inequalities in Latin America*. Latin American Population Association. Rio de Janeiro, Brazil. http://www.alapop.org/alap/SerieInvestigaciones/InvestigacionesSI1aSi9/DemogTransformations_ParteI-4.pdf.

Burges, Katrina, 2006. "El impacto del 3x1 en la gobernanza local". In R. Fernández de Castro, R. García Zamora & A. Vila Freyer (coords.), *El programa 3x1 para migrantes. ¿Primera política transnacional en México?*, México, Miguel Ángel Porrúa Editores, Universidad Autónoma de Zacatecas and Instituto Tecnológico Autónomo de México, pages 99–118.

Bustamante, Jorge A., 2002 "Immigrant's Vulnerability as Subjets of Human Rights". *International Migration Review*. Volume 36, Number 2, 333–354.

Bustamante, Jorge. 1973. *Espaldas mojadas: materia prima para la expansión del capitalismo*. México, El Colegio de México. Cuadernos del CES.

Cabré, Anna, 1999. *El sistema català de reproducció*. Proa, Barcelona.

Cagan, Phillip (1956). "The Monetary Dynamics of Hyperinflation". In Friedman, Milton (ed.). *Studies in the Quantity Theory of Money*. Chicago: University of Chicago Press.

Caicedo, Maritza. 2010. *Migración, trabajo y desigualdad. Los inmigrantes latinoamericanos y caribeños en Estados Unidos*. México. El Colegio de México, Centro de Estudios Demográficos, Urbanos y Ambientales.

Cain, Glen G. 1986. "The Economic Analysis of Labor Market Discrimination: a Survey". *Handbook of Labor Economics*, Volume L Edited by O. Ashenfelter and R. Layard. Elsevier Science Publishers B v.

Camarillo, Albert M. and Frank Bonilla. 2001. "Hispanics in a Multicultural Society. A New American Dilemma?" In Neil Smelser, William Julius Wilson, and Faith Mitchell, editors. *America becoming. Racial trends and their consequences*. US National Academy of Sciences. National Academy Press.

Canales, Alejandro I. 2017. "Migración y trabajo en Estados Unidos. Polarización ocupacional y racialización de la desigualdad social en la postcrisis". *REMHU, Revista Interdisciplinar da Mobilidade Humana, v. 25, n. 49*, abril 2017, p. 13–34, http://www.scielo.br/pdf/remhu/v25n49/1980-8585-REMHU-25-49-013.pdf.

Canales, Alejandro I. 2015. "El papel de la migración en el sistema global de reproducción demográfica". *Notas de Población*, Vol. XLII, No. 100. CELADE, Population Division of ECLAC. Pages. 91–123. Santiago, Chile. http://repositorio.cepal.org/bitstream/handle/11362/38514/S1500199_es.pdf?sequence=1.

Canales, Alejandro I. 2015b. "El debate Migración y Desarrollo. Evidencias y aportes desde América Latina". *Latin American Research Review*. Vol. 50, no. 1. Pages. 29–53. Latin American Studies Association, USA. https://lasa.international.pitt.edu/LARR/prot/fulltext/vol50no1/50-1_29-53_canales.pdf.

Canales, Alejandro I. 2014. "La centralidad de la migración en las sociedades avanzadas. Intersecciones entre demografía, economía y sociedad". *Revista Trabajo*, Vol. 8, No. 11. Page. 61–87. Metropolitan Autonomous University, México. http://www.izt.uam.mx/sotraem/Documentos/Revistadetrabajo11final.pdf.

Canales, Alejandro I. 2013. "Migración y desarrollo en las sociedades avanzadas. Una mirada desde América Latina". *POLIS, Revista Latinoamericana*. Num. 35. Santiago, Chile.

Canales, Alejandro I. 2011. "Las profundas contribuciones de la migración latinoamericana a los Estados Unidos". In Jorge Martínez Pizarro (Editor) *Migración internacional en América Latina y el Caribe. Nuevas tendencias, nuevos enfoques*. ECLAC, Santiago, Chile. Pages 257–331, LC/R.2170

Canales, Alejandro I. 2008. *Vivir del norte. Remesas, desarrollo y pobreza en México*. National Population Council (CONAPO) México.

Canales, Alejandro I. 2007. "*Inclusion and Segregation: The Incorporation of Latin American Immigrants into the U.S. Labor Market*". Latin American Perspectives. Issue 152, Volume 34 Number 1, January. Pages 73–82.

Canales, Alejandro I. 2003. "Demografía de la desigualdad. El discurso de la población en la era de la globalización". In Alejandro I. Canales and Susana Lerner Sigal (Coords.) *Desafíos teórico-metodológicos en los estudios de población en el inicio del milenio*. México, El Colegio de México, Universidad de Guadalajara and SOMEDE, pages 42–84.

Canales, Alejandro I. 2001. "La población en la era de la información. De la transición demográfica al proceso de envejecimiento". *Estudios Demográficos y Urbanos*. Vol. 16, No. 3. México, El Colegio de México. Pages. 485–518.

Canales, Alejandro I., and Meza, Sofía. 2016. "Fin del colapso y nuevo escenario migratorio México-Estados Unidos". *Migración y Desarrollo No. 27, Segundo Semestre 2016*. International Network on Migration and Development. Pages 65–107. http://www.estudiosdeldesarrollo.mx/revista/rev27/3.pdf.

Canales, Alejandro I., and Montiel Armas, Israel. 2010. "Migration, transnationalism and post-modernity. Keys to understand immigration in the United States". In Richard Dello Buono and David Fasenfest (Eds.) *Social Change, Resistance and Social Practices*. Critical Sociology, Koninklijke Brill NV, Leiden, The Netherlands.

Cassarino, Jean-Pierre "Theorising Return Migration.The Conceptual Approach to Return Migrants Revisited". *International Journal on Multicultural Societies* (IJMS), Vol. 6, No. 2, 2004: 253–279. www.unesco.org/shs/ijms/vol6/issue2/art4.

Castells, Manuel. 1996. *The rise of the network society. The Information Age: Economy, Society, and Culture Volume I*. Cambridge, Mass., Blackwell Publishers.

Castillo Fernández, Dídimo. 2016. "La deslocalización del trabajo y la migración hacia Estados Unidos. La paradoja de la 'migración de los puestos'". In Castillo, Dídimo; Baca, Norma; Todaro, Rosalba (Coords.) *Trabajo y desigualdades en el mercado laboral*. CLACSO, CEM, UAEM, México, 2016, p. 57–81. http://biblioteca.clacso.edu.ar/clacso/se/20160225024249/TrabajoGlobal.pdf.

Castles, Stephen and Mark J. Miller. 1993. *The Age of migration. International Population Movements in the Modern World*. Nueva York, Guilford Press.

Castro, Antonio and Carlos F. Lessa, 1991. (1969). *Introducción a la economía: un enfoque estructuralista*. México, Siglo XXI Editores. 50th. Edition.

Catarino, Christine and Laura Oso, 2000. "La inmigración femenina en Madrid y Lisboa: hacia una etnización del servicio doméstico y de las empresas de limpieza". *PAPERS, Revista de Sociología*, Num. 60. Pages 183–207. Universidad Autónoma de Barcelona.

Cavalcanti, Leonardo and Parella, Sonia. 2013. "Entre las políticas de retorno y las prácticas transnacionales de los migrantes brasileños: re-pensando el retorno desde una perspectiva transnacional". *REMHU – Rev. Interdiscipl. Mobil. Hum. Brasília*, Ano XXI, n. 41, p. 9–20, jul./dez.

Chami, Ralph, Connel Fullenkamp and Samir Jahjah. 2003. *Are Immigrant Remittances Flows a Source of Capital for Development?* International Monetary Fund. Working Paper WP/03/189. Washington D. C.

Chang, Ha-Joon. 2011. "Institutions and economic development. Theory, policy and history". *Journal of Institutional Economics*, Vol. 7, No. 4. Pages 1 of 26. Cambridge University.

Chávez, Leo. 1988. "Settlers and Sojourners: The Case of Mexicans in the United States". *Human Organization*, Vol. 47, No. 2, pp. 95–198.

Chávez, Leo. 1994. "The power of the imagined community: a logistic analysis of settlement by undocumented Mexicans and Central Americans", *American Anthropologist*, vol. 96, No 1, Pages 52–73.

Chayanov, Alexander. 1986 (1925). *The Theory of Peasant Economy*. Manchester, Manchester University Press.

Chernilo, Daniel. 2011. *La pretensión universalista de la teoría social*. Chile, LOM Editores and Universidad de Chile.

Clark, John Bates, 1899. *The distribution of Wealth. A theory of wages, interest and profits*. New York and London, The Macmillan Company.

Coale, Ansley. 1973. "The Demographic Transition". In IUSSP, *International Population Conference*, Vol. I, Lieja, pp. 53–73.

Coleman, David. 2009. "Divergent patterns in the ethnic transformation of societies", *Population and Development Review*, vol. 35, N° 3.

Coleman, David. 2006. "Immigration and ethnic change in low-fertility countries: A third demographic transition", *Population and Development Review*, vol. 32, N° 3.

Coleman, Roger. 1993. "A demographic overview of the ageing of First World populations". *Applied Ergonomics* 24 (1), 5–8.
CONAPO, 2015. *Yearbook of migration and remittances, Mexico 2016*. México, National Population Council and BBVA Bancomer Foundation. https://www.bbvaresearch.com/wp-content/uploads/2016/06/1606_Mexico_AnuarioMigracion_2016.pdf.
Cooke, M. (2003), "Population and Labour Force Ageing in Six Countries", in *Workforce Aging in the New Economy*, Working Paper (4).
Cortés, Fernando. 1980. "Conciencia teórica y metodológica: a propósito de la cuestión agraria". In I. Restrepo (coord.) *Conflicto entre Campo y Ciudad en América Latina*. Centro de Ecodesarrollo and Ed. Nueva Imagen. México, D.F. Pages. 37–51.
Cortina, Jerónimo, Rodolfo de la Garza and Enrique Ochoa-Reza, 2004. "Remesas: límites al optimismo". *Foreign Affairs en Español*, Vol. 5, Num. 3: 27–36.
CPS. 2016. *Current Population Survey 2016*. U.S. Department of Commerce, U.S. Census Bureau.
CPS. 2015. *Current Population Survey 2015*. U.S. Department of Commerce, U.S. Census Bureau.
Cypher, James. 2009. "El auge actual de los *commodities* y el proceso de primarización en América Latina ¿retorno al siglo XX?". *Foro Internacional*, Vol. 49, Num. 1, Pages 119–162.
Cypher, James and Raúl Delgado Wise. 2010. *Mexico's Economic Dilemma: The Developmental Failure of Neoliberalism*. United States of America, Rowman & Littlefield Publisher Inc.
Dahinden, Janine. 2017. "Transnationalism reloaded: the historical trajectory of a concept". *Ethnic and Racial Studies* 40(9):1474–1485.
Davis, Kinsley. 1945. "The world demographic transition", *Annals of the American Academy of Political and Social Science*, 273 (Jan.), 1–11.
De Haas, Hein. 2008. "Migration and development. A theoretical perspective". *Workings Papers*, No. 9. International Migration Institute, University of Oxford.
De Haas, Hein. 2007. *Remittances, Migration and Social Development. A Conceptual Review of the Literature*. United Nations, Research Institute for Social Development. Social Policy and Development Programme Paper Number 34.
De Haas, Hein. 2005. "International Migration, Remittances and Development: myths and facts". *Third World Quaterly*. Vol. 26, No. 8, pp. 1269–1284.
De la Garza, Enrique. 1998. "El concepto de economía y su transformación". In E. de la Garza (coord.), *Ciencia económica. Transformación de conceptos*. México, Siglo XXI Editores and UNAM, Centro de Investigaciones Interdisciplinarias en Ciencias y Humanidades.
De la Garza, Enrique. 1998b. "Economía y totalidad". In E. de la Garza (coordinador), *Ciencia económica. Transformación de conceptos*. México, Siglo XXI Editores and UNAM, Centro de Investigaciones Interdisciplinarias en Ciencias y Humanidades.

Delauney, Daniel and Françoise Lestage. 1998. "Hogares y fratrías mexicanas en Estados Unidos: varias historias de vida, una historia de familia". *Estudios Demográficos y Urbanos*, Vol. 13, Num. 3 El Colegio de México.

Delgado, R., H. Márquez Covarrubias and R. Puentes. (2010). *Reframing the debate on migration, development and human rights: Fundamental elements*. People's Global Action on Migration, Development and Human Rights. IV Global Forum on Migration and Development. November 2010.

De Soto, Hernando, 2002. *The Other Path: The Economic Answer to Terrorism*. Basic Books, New York, NY.

De Souza Martins, José. 1998. "O problema das migrações no limiar do terceiro milênio". In *O fenômeno migratório no limiar do terceiro milenio. (Desafios Pastorais)*. Editora Vozes. Brasil.

Djajić, Slobodan. 1998. "Emigration and welfare in an economy with foreign capital". *Journal of Development Economics*, 56: 433–445.

Domingo i Valls, Andreu. 2006. "Tras la retórica de la hispanidad: la migración latinoamericana en España. Entre la complementariedad y la exclusión". In Alejandro I. Canales (Editor) *Panorama actual de las migraciones en América Latina*. University of Guadalajara and Latin American Population Association. México.

Durand, Jorge. 1994. *Más allá de la línea: patrones migratorios entre México y Estados Unidos*. Federal District, México. National Council for Culture and Arts.

Durand, Jorge and Douglas Massey, 2003. *Clandestinos. Migración México-Estados Unidos en los albores del siglo XXI*. M. A. Porrúa and Universidad Autónoma de Zacatecas, México.

Durand, Jorge, Emilio A. Parrado and Douglas S. Massey. 1996. "Migradollars and Development: A Reconsideration of the Mexican Case". *International Migration Review* 30 (2):423–444.

ECLAC, 2010. *Time for equality: closing gaps, opening trails. Thirty-third session of ECLAC*. Santiago, Chile. United Nations, Economic Commission for Latin America and the Caribbean. LC/G.2432(SES.33/3)

ECLAC, 2006. *International Migration, Human Rights and Development in Latin America and the Caribbean. Summary and Conclusions*. Montevideo, Uruguay. Thirty First Session of Economic Commission for Latin America and the Caribbean, 20–24 March.

ECLAC, 2005. *Social Panorama of Latin America, 2005*. Santiago, Chile, United Nations, Economic Commission for Latin America and the Caribbean. LC/G.2288-P.

ECLAC, 2000. *Uso productivo de las remesas familiares y comunitarias en Centroamérica*. United Nations, Economic Commission for Latin America and the Caribbean, México. (LC/MEX/L.420),

Ehrenteich, Barbara and Hochschild, Arlie Russel. 2004. *Global Woman. Nannies, Maids and Sex Workers in the New Economy*. New York, Henry Holt and Company.

ENIGH, 2014. *Encuesta Nacional de Ingresos y Gastos de los Hogares, 2014*. México, Instituto Nacional de Estadística y Geografía.

Escrivá, Ángeles M. 2000. "¿Empleadas de por vida? Peruanas en el servicio doméstico en Barcelona". *PAPERS, Revista de Sociología*, Num. 60. Pages 327–342. Universidad Autónoma de Barcelona.

Fernández, Juan Carlos. 2006. "Experiencia de campo: programas de CIDEAL en Ecuador". In *Crisis, migración y remesas en ecuador. ¿Una oportunidad para el codesarrollo?*. CIDEAL, Fundación Asistencia Técnica para el Desarrollo, Madrid, Spain, pages 153–164.

FMI. 2005. *World Economic Outlook, April 2005*. International Monetary Fund. Washington, DC, United Sates.

FOMIN. 2004. *Remittances to Latin America and the Caribbean: Goals and Recommendations*. Washington D.C. Multilateral Investment Fund, Inter-American Development Bank.

Fritz, Catarina; Stone, John. 2009. "A Post-Racial America: Myth or Reality?", *Ethnic and Racial Studies*, 32:6, p. 1083–1088, DOI: 10.1080/01419870902975068.

García Canclini, Néstor. 2014. *The Imagined Globalization*. Durham, Duke University Press.

Germani, Gino. 1981. *The Sociology of Modernization. Studies on its Historical and Theoretical Aspects with Special Regard to the Latin American Case*. New Brunswick, N.J., Transaction Books

Ghosh, Bimal. 1992. "Migration-Development linkages. Some specific issues and practical policy measures". *International Migration*, Vol. 30, Num. 3–4, pp. 423–456. International Organization for Migration, Geneva.

Gibson, Campbell & Young, Kay. 2002. *Historical Census Statistics on Population Totals by Race, 1790 To 1990, and by Hispanic Origin, 1970 to 1990, for The United States, Regions, Divisions, and States*. US Census Bureau, Population Division, Working Paper No. 56. Washington, DC.

Giddens, Anthony. 1986. *The Constitution of Society. Outline of the Theory of Structuration*. Berkeley, CA, University of California Press.

Glick Schiller, Nina; Linda Basch and Cristina Szanton-Blanc. 1992. "Transnationalism: a New Analytical Framework for Understanding Migration". In *Towards a Transnational Perspective on Migration*. N. Glick Schiller; L. Basch and C. Szanton-Blanc, eds. p. 1–24. New York Academy of Sciences, N.Y.

Glick Schiller, N. and P. Levitt. 2006. *Haven't We Heard this Somewhere Before? A Substantive Review of Transnational Migration Studies by Way of a Reply to Waldinger and Fitzgerald*, Princeton, New Jersey, Center for Migration & Development, Princeton University (Working Paper 0601).

Goic, Ramón Llopis. 2007. "El "nacionalismo metodológico" como obstáculo en la investigación sociológica sobre migraciones internacionales". *Empiria. Revista de Metodología de Ciencias Sociales*, Num. 13, Spain.

Goldring, Luin. 1997."Difuminando fronteras: construcción la comunidad transnacional en el proceso migratorio México-Estados Unidos". In Saúl Macías Gamboa and Fernando Herrera Lima (Coordinadores) *Migración laboral internacional.: Transnacionalidad del espacio social*. Benemérita Universidad Autónoma de Puebla, Mexico.

Gregson, Nicky and Michelle Lowe. 1994. *Servicing the Middle Classes. Class, Gender and Waged Domestic Labor in Contemporary Britain*. London, Routledge.

Gutiérrez, Alicia B. 2011. "Clases, espacio social y estrategias. Una introducción al análisis de la reproducción social en Bourdieu". In Pierre Bourdieu *Las estrategias de la reproducción social*. Buenos Aires, Siglo XXI Editores, Pages. 9–27.

Guzmán, José Miguel. 2002. "Envejecimiento y desarrollo en América Latina y el Caribe". *Serie Población y Desarrollo*, 28. Santiago, Chile. CELADE/Population división of ECLAC.

Hayes-Bautista, David. 2017. *La Nueva California: Latinos from pioneers to post-millennials*. Oakland, California: University of California Press.

Herrera C., Roberto. 2006. *La perspectiva teórica en el estudio de las migraciones*. México, Siglo XXI Editores.

Herrera Ponce, María Soledad. 2007. *Individualización social y cambios demográficos:¿hacia una segunda transición demográfica?* Madrid, Spain. Sociological Research Center, CIS, Monographs 232.

Herrera, Gioconda. 2005. "Mujeres ecuatorianas en las cadenas globales del cuidado". In G. Herrera, M.C. Carrillo and A. Torres (Editors.) *La migración ecuatoriana. Transnacionalismo, redes e identidades*. Equator, FLACSO, Latin American Social Sciences Institute.

Heuser, Robert L. 1976. *Fertility tables for birth cohorts by color. United States, 1917–73*. National Center for Health Statistics (U.S.). Division of Vital Statistics. 1976.

Hirst, Paul, &, Zeitlin, Jonathan. (1991). Flexible specialization versus post-Fordism: theory, evidence and policy implications. *Economy and Society*, 20(1), 5–9.

Hobbs, Frank and Nicole Stoops. 2002. *Demographic Trends in the 20th Century*. Census 2000 Special Reports, #4. U.S. Department of Commerce. Economics and Statistics Administration, U.S. Census Bureau.

Hobsbawm, Eric. 2000. *Entrevista sobre el siglo XXI*. Barcelona, Editorial Crítica.

Hodgson, Geoffrey M. 1998. "The Approach of Institutional Economics". *Journal of Economic Literature*. Vol. XXXVI (March), pp. 166–192.

Hondagneu-Sotelo, Pierrete. 2007. *Doméstica: Immigrant Workers Cleaning and caring in the Shadows of Affluence*. Los Angeles, CA: University of California Press.

Hondagneu-Sotelo, Pierrete. 1994. *Gender Transitions. Mexican Experiences of Immigration*. Los Angeles, CA: University of California Press.

Hondagneu-Sotelo, Pierrete, and E. Ávila. 1999. *"I'm Here, but I'm There*. Yhe Meaning of latina Transnational Motherhood". In Katie Willis and Brenda Yeoh (eds.) *Gender and Migration*. Cheltenham, UK and Northampton, MA: an Elgar Reference Collection.

Hugo, Graeme. 2005. "Asian Experience with Remittances". In Donald F. Terry and Steven R. Wilson (ed.), *Beyond Small Change: Making Migrant Remittances Count*. Washington, DC, Inter-American Development Bank.

Huntington, Samuel. 2004. *Who are we? The Challenges to America's National Identity*. New York: Simon and Schuster.

Ianni, Octavio. 1996. *Teorías de la Globalización*. México. Editorial Siglo XXI and National Autonomous University of Mexico.

Izquierdo E., Antonio. 2011. "Time of Loss: A False Awareness of the Integration of Immigrants". *Migraciones Internacionales*, Vol. 1 Num. 6, El Colegio de la Frontera Norte. México. Pages 145–184.

Jones, Richard C. 1998. "Remittances and Inequality: A Question of Migration Stage and Geographic Scale". *Economic Geography* 74 (1):8–25.

Jones, Richard C. 1995. *Ambivalent Journey: U.S. Migration and Economic Mobility in North-Central Mexico*. Tucson, United States. University of Arizona Press.

Kapur, Devesh. 2004. *Remittances: The New Development Mantra?*. United Nations, G-24 Discussion Paper Series.

Kearney, Michael and Carole Nagengast. 1989. *Anthropological Perspectives on Transnational Communities in Rural California*. California Institute for Rural Studies. United States.

Khagram, S. and P. Levitt. 2007. *The Transnational Studies Reader*, New York/London: Routledge Press.

Kirk, Dudley. 1996. "Demography Transition Theory". *Population Studies*, num. 50, pages 361–387.

Koch, M. 2017. *Roads to post-Fordism: labour markets and social structures in Europe*. Routledge.

Krugman, Paul and Robin Wells. 2006. *Introducción a la Economía. Microeconomía*, Barcelona, Editorial Reverté.

Kumar, Kishan. 1995. *From Post-Industrial to Post-Modern Society. New Theories of the Contemporary World*. MA: Blackwell Publishers Ltd.

Kwong, Peter. 1997. *Forbidden Workers. Illegal Chinese Immigrants and American Labor*. New York: The New Press.

Landry, Adolphe. 1934. *La révolution démographique*. Paris, France. Librairie Sirey.

Lash, Scott, and John Urry. 1994. *Economies of signs and space*. Sage, London, Thousand Oaks, CA.

Lee, Ronald. 2003. *Demographic Change, Welfare, and Intergenerational Transfers: A Global Overview*. CEDA Papers, Center for the Economics and Demography of Aging. University of California.

Leguina, Joaquín. 1981. *Fundamentos de demografía*. Madrid, Spain. Siglo XXI de España Editores.

Levitt, Peggy. 2011. "A Transnational Gaze". *Migraciones Internacionales*, Vol. 1 Num. 6. El Colegio de la Frontera Norte. México. Pages 9–44.

Levitt, P. and N. Glick Schiller. 2004. "Conceptualizing Simultaneity: A Transnational Social Field Perspective on Society", *International Migration Review*, vol. 38, num. 3, pp. 1002–1039.

Lewis, W.A. 1954. "Economic Development with Unlimited Supplies of Labour", *The Manchester School* Vol. 28, No. 2, pp. 139–191.

Lewis, Oscar. 1961. *The Children of Sánchez. Autobiography of a Mexican Family*. New York, Vintage.

Lindstrom, D.P. and E. Muñoz-Franco. 2005. "Migration and the Diffusion of Modern Contraceptive Knowledge and Use in Rural Guatemala", *Studies in Family Planning*, vol. 36, num. 4, pp. 277–288.

Lipietz, Alain. 1997. *El mundo del post-fordismo*. Jalisco, México. Cuadernos del CUSCH. Universidad de Guadalajara. On line: http://www.revistas.unal.edu.co/index.php/ede/article/viewFile/23729/24410.

Livi-Bacci, Massimo. 2012. *A Concise History of World Population*. 5th edition. Malden MA: Wiley-Blackwell.

Livi Bacci, Massimo. 1994. "Notas sobre la Transición Demográfica en Europa y América Latina". *La Transición Demográfica en América Latina y El Caribe*. Acts of IV Latin American Population Conference. Vol. 1, First Part, Mexico. ABEP, CELADE, IUSSP, PROLAP, SOMEDE.

Livi Bacci, Massimo. 1993. *Introducción a la Demografía*. Barcelona, Spain, Editorial Ariel.

Lomnitz, Larissa. 1977. *Networks and Marginality. Life in a Mexican Shantytown*. New York. Academic Press

Love, Bettina L. & Tosolt, Brandelyn. 2010. "Reality or Rhetoric? Barack Obama and Post-Racial America". *Race, Gender & Class, Vol. 17, No. 3/4*, pp. 19–37.

Lozano, Fernando. 2005. "De excluidos sociales a héroes sexenales. Discurso oficial y remesas en México". In Raúl Delgado Wise and Beatrice Knerr (coords.), *Contribuciones al análisis de la migración internacional y el desarrollo regional en México*. Universidad Autónoma de Zacatecas and Miguel Ángel Porrúa. Mexico.

Lucas, Robert Jr., 1972. "Expectations and the Neutrality of Money". *Journal of Economic Theory*, 4; 193–124.

Maldonado, Marta María. 2009. "'It is their nature to do menial labour': the racialization of 'Latino/a workers' by agricultural employers", *Ethnic and Racial Studies*, 32:6, p. 1017–1036, DOI: 10.1080/01419870902802254.

Martin, Joyce A.; Hamilton, Brady E.; Osterman, Michelle J.K.; Driscoll, Anne K. and T.J. Mathews. 2017. *Births: Final Data for 2015*. National Vital Statistics Report, Vol. 66, Number 1. US Department of Health and Human Services. Center for Disease Control and Prevention, National Vital Statistics System.

Martin, Philip. 2009. "International Labor Migration: The Numbers-Rights Dilemma", Paper presented in *Global Mobility Regimes Conference*, 27 and 28 de april, New York, http://globalmobility.info/pdfs/PMartin.pdf.

Martin, Philip. 2002. "Mexican Workers and U.S. Agriculture: The Revolving Door". *International Migration Review*; Vol. 36, No. 4. New York, Center for Migration Studies.

Martin, Philip and Manolo Abella. 2009. "Migration and development: the elusive link at the GFMD", *International Migration Review*, Vol. 43, N° 2, New York, Center for Migration Studies.

Martínez Pizarro, Jorge. 2008. *América Latina y el Caribe: migración internacional, derechos humanos y desarrollo*. Economic Commission for Latin America and the Caribbean. ECLAC Books Serie Num. 97. Santiago, Chile.

Martínez Pizarro, Jorge. 2003. "Panorama regional de las remesas durante los años noventa y sus impactos macrosociales en América Latina". *Migraciones Internacionales*, Num. 5, pages 40–76. Mexico, El Colegio de la Frontera Norte.

Martínez Pizarro, Jorge; Leandro Reboiras Finardi and Magdalena Soffia Contrucci. 2009. *Los derechos concedidos: crisis económica mundial y migración internacional*. Population and Development Series, Num. 89. CELADE, Population Division of ECLAC. Santiago, Chile.

Marx, Karl. 1971. *Critique of Political Economy (Grundrisse)*. London, Lawrence and Wishart.

Marx, Karl. 1967. *Capital. A critique of political economy*. New York, N. Y., International.

Massey, Douglas S. 2007. *Categorically Unequal: The American Stratification System*, New York: Russell Sage.

Massey, Douglas S. 1990. "Social Structure, Household Strategies, and Cumulative Causation of Migration". *Population Index*, Vol. 56, Num. 1, pages. 3–26.

Massey, Douglas S. and Emilio Parrado. 1998. "International Migration and Business Formation in Mexico". *Social Science Quarterly* 79 (1):1–20.

Massey, Douglas S. and Emilio Parrado. 1994. "Migradollars: The Remittances and Savings of Mexican Migrants to the United States". *Population Research and Policy Review* 13 (1):3–30.

Massey, Douglas S., Jorge Durand and Nolan J. Malone, 2002. *Beyond Smoke and Mirrors. Mexican Immigration in an Era of Economic Integration*. New York, Russell Sage Foundation.

Massey, Douglas; Arango, Joaquin; Hugo, Graeme; Kouaouci, Ali; Pellegrino, Adela and Taylor, J. Edward. 1993. "Theories of International Migration: A Review and Appraisal". *Population and Development Review*, Vol. 19, No. 3, Septiembre.

Mattelart, Armand. 1998. *La mundialización de la comunicación*. España, Paidós.

Maturana, Humberto. 2002. "Autopoiesis, Structural Coupling and Cognition: A history of these and other notions in the biology of cognition". *Cybernetics & Human Knowing*, Vol.9, Num.3–4, pages. 5–34.

Maturana, Humberto and Francisco Varela. 1987. *The Tree of Knowledge. The Biological Roots of Human Understanding*. Shambhala Publications. Boston, MA. United States.

Meek, Ronald L. 1956. *Studies in Labor Theory of Value*. Monthly Review Press. New York and London.

Meller, Patricio. 1982. "Las diferencias (económicas) entre el mercado del trabajo y el mercado de las papas". *Colección Estudios CIEPLAN*, No. 9, pp. 75–105. Santiago, Chile. http://www.cieplan.org/media/publicaciones/archivos/123/Capitulo_4.pdf. Consultado 28 de febrero de 2013.

Mendieta, Eduardo. 2007. *Global fragments. Globalizations, Latinamericanisms, and critical theory*. Albany, NY: State University of New York Press.

Mines, Richard. 1981. *Developing a Community Tradition of Migration to the United States: A Field Study in Rural Zacatecas, Mexico, and California Settlement Areas*. Monographs in U.S.-Mexican Studies, 3. Program in United States-Mexican Studies. San Diego, CA: University of California at San Diego.

Mires, Fernando. 2000. *Teoría política del nuevo capitalismo, o el discurso de la globalización*. Venezuela, Editorial Nueva Sociedad.

Moctezuma, Miguel. 2016. "El sujeto transnacional migrante". In Alejandro I. Canales (Coord.) *Debates contemporáneos sobre migración internacional. Una mirada desde América Latina*. México, M.A. Porrúa and Universidad de Guadalajara, pages 177–209.

Moore, Joan W. 2008. "Presentation". In Edward Téllez and Vilma Ortíz, Telles, *Generations of Exclusion. Mexican Americans, Assimilation, and Race*. New York, Russell Sage Foundation.

Mora y Araujo, Manuel. 1982. "Teoría y datos. Comentarios sobre el enfoque histórico-estructural". In *Reflexiones Teórico-Metodológicas sobre Investigaciones en Población*. México, Latin American Council of Social Sciences (CLACSO) and The College of Mexico (COLMEX).

Moré, Íñigo. 2005. "Las remesas de los inmigrantes y su contribución al desarrollo". In *Codesarrollo: migraciones y desarrollo mundial*. CIDEAL, Fundación Asistencia Técnica para el Desarrollo, Madrid, Spain, pages. 95–121.

Moser, Caroline. 1998. "The Asset Vulnerability Framework: Reassessing Urban Poverty Reduction Strategies". *World Development*, Vol. 26, Num. 1., Great Britain, Elsevier Science.

Muth, John F. 1961. "Rational Expectations and the Theory of Price Movements". *Econometrica*, 29. Julio, pp. 315–335.

Myrdal, Gunnar. 1957. *Economic Theory and Underdeveloped Regions*. London, G. Duckworth.

Myrdal, Gunnar. 1944. *An American dilemma. The Negro problem and modern democracy*. New York and London, Harper and Brothers Publishers.

Nair, Sami. 2006. *Y vendrán ... Las migraciones en tiempos hostiles*. Barcelona, Spain. Editorial Planeta.

Negroponte, Nicholas. 1995. *Being Digital*. New York: Alfred A. Knopf.

Newland, Kathleen. 2007. "A New Surge of Interest in Migration and Development". *Migration Information Source*. (Special Issue on Migration and Development). Washington, DC: Migration Policy Institute.

Noriega Ureña, Fernando A. 1994. *Teoría del desempleo, la distribución y la pobreza*. México, Editorial Ariel.

Nosthas, Ernesto. 2006. "El caso de El Salvador: Programa unidos por la solidaridad". En R. Fernández de Castro. R. García Zamora & A. Vila Freyer (Coords.) *El programa 3x1 para migrantes. ¿Primera política transnacional en México?*, México, M.A. Porrúa Editores, Universidad Autónoma de Zacatecas and Instituto Tecnológico Autónomo de México, pages 45–59.

Notestein, Frank W. 1945. "EPopulation tje Long View". In T. Shultz, (ed.). *Food for the World. Chicago*. Chicago, IL: University of Chicago Press.

Ohmae, Kenichi. 1995. *The End of the Nation State. The Rise of Regional Economies*. New York, NY: Free Press.

OIM, 2006. *Migration for Development: Within and Beyond Frontiers*. International Organization for Migration. Geneva.

OIM, 2003. *The Migration-Development Nexus: Evidence and policy Options*. International Organization for Migration. Geneva.

Omi, Michael; Winant, Howard. 2015. *Racial Formation in the United States*. New York, Routledge/Taylor & Francis Group, Third edition.

Ono, Kent A. 2010. "Postracism: A Theory of the "Post"- as Political Strategy". *Journal of Communication Inquiry* 34(3) p. 227–233.

Orozco, Manuel and Steven R. Wilson. 2005. "Making Migrant Remittances Count". In D. Terry and S.R. Wilson (editors), *Beyond Small Change: Making Migrant Remittances Count*. Washington, D.C. Inter-American Development Bank.

Ortman, Jennifer M.; Victoria A. Velkoff. and Howard Hogan. 2014. *An Aging Nation: The Older Population in the United States. Population Estimates and Projections*. U.S. Census Bureau Current Population Reports.

Parella Rubio, Sonia. 2003. *Mujer, inmigrante y trabajadora: la triple discriminación*. Spain, Editorial Anthropos.

Patarra, Neide. 1973. "Transición demográfica: resumen histórico o teoría de la población?". *Demografía y Economía*. Vol. VII, Num. 1. México. The College of Mexico (COLMEX).

Pérez, Julio. 2013. *Qué es la Demografía*. In Curso de Demografía. CSIC, Grupo de Investigación de Dinámicas Demográficas (IEGD, CCHS), Madrid, consulted on line, February 15th, 2013. http://apuntesdedemografia.wordpress.com/curso-de-demografia/que-es-la-demografia/.

Pérez Díaz, Julio. 2002. *La Madurez de Masas*. www.ced.uab.es/jperez/PDFs/Madurez Masas.pdf.

Pino Arriagada, Osvaldo. 2004. "Análisis de encadenamientos productivos para la economía regional. Base 1996". *Theoría*, Vol. 13: 71–82. Universidad del Bío Bío, Chillán, Chile.

Piore, Michael. 1979. *Birds of Passage. Migrant Labor and Industrial Societies*. Cambridge, Cambridge University Press. UK.

Popper, Karl. 1968. *The logic of scientific Discovery*. London. Hutchinson.

Popper, Karl. 1965. *Conjectures and refutations. The growth of scientific knowledge*. London, Routledge and K. Paul.

Portes, Alejandro. 2007. "Migración y desarrollo. Una revisión conceptual de la evidencia". In S. Castles and R. Delgado Wise (coords.) *Migración y desarrollo: perspectivas desde el sur*. México, M. A. Porrúa.

Portes, Alejandro. 2001. "Introduction: the debates and significance of immigrant transnationalism". *Global Networks* 1 (3): 181–193.

Portes, Alejandro. 1997. "Immigration theory for a new century: some problems and opportunities". *International Migration Review*. Winter 1997, v31, n4, p 799(27).

Portes, Alejandro. 1998. "Social Capital: Its Origins and Applications in Modern Sociology". *Annual Review of Sociology*, Vol. 24. 1–24. DOI: 10.1146/annurev.soc.24.1.1.

Portes, Alejandro. 1995. "Economic Sociology and the Sociology of Immigration: A Conceptual Overview". En Alejandro Portes, Ed. In *The Economic Sociology of Immigration*. New York: Russell Sage Foundation, pp. 1–41.

Portes, Alejandro and Josh deWind. 2006. "Un diálogo transatlántico: el progreso de la investigación y la teoría el estudio de la migración internacional". In A. Portes and J. DeWind (Coords.) *Repensando las migraciones. Nuevas perspectivas teóricas y empíricas*. México, M.A. Porrúa, Universidad Autónoma de Zacatecas.

Portes, Alejandro; Luis Eduardo Guarnizo and Patricia Landolt. 2003. "El estudio del transnacionalismo: peligros latentes y promesas de un campo de investigación emergente". In A. Portes, L.E. Guarnizo and P. Landolt (Coords.) *La globalización desde abajo: Transnacionalismo inmigrante y desarrollo. La experiencia de Estados Unidos y América Latina*. México, M.A. Porrúa.

Portes, Alejandro; Guarnizo, Luis Eduardo; Landolt, Patrícia. (Eds.) 1999. *Transnational Communities. Special Issue of Ethnic and Racial Studies*, 22 (2), 217–463.

Portes, Alejandro; Guarnizo, Luis Eduardo; Landolt, Patrícia. 1999. "The Study of Transnationalism: Pitfalls and Promise of an Emergent Research Field". *Ethnic and Racial Studies*, 22 (2), 217–237.

Portes, Alejandro and Rubén G. Rumbaut. 1996. *Immigrant America. A Portrait*. University of California Press. California, United States.

Prebisch, Raúl. 1950. *The economic development of Latin America and its principal problems*. Lake Success, NY: United Nations, 59 p. E/CN.12/89/Rev.1

Przeworski, Adam. 1982. "Teoría sociológica y el estudio de la población: reflexiones sobre el trabajo de la Comisión de Población y Desarrollo de CLACSO". In

*Reflexiones Teórico-Metodológicas sobre Investigaciones en Población*. México, Latin American Council of Social Sciences (CLACSO) and The College of Mexico (COLMEX).

Puentes, R., A. Canales, H. Rodríguez, R. Delgado-Wise and S. Castles. 2011. *Towards an assessment of migration, development and human rights links: Conceptual framework and new strategic indicators*. People's Global Action on Migration, Development and Human Rights. IV Global Forum on Migration and Development. November 2010.

Ratha, Dilip. 2003. "Worker's Remittances: An Important and Stable Source of External Development Finance". *Global Development Finance 2003*. Washington, D. C., United States. World Bank.

Redondo, Nélida and Sagrario Garay. 2012. *El envejecimiento en América Latina. Evidencia empírica y cuestiones metodológicas*. Latin American Population Association, Publications Serie, Num. 13. Río de Janeiro, Brazil.

Reichert, Joshua. 1981. "The Migration Syndrome: Seasonal U.S. Wage Labor and Rural Development in Central Mexico", In *Human Organization* 40 (1): 56–66.

Reisman, George. 1990. *Capitalism. A Treatise on Economics*. Illinois, Jameson Books.

Requena, Felix. 1991. "Social Resources and Occupational Status Attainment in Spain: A Cross-National Comparison with the United States and the Netherlands". *International Journal of Comparative Sociology*, 32:3/4 (1991,Sept.) p.233–242.

Ritchey, Neal. 1976. "Explanations in migration". *Annual Review of Sociology*, Alex Inkeles (Ed.), Vol. 2, Annual Review, California.

Rivera Sánchez, Liliana. 2004. "Expressions of Identity and Belonging: Mexican Immigrants in New York", in Jonathan Fox and Gaspar Rivera-Salgado (eds.), *Indigenous Mexican Migrants in the United States*, La Jolla, California, Center for U.S. Mexican Studies, UCSD, pages. 417–446.

Robertson, Roland. 1992. *Globalization. Social Theory and Global Culture*. London, UK. SAGE Publications.

Robinson, Joan. 1979. *Aspects of development and underdevelopment*. New York, Cambridge University.

Robinson, Joan. 1969. *The Economics of Imperfection Competition*. London, MacMillan.

Robinson, Joan. 1956. *The accumulation of capital*, London, UK. Macmillan Company. Palgrave Classics in Economics.

Rodríguez, Daniel. 1981. "Discusiones en torno al concepto de Estrategias de supervivencia". *Demografía y Economía*, No. 46. El Colegio de México.

Rodríguez, Josep A. 1994. *Envejecimiento y familia*. Madrid. Spain. Centro de Investigaciones Sociológicas.

Rouse, Roger. 1991. "Mexican Migration and the Social Space of Postmodernism". *Diaspora Spring*, Vol. 1. Num.1.

Ruhs, Martin. 2009. "Migrant Rights, Immigration Policy and Human Development", *Human Development Research Paper* 2009/23, United Nations Development

Programme (UNDP), http://hdr.undp.org/en/reports/global/hdr2009/papers/HDRP_2009_23.pdf.

Ruhs, Martin and Phillip Martin. 2008. "Numbers vs. Rights: Trade-offs and Guest Worker Programs", *International Migration Review*, vol. 42, 1, pages. 249–265, New York, Center for Migration Studies.

Rumbaut, Ruben G. 1997. "Assimilation and its Discontents: Between rethoric and Reality". *International Migration Review*. Winter, Vol. 31, n4. Pages 923(38).

Russell, Sharon Stanton. 1992. "Migrant remittances and development". *International Migration: Quarterly Review*, 30 (3/4):267–287.

Salles, Vania. 2003. "El debate micro-macro: dilemas y contextos". In Alejandro I. Canales and Susana Lerner Sigal (Coords.) *Desafíos teórico-metodológicos en los estudios de población en el inicio del milenio*. México, El Colegio de México, Universidad de Guadalajara and SOMEDE, pages. 99–134.

Salles, Vania and Rodolfo Tuirán. 2003. *Dentro del laberinto*. Jornadas No. 140. México, el Colegio de México.

Samuelson, Paul and William Nordhaus, 2005. *Economía*. (18th Edition). México, McGraw Hill.

Santos, Milton. 1994. *Técnica, espaço, tempo (Globalização e Meio técnico-científico informacional)*. São Paulo, Hucitec.

Sassen, Saskia. 2007. *Sociology of Globalization*. New York : W.W. Norton.

Sassen, Saskia. 1998. *Globalization and its Discontents*. New York. The New Press.

Sassen, Saskia. 1995. "Immigration and Laboor Market". In Alejandro Portes, Ed. In *The Economic Sociology of Immigration*. New York: Russell Sage Foundation, pages 87–127.

Sassen, Saskia. 1991. *The Global City. New York, London and Tokyo*. Princeton, N.J. Princeton University Press.

Sassone, Susana and Carolina Mera. 2007. "Barrios de migrantes en Buenos Aires: Identidad, cultura y cohesión socioterritorial". Paper presented at *V Congreso Europeo CEISAL de Latinoamericanistas: Las relaciones triangulares entre Europa y las Américas en el siglo XXI: expectativas y desafíos*. Bruselas, 11th to 14th, Abril.

Shannon, Amy. 2006. "Las organizaciones transnacionales como agentes del desarrollo local. Retos y oportunidades del programa 3x1 para migrantes". In R. Fernández de Castro, R. García Zamora and A. Vila Freyer (Coords.) *El Programa 3x1 para migrantes. ¿Primera políticas transnacional en México?*. México, M.A. Porrúa.

Sjaastad, Larry A. 1962. "The costs and returns of human migration". *Journal of Political Economy*, 70S : 80–93.

Smart, Alan. 1999. "Participating in the Global: Transnational Social Network and Urban Anthropology". *City and Society*. vol. XI, Num. 1–2. Washington.

Smith, James P. and Barry Edmonston, Editors. 1997. *The New Americans: Economic, Demographic, and Fiscal Effects of Immigration*. Panel on the Demographic and Economic Impacts of Immigration, National Research Council. United States.

Smith, Robert. 2006. *Mexican New York. Transnational Lives of New Immigrants*, Berkeley, University of California Press. United States.

Smith, Robert. 1995. *Los Ausentes Siempre Presentes: The Imagining, Making, and Politics of a Transnational Community Between New York and Ticuani, Puebla*. Ph.D. Dissertation in Political Science. Columbia University. NY, United States.

Sorensen, Ninna Nyberg. 2004. "Globalización, género y migración transnacional. El caso de la diáspora dominicana". In A. Escrivá and N. Rivas (Coords.). *Migración y Desarrollo*. Córdoba, Spain. Spanish National Research Council (CSIC).

Stahl, Charles W. and Fred Arnold. 1986. "Overseas Workers' Remittances in Asian Development". *International Migration Review* 20 (4): 899–925.

Stalker, Peter. 2000. *Workers Without Frontiers. The Impact of Globalization on International Migration*. Boulder, Colorado. Lynne Rienner Publisher, International Labour Office.

Stark, Oded. 1991. *The Migration of Labor*. Cambridge, Basil Blackwell.

Stark, Oded. 1984. "Migraton decision making: a review article". *Journal of Development Economics*, 14: 251–259.

Stefoni, Carolina. 2009. "Gastronomía peruana en las calles de Santiago y la construcción de espacios transnacionales y territorios". In Susana Novick (Comp.) *Las migraciones en América Latina. Políticas, culturas y estrategias*. Buenos Aires, Editorial Catálogos and Latin American Council of Social Sciences (CLACSO).

Stiglitz, Joseph E. 2012. *The Price of Inequality*. New York, W.W. Norton & Co.

Stiglitz, Joseph E. 2002. *Globalization and its discontents*. New York. W.W. Norton & Co.

Storper, Michael & Richard Walker. 1983 "La división espacial del trabajo". *Cuadernos Políticos*, No. 38, México, Editorial Era, pages 4–22.

Straubhaar, Thomas and Florin P. Vâdean, 2005. "International Migrant Remittances and their Role in Development". In OECD, *Migration, Remittances and Development*. Organisation for Economic Cooperation and Development.

Suárez, Liliana. 2008. "La perspectiva transnacional en los estudios migratorios. Génesis, derroteros, y surcos metodológicos". En Joaquín García Roca, Joan Lacomba Vázquez (Coords.) *La inmigración en la sociedad española: una radiografía multidisciplinar*. España, editorial Bellaterra, págs. 771–796

Tapinos, Georges and Daniel Delaunay. 2000. «Peut-on parler d'une mondialisation des migrations internationales?», *Mondialisation, migrations et développement*. Conférences de l'OCDE. Francia.

Taylor, J. Edward. 1999. "The new Economics of Labour Migration and the Role of Remittances in the Migration Process". *International Migration Quarterly Review* 37 (1).

Taylor, J. Edward. 1992. "Remittances and Inequality Reconsidered: Direct, Indirect and Intertemporal Effects". *Journal of Policy Modeling* 14 (2):187–208.

Taylor, J. Edward and T.J. Wyatt. 1996. "The shadow value of migrant remittances, income and inequality in a household-farm economy". *Journal of Development Studies*, Vol. 32, No. 6, pp. 899–912.

Teitelbaum, Michael S. and Jay M. Winter. 1985. *The Fear of Population Decline*. Orlando, FL., Academic Press Inc.

Telles, Edward and Vilma Ortiz. 2008. *Generations of Exclusion. Mexican Americans, Assimilation, and Race*. New York, Russell Sage Foundation.

Terry, Donald. 2005. "Remittances as a Development Tool". In Donald F. Terry and Steven R. Wilson (editors), *Beyond Small Change: Making Migrant Remittances Count*. Washington, D.C. Inter-American Development Bank.

The New York Times (2017, January 10th). *President Obama's Farewell Address: Full Video and Text*. Recovered on March, 21, 2017, from https://www.nytimes.com/2017/01/10/us/politics/obama-farewell-address-speech.html?_r=0.

Thompson, Warren S. 1929. "Population". *American Sociological Review* 34 (6): 959–975.

Thumerelle, Pierre-Jean. 1996. *Las poblaciones del mundo*. Madrid. Ediciones Cátedra.

Tilly, Charles. 1990. "Transplanted Networks". In Virginia Yans-McLaughlin (Eds.). *Immigration Reconsidered. History, Sociology and Politics*. New York. Oxford University Press.

Todaro, Michael P. 1976. *Internal Migration in Developing Countries*. Geneva, International Labor Office.

Todaro, Michael, P. 1969. "A model of labor migration and urban unemployment in less developed countries". *The American Economic Review*, 59, 138–148.

United Nations. 2001. *Replacement Migration: Is It a Solution to Declining and Ageing Populations?*. United Nations, Population Division. United Nations Publication, ST/ESA/SER.A/206.

U.S. Census Bureau. 1975. *Historical Statistics of the United States, Colonial Times to 1970*, Bicentennial Edition, Part 1 and 2. Washington, D.C., 1975.

U.S. Census Bureau. 1980. *US Population Census, 1980*. U.S. Department of Commerce Economics and Statistics Administration, U.S. Census Bureau.

U.S. Census Bureau. 2000. *US Population Census 2000*. U.S. Department of Commerce Economics and Statistics Administration, U.S. Census Bureau.

U.S. Census Bureau. 2014. *2014 National Population Projections*. U.S. Census Bureau, Population Division.

Van de Kaa, Dirk. 2002. "The idea of a Second Demographic Transition in Industrialized Countries". Paper presented at the *Sixth Welfare Policy Seminar of the National Institute of Population and Social Security*, Tokyo, Japan, 29 January.

Van de Kaa, Dirk. 1987. "Europe's second demographic transition". *Population Bulletin*, 42(1).

Vershuur, Christine. 2007; "Inmigrantes y nueva división internacional del trabajo y de los cuidados". In Isabel Yépes del Castillo and Gioconda Herrera (Editors.) *Nuevas migraciones latinoamericanas a Europa Balances y desafíos*. FLACSO Ecuador, OBREAL, GRIAL and Universidad of Barcelona.

Wahba, Jackline. 2005. "What is the Macroeconomic Impact of International Remittances on the Home Country?". In OECD, *Migration, Remittances and Development*. Organization for Economic Cooperation and Development.

Wallerstein, Immanuel. 1995. *After Liberalism*. New York, New Press.

Wallerstein, Immanuel. 1991. *Unthinking the Social Sciences. The Limits of Nineteenth-Century Paradigms*. Oxford, England. Polity Press.

Wickramasekara, Piyasiri. 2008. "Globalization, International Labour Migration and the Rights of Migrant Workers", *Third World Quarterly* 29(7), pp. 1247–1264.

Wiest, Raymond E. 1984. "External Dependency and the Perpetuation of Temporary Migration to the United States". In Richard C. Jones (ed.), *Patterns of Undocumented Migration: Mexico and the United States*. Totowa, United States. Rowman & Allanheld.

Wievorka, Michel. 2011. "A World in Movement". *Migraciones Internacionales*, 20, Vol. 1 No. 6, El Colegio de la Frontera Norte. México. Pages 45–60.

Wimmer, Andreas and Nina Glick-Schiller. 2002. "Methodological nationalism and beyond: nation-state building, migration and the social sciences". *Global Networks. A Journal of Transnational Affairs*, Vol. 2, Num. 4, pages. 301–334.

Zárate, Germán. 2007. "A Mutiplier Analysis of Remittances in the Mexican Economy". G. Zárate-Hoyos. *Multidisciplinary Perspectives on Remittances from Migrant Workers in the United States*. Kassel University Press, Germany. pages. 102–129.

Zemelman, Hugo. 1992. *Los horizontes de la razón. Uso crítico de la teoría.* Barcelona, Anthropos Editorial.

Zemelman, Hugo. 1982. "Problemas en la Explicación del Comportamiento Reproductivo (sobre las mediaciones)". In *Reflexiones Teórico-Metodológicas sobre Investigaciones en Población*. México, Latin American Council of Social Sciences (CLACSO) and The College of Mexico (COLMEX).

Zlolniski, Christian. 2006. *Janitors, Street Vendors, and Activists: The Lives of Mexican immigrants in Silicon Valley*. Berkeley. University of California Press.

# Index

accumulation   1, 8, 25, 72, 73, 74, 76, 79, 99, 136n, 139, 140, 141, 143, 146, 151, 153, 154, 155, 163, 164, 165, 166, 167, 175, 194, 195, 106, 200, 212, 236
active age   73, 99, 108, 118, 119, 121, 123, 125
active population   8, 13, 102, 118n, 119, 120, 122, 123, 124, 126, 133, 148, 187, 206, 209, 220
adolescent   109, 128, 218, 219
adults   109, 110, 111, 112n, 128, 171, 185, 186, 213, 219
advanced societies   13, 76, 102, 106, 107, 131, 133, 136, 148, 151, 154, 155, 173, 174, 175, 177, 179, 185, 194, 196, 204, 206, 210, 212, 232
Africa   72, 120, 120n
African American   24, 26, 121
age of globalization   6, 7, 87, 94, 100, 161
age structure   108, 109, 110, 112, 116, 118, 123, 205, 218
ageing   8, 9, 11, 12, 73, 76, 98, 102, 106, 108, 109, 110, 112, 116, 119, 122, 124, 130, 147, 148, 150, 186, 188, 192, 196, 204, 207, 208, 210, 219, 220, 235
agencies   52, 67
agent   20, 37, 41, 55, 60, 67, 90, 137, 202
ahistoricism   39, 46, 47
alienate   165
American   10, 12, 57, 58n, 93, 104n, 121, 208, 217, 231
American dilemma   10, 210, 220, 233, 234, 236
American dream   173
American way of life   57
Americanization   57, 92
Amin, Samir   41, 142
Appadurai, Arjun   6, 14, 82, 84, 884
apprehension   94
Argentina   2, 52, 64, 73, 105, 107, 155n
Arians   211
Asia   120
Asian   63, 121, 174n, 182
assimilation   5, 57, 91, 198

Australia   3, 52, 73, 195, 107, 155n

Bauman, Zygmunt   114, 142, 162, 166, 173, 176, 194, 206
Beck, Ulrich   5, 14, 138, 78, 80n, 82, 83, 84, 167, 175, 179, 226
Becker, Gary S.   38, 226
Bell, Daniel   142
belonging   8, 21, 89, 92, 93, 165, 170, 179, 182, 198
birth rates   9, 102, 114, 117, 196, 214
borders   2, 4, 6, 14, 34, 58, 79, 81, 83, 123, 141, 165, 197, 217
boundaries   83, 89, 91, 160, 162, 169, 194
Bourdieu, Pierre   17, 20, 21, 22, 23, 27, 43
Bustamante, Jorge A.   41, 155, 191

Cabré, Anna   107n, 130
California   12n, 129, 182, 215, 216, 225, 226, 233
Canada   2, 52, 73, 105, 107, 155n
capital   3, 8, 9, 16, 24, 42, 43, 44, 67, 68, 71, 72, 73, 82, 88, 97, 98, 101, 136, 137, 138, 139, 139n, 140, 140n, 141, 143, 155, 156, 161, 162, 163, 164, 165, 166, 167, 168, 172, 173, 183, 204, 234
capital accumulation   8, 74, 139, 140, 141, 151, 163, 196
capital reproduction   8, 72, 98, 136, 138, 139, 140, 148, 151, 153, 163, 165
capitalism   18, 39, 47, 70, 72, 79n, 81, 136n, 139, 139n, 140n, 166, 167, 195, 231
capitalist   48, 52, 72, 73, 81, 107, 136n, 139, 140n, 141, 164, 199
capitalist society   50, 68, 139n, 154, 186
capital-labor   142, 175
care industry   131, 187, 189, 193, 206, 234
Castells, Manuel   80n, 82, 143, 176
Castles, Stephen   3n, 56, 67
CELADE, Population Division of ECLAC   104, 117, 125n
Central America   3, 61, 62, 174n
central countries   36, 56, 104n, 108, 146, 156, 157, 157n, 174n, 190, 191, 208, 209

children   17, 38, 38n, 103, 109, 110, 111, 112, 112n, 114, 115, 116, 117, 119, 120, 121, 126n, 170, 174, 185, 186, 186n, 188n, 190, 190n, 196, 207, 213, 216, 218, 219, 234
children care   189
circular and cumulative causation   17, 24, 25, 26, 27, 29, 30, 32, 100
circularity   25, 31, 32
citizenship   4, 90, 93, 197, 234
class structure   7, 17, 20, 75, 76, 83n, 99, 100, 101, 138, 168, 169, 175, 180, 186, 193, 194, 195, 212, 225, 231, 232, 233, 235
class struggle   10, 234, 235, 236
Coale, Ansley   241
cohesion   179, 233
Coleman, David   9, 12
collective identities   132
colonization   107n, 136
commodities   74, 138, 166, 195
Compadrazgo   22, 29, 169, 172
competitiveness   66, 155
consensus   4, 55, 70, 80, 197
consumer society   48
consumption   38, 38n, 61, 62, 62n, 63n, 138, 139, 139n, 143, 148, 154, 155n, 156, 159, 160, 174, 174n, 185, 187, 192, 196, 206, 207, 212, 232, 234, 235
contraception   115
contractual deregulation   147, 161, 174, 176, 192, 207
cosmopolitanism   79n, 95
country of origin   2, 3, 36, 90, 91, 200
crisis   3n, 64, 140, 148, 150, 152, 153, 156, 157, 202, 210, 220, 221
critical perspective   34, 65, 66
criticism   39, 43, 46, 47
critique   23, 68, 75, 85, 88, 94, 95, 105, 197
critique of methodological nationalism   77, 78, 80, 87
Cuba   122, 123, 126, 126n
cultural capital   93, 172
cumulative causation   16, 17, 24, 25, 26, 27, 28, 29, 30, 31, 32, 100, 155, 192, 201
Cypher, James   74, 174n

daily life   2, 91, 114, 187, 188, 190, 234
Delgado Wise, Raúl   4n, 55, 56, 66, 71, 74
demographic ageing   106, 112, 213

demographic bonus   73, 98, 118
demographic change   10, 12, 56, 103, 104, 104n, 107, 108, 117, 119, 119n, 123, 124, 129, 131, 148, 180, 181, 185n, 192, 197, 205, 212, 218, 219, 236
demographic complementarity   98, 107, 123
demographic decline   9, 12, 126, 181, 214, 219, 235
demographic deficit   12, 130, 174
demographic dependence   117, 118, 119
demographic dividend   73, 102, 108, 116, 118, 122, 123, 124, 125, 126, 130
demographic gap   149, 207
demographic growth   48, 136n, 150, 181, 205, 214, 222, 226
demographic imbalances   52, 73, 107n, 123, 124, 166n
demographic minority   11, 129, 132, 182, 233
demographic regime   103, 104n, 113, 148, 206, 208
demographic replacement   9, 10, 102, 117, 121, 126, 128, 150, 207, 212, 216, 218, 224, 225, 231, 233
demographic reproduction   8, 9, 12, 18, 19, 20, 76, 98, 102, 105, 106, 107, 108, 113, 113n, 119, 120, 123, 130, 131, 133, 149, 168, 173, 196, 208
demographic structures   19, 106, 108, 130, 212
demographic transition   8, 9, 12, 19, 52, 73, 98, 102, 103, 104, 104n, 105, 105n, 106, 107, 108, 112, 113, 114, 115, 116, 119, 122, 123, 126, 127n, 130, 131, 133, 148, 163, 186, 188, 192, 204, 205, 207, 213
demography   8, 13, 17, 18, 19, 20, 27, 73, 98, 100, 105, 113n, 119, 130, 131, 148, 151, 162, 168, 206, 207, 209, 212
deportations   4, 197, 234
deregulation   73, 142, 143, 147, 161, 167, 174, 175, 176, 178, 179, 192, 199, 207, 212
descendants   13, 107, 121, 222
deterritorialization   6, 14, 79, 82, 84, 86, 165, 200
developed countries   4n, 9, 12, 36, 73, 74, 108, 113, 119, 120, 121, 123, 124, 133, 136n, 142, 143, 153, 156, 165, 186, 188, 192, 197, 207, 208
discrimination   26, 41, 182, 188, 223, 226n, 227, 228, 229, 230, 232, 235

INDEX

displacement 96, 147, 150, 155, 164, 165, 169, 170, 200
diversity 5, 11, 92, 114
domestic service 131, 174, 186, 188n, 189n, 190, 190n, 206, 207, 234
domestic units 39, 43, 44, 137
Dominican Republic 123
dual life 91, 109
duality 31, 85
Durand, Jorge 16, 29, 61n, 63

economic activity 63, 138, 139, 221, 232
economic asymmetries 31, 56, 74
economic capital 22, 61
economic crises 64, 140n
economic development 2n, 24, 49, 56, 60, 65, 67, 74, 104n, 174, 207
economic discrimination 154, 180, 226, 227, 230
economic growth 8, 24, 55n, 56, 66, 71, 73, 74, 136, 136n, 139, 148, 151, 154, 167, 206, 223, 234
economic inequality 25, 31, 63, 231
economic rationality 35, 38
economic reproduction 91, 119, 131, 164, 169, 208, 209
economic structures 61, 225
economic system 31, 88, 137, 138, 139, 163
economic transfers 135, 141
economically active population 149, 150, 220
Ecuador 164, 123
El Salvador 123
elderly 110, 111, 112, 117, 150, 170, 171, 174, 188n, 207
emancipation 174, 191, 207
emigration 2, 19, 62n, 63, 64, 74, 86, 106, 107, 123, 124, 125, 126
employment 3, 36, 40, 41, 42, 44, 73, 142, 143, 144, 146, 148, 150, 151, 161, 172, 175, 176, 177, 178, 179, 180, 181, 182, 187, 212, 221, 223, 230, 231, 232
equity 227, 228, 230
ethnic composition 10, 12, 121, 126, 127, 128, 129, 133, 150, 181, 182, 208, 212, 214, 216, 217, 218, 219, 220, 233
ethnic differentiation 132, 182, 211
ethnic discrimination 26, 59, 60, 183, 211, 230

ethnic minorities 60, 120, 129, 134, 153, 180, 185, 214, 216, 217, 218, 222, 223, 228, 236
ethnicity 120, 130
Europe 47, 52, 72, 73, 74, 105, 114, 121, 143, 144, 155n, 177, 178, 179, 189, 207, 210, 212, 235, 236
European Union 120n, 176, 177, 179
exchange value 137, 143n, 154
exclusion 161, 166, 167, 171, 231, 232
exile 96
exploitation 107, 167
explosive growth 104n

family 16, 21, 22, 23, 26, 35, 36, 38, 42, 43, 44, 50, 86, 87, 89, 91, 104n, 114, 116, 154, 156, 159, 161, 162, 164, 169, 170, 171, 172, 174, 192, 200, 201, 204, 207, 211n, 213
family networks 42, 86, 131, 155, 166, 169, 170, 172, 189, 190, 192, 193, 199
family patterns 114
female 171, 190n
female emancipation 114, 234
female migrants 170
fertility 9, 12, 38, 38n, 73, 98, 103, 104n, 108, 109, 110, 113, 113n, 114, 115, 116, 117, 119, 120, 121, 126, 126n, 148, 186, 205, 207, 208, 213, 214, 218
fertility transition 116
feudal 4, 139n, 182
First World 2, 7n, 122, 159, 208
flexibility 73, 143, 147, 154, 172, 175, 176, 179, 199
Florida 12n, 129, 182, 216
forced migration 55, 72, 96
Fordism 141, 175, 175n, 179
free movement 37, 71, 197
friendship 22, 91

García Canclini, Néstor 87, 194
gender 19, 110, 171, 173, 191, 211, 212, 232, 235
gender equity 114
generations 17, 154
ghettos 165, 231
Giddens, Anthony 15, 72, 94
Glick Shiller, Nina 5, 79, 80n
global capitalism 69, 90, 136n, 156, 169
global economy 24, 74, 81, 82, 84n, 136, 141, 142, 212, 164, 167

global factory 82, 82n, 142
global society 7, 8, 15, 16, 47, 51, 55, 72, 76, 78, 79, 79n, 80, 83, 84, 85, 97, 100, 113, 163, 167, 169, 193
globalization 1, 2, 4, 6, 7, 8, 14, 15, 18, 33, 69, 71, 72, 73, 75, 78, 79, 80, 80n, 81, 82, 83, 84, 85, 87, 88, 94, 95, 97, 98, 100, 106, 136, 140, 141, 142, 147, 148, 160, 161, 162, 163, 164, 165, 166, 167, 167n, 173, 174, 174n, 175, 179, 188, 190n, 191, 192, 193, 194, 195n, 196, 198, 199, 201, 203, 204, 206, 232
glocalization 85, 166, 194
gross domestic product 62n, 63, 66, 139, 151, 152, 222
Guatemala 123

haciendas 72, 139n
Herrera, María Soledad 114, 116, 188, 192
Hispanic 12n, 92
historical-structural approaches 23
Hobsbawm, Eric 81, 175
homo economicus 39, 43
Hondagneu-Sotelo, Pierrete 170, 171, 180, 188, 189
host country 1, 3, 86, 189
household 35, 38, 39, 42, 43, 44, 45, 50, 103, 160, 170, 174, 178, 186, 186n, 190, 207
household consumption 61, 63n
human capital 38, 61, 64, 176, 198, 230
human rights 11, 12, 59
humanity 102, 112
Huntington, Samuel 11, 57, 58n

Ianni, Octavio 78, 79n, 82
imagined communities 93
immigrant 57, 60, 90, 92, 120, 121, 170, 174, 186, 187, 188, 190, 191, 193, 206, 207, 211, 212, 228, 235
immigrant labor 150, 151, 153
immigration 4, 8, 9, 11, 12, 12n, 13, 19, 55, 56, 57, 58, 58n, 66, 71, 73, 76, 97, 106, 107n, 121, 131, 132, 133, 136n, 147, 148, 149, 150, 151, 152, 174, 188, 192, 204, 205, 206, 207, 208, 209, 210, 211, 212, 213, 214, 217, 218, 219, 221, 234, 235
inactive ages 1, 18
inactive population 118, 119, 122
inclusion 92, 142, 161, 167, 171, 231

income distribution 63, 64, 66, 138, 184
individuation 33, 87, 99, 114, 116, 174, 185, 186, 188, 204, 205, 207, 213, 234
Industrial Reserve Army 166, 167
industrial society 102, 142, 143, 199
industrialization 48, 146, 177, 179
inequality 7, 20, 21, 24, 25, 26, 28, 31, 32, 33, 36, 41, 49, 50, 52, 59, 63, 64, 67, 70, 71, 74, 76, 97, 97n, 99, 100, 132, 142, 161, 166, 166n, 167, 167n, 169, 171, 172, 172n, 176, 178, 179, 180, 181, 182, 184, 185, 185n, 191, 194, 195, 212, 220, 223, 224, 225, 231, 233, 234, 235, 236
informal sector 166
information economy 143, 143n, 144, 146
informational society 143, 176, 199
inheritance 5, 14, 21, 22, 83
insecurity 41, 71, 160, 161, 163, 164, 172, 174n, 206
instability 61, 119, 123, 124, 154, 157, 163, 206
integration 4, 18, 21, 30, 57, 69, 74, 84, 92, 94, 98, 116, 161, 170, 179, 193, 194, 195, 203, 205
intergenerational exchanges 117
internal mobility 72
international agencies 54, 77
international cooperation 1, 60
international division of labor 81
international inequalities 74
international migration 1, 2, 4, 5, 6, 7, 8, 9, 14, 15, 16, 27, 28, 29, 32, 33, 34, 34n, 35, 37, 38, 39, 41, 43, 45, 47, 49, 51, 52, 53, 54, 54n, 55, 56, 66, 71, 72, 73, 74, 75, 78, 79, 80, 83, 86, 94, 95, 96, 97, 97n, 98, 100, 102, 105, 106, 107, 107n, 108, 119, 120, 122, 123, 124, 130, 136n, 140, 141, 155, 156, 160, 163n, 166, 169, 174, 191, 193, 196, 197, 201, 203, 205, 207
international trade 24, 81, 88
irregular 58, 96, 229

janitors 187, 189n, 199
Jones, Richard C. 61n, 63, 67
just in time 142, 175

Kabila 21, 22
knowledge 17, 37, 46, 60, 64, 65n, 87, 143, 176, 199

INDEX    261

labor   4n, 18, 34, 36, 40, 41, 42, 43, 58, 59, 72, 81, 86, 91, 99, 100, 101, 114, 122, 124, 131, 135, 136, 138, 139, 140, 141, 142, 143, 143n, 144, 146, 147, 148, 149, 150, 151, 153, 154, 155, 157, 158, 159, 161, 162, 163, 164, 165, 166, 168, 172, 174, 174n, 175, 178, 179, 182, 183, 184, 187, 187n, 188, 190, 191, 192, 193, 196, 197, 199, 205, 206, 207, 208, 212, 221, 222, 223, 225, 229, 231, 232, 234, 235
labor deficit   147, 148, 149, 150, 153, 220, 222
labor discrimination   41, 43
labor flexibility   142, 146, 161, 163, 167, 174, 175n, 178, 192, 199, 207
labor force   8, 9, 50, 66, 71, 73, 80, 82, 93, 98, 100, 107, 119, 131, 135, 137, 138, 139n, 140, 141, 146, 147, 148, 149, 150, 151, 152, 153, 154, 155, 156, 159, 160, 161, 162, 163, 165, 166n, 168, 174, 191, 196, 220, 222, 226, 226n, 227n
labor force reproduction   8, 139, 139n, 140, 154, 155, 156, 160, 162, 164, 165, 166, 174n, 189
labor insertion   23, 98, 103, 142, 159, 161, 170, 172, 191, 199
labor market   4, 33, 37, 40, 41, 42, 43, 58, 66, 91, 116, 136, 136n, 142, 147, 163, 166, 167, 170, 175, 180, 186, 188, 204, 206, 221, 225
labor markets segmentation   142, 174
labor migration   8, 38, 52, 80, 98, 136, 136n, 141, 151, 154, 162, 170, 189
labor relations   142, 162, 175, 199
labor rights   56, 58, 59, 226
labor risk regime   175, 176, 179
Latin America   2, 11, 12n, 17, 22, 23, 39n, 47, 57, 58n, 61, 67, 74, 91n, 104n, 116, 119n, 120, 120n, 122, 123, 125, 126, 126n, 149, 150, 155, 158, 186, 187, 188, 213, 124, 221, 226n, 227, 228, 229, 230
Latinos   9, 11, 128, 129, 132, 133, 150, 151, 180, 181, 182, 183, 184, 185, 187n, 188n, 210, 211, 213, 214, 215, 217, 219, 220, 221, 222, 223, 224, 225, 226, 227, 229, 231, 232, 233, 234, 235, 236
liberation   174, 191, 207
life cycle   109, 116, 128
life expectancy   109, 110, 113
lifestyle   38n, 91, 154, 174, 207
Livi Bacci, Masimo   17, 103, 104, 113n

living conditions   31, 42, 63, 154, 155, 157, 166, 195n, 231
local economy   44, 98
local spaces   82, 170, 174n, 191, 195n
localization   82, 85, 166, 174n, 194
longevity   109, 213
Los Angeles   1, 84n, 92
low-skilled   154, 175, 176, 188, 206

maids   144, 178n, 187, 199, 223, 234
male   171
marginalism   20, 38n
marginality   22, 67
Martínez, Jorge   56
Marx, Karl   72, 88, 138, 139n, 140n
Marxists   136
Massey, Douglas   2, 16, 29, 35n, 39, 42, 61n, 63, 70, 100, 155, 182, 193
maternity   170
matrimonial strategies   21, 22
Maturana, Humberto   201, 202
means of production   138, 139
membership   93, 94, 171
men   60, 113n, 174, 186, 191, 207
merchandise   41, 59, 89, 164, 165, 174n, 132
methodological dualism   5, 198
methodological individualism   20, 22, 35
methodological nationalism   5, 14, 15, 19, 72, 77, 78, 80, 83, 84, 85, 87, 88, 94, 95, 105, 197, 203
Mexican   11, 12n, 57, 58n, 63, 66, 92, 93, 158, 160
Mexico   3, 11, 12n, 22, 51, 52, 58n, 61, 62, 63, 64, 66, 84n, 92, 104n, 123, 126, 126n, 129, 157, 157n, 158, 160, 174n, 182, 216, 220
Middle Ages   4, 58, 129
middle classes   179
migrant   3, 12, 14, 16, 29, 41, 59, 64, 70, 86, 89, 90, 91n, 92, 93, 95, 98, 101, 102, 121, 135, 140, 141, 147, 149, 150, 151, 154, 155, 156, 158, 159, 160, 161, 162, 162n, 163, 164, 168, 171, 172, 173, 185, 188, 189, 190, 190n, 191, 193, 199, 200, 201, 211n, 223, 235
migrant workers   41, 42, 58, 142, 146, 161, 162, 163, 164, 167, 172, 175, 188, 189, 199, 230
migrants networks   155
migration policy   13, 59

migration reproduction   21, 27, 29, 100, 155, 156, 163, 189
migratory system   72
migratory wave   106, 107, 130, 154, 154n
minimizing risk   39, 44, 45
minority   10, 11, 12n, 129, 132, 133, 161, 167, 181, 182, 219, 228, 231, 233
modern society   14, 20, 78, 103, 105, 106, 130, 198
modernity   5, 14, 78, 79, 79n, 83, 83n, 87, 104, 105, 106, 176, 192, 197, 197n, 198, 232
modernization theory   104n
mortality   19, 103, 104n, 108, 110, 113, 116, 118
mortality rates   19, 113
mortality transition   116
Moslem   211, 235
motherhood   116, 170, 189, 190, 193
mothers   115, 121, 208, 216
movement of society   15, 18, 23
multiculturalism   14, 34
multiplier effects   62, 63, 63n
mundialization   7
Myrdal, Gunnar   2n, 17, 25, 25, 26, 27, 29, 30, 31, 32, 100, 101, 234

nation state   5, 15, 58, 79, 83, 83n, 87, 88, 93, 95, 198, 203
national boundaries   89, 160, 162, 194
national economy   63, 63n, 74
national society   51, 79, 79n, 84
Native American Indians   182, 216
native population   8, 9, 11, 13, 32, 59, 73, 95, 100, 119, 121, 126, 149, 150, 152, 174, 174n, 185, 187, 188, 189, 192, 204, 205, 207, 208, 221
natural growth   19, 107, 126
neoclassical   38, 39, 40, 42, 43, 44, 45, 46, 47, 49, 50, 52, 138, 166
neo-liberalism   83n, 175
new economy   166, 199, 242, 243
New Home Economics   35, 38, 39, 42, 44, 49, 50, 198
New Mexico   12n, 129, 131, 182, 183, 216
New World   105, 175, 238
Non-Latino White Population   10, 126, 128, 129, 132, 189
north   51, 91, 135

Obama, Barack   12n, 13, 73n, 210, 211
occupations structure   175, 206
old   23, 39n, 58, 59, 68, 84, 102, 103, 111, 183, 218
older adults   110, 11, 112n, 128, 186
oligopolistic   40, 81, 199
optimization   35, 39, 43, 44
origin communities   33, 62, 86, 91, 94, 135, 156, 163, 164, 169, 170, 189

Paisanos   155, 172, 200
people caring   189n, 190
people displacement   99, 107, 156
perfect competition   35, 37, 39, 43, 226n
peripheral countries   56, 106, 108, 116, 121, 123, 131, 149, 174n, 186
personal services   8, 144, 146, 147, 178, 178n, 186, 190, 206, 223, 225, 235
Piore, Michael   3n, 42, 43, 176
polarization   73, 100, 142, 146, 147, 174, 175, 176, 177, 179, 180, 188, 194, 206, 223, 231
political balances   12, 133, 232, 233
political economy   20, 81, 199
poor   22, 26, 27, 31, 60, 61, 65, 154, 184, 185, 191, 194, 199, 224, 231, 235
Popper, Karl   46
population dynamics   102, 103, 105, 106, 107, 113, 119, 123, 130, 136, 150, 168
population growth   10, 11, 19, 73, 104, 105, 106, 108, 123, 125, 126, 130, 132, 148, 207
population movements   3, 85
population pyramid   110, 111, 128, 129, 131, 219, 232
population reproduction   12, 17, 18, 19, 23, 23n 27, 76, 102, 103, 106, 107, 113n, 119, 123, 125, 130, 135, 193, 207, 208
population structure   19, 106, 129
population surplus   107n, 108, 123, 130
Portes, Alejandro   3n, 43, 55, 58, 60, 80n, 86, 89, 90, 91, 162
post-Fordism   142, 175, 212
post-industrial societies   174, 207
postmodern society   49, 53, 78, 106, 179, 185, 188, 192, 204
postmodernity   100, 232
post-racial   211

poverty    22, 26, 27, 55, 60, 61, 63, 64, 65, 66, 67, 70, 71, 74, 158, 159, 160, 167, 167n, 184, 190, 194, 224, 226, 232
power relations    21, 41, 70, 171
precarious    50, 73, 98, 142, 144, 146, 147, 154, 158, 159, 160, 161, 167, 172, 175, 176, 178, 179, 186, 188, 190, 223, 230, 131, 232
production factors    24, 37, 137, 138
productive forces    82, 119, 133, 234
productive moment    98, 138, 140, 141, 164
productive services    139, 188, 191
productive system    17, 18, 135, 136, 141, 202
productive transformation    148, 193, 206
productivity    36, 38n, 41, 146, 226, 227, 227n, 228, 229, 230, 232
professional services    144, 146
profits    37, 137, 138
progress    4n, 36, 57, 80, 91, 92, 104n, 105, 106, 110, 126, 192, 197, 203
proletarian    199
proximity services    186

qualifications    77n, 144, 188, 223, 229, 230
quality of life    36, 49, 99, 190n

race    210
racialization    188, 194, 220, 225, 231, 233, 235
racism    13, 92, 183, 210, 211, 212, 231, 232, 234, 235, 3236
radicalism    29, 42
rational choice    35, 36, 37, 38, 38n, 39, 41, 42, 43, 44, 45, 46
rationality    35, 38, 43, 45n, 104n
reciprocity    29, 91, 155, 161, 163, 169, 200
reflexivity    1, 143, 144
refugees    96
regulation    140n, 143, 175
relocation    143, 154, 161, 177, 200
remittances    3, 5, 55, 55n, 56, 60, 61, 62, 62n, 63, 64, 65, 65n, 66, 67, 68, 70, 71, 77, 89, 91n, 96, 98, 99, 100, 135, 136, 141, 154, 156, 157, 157n, 158, 159, 160, 164, 189, 190, 198
rents    137, 138
replacement    9, 10, 13, 102, 121, 126, 128, 129, 133, 150, 207, 212, 213, 216, 217, 218, 219, 224, 225, 231, 233, 234, 235
replacement level    115, 117

reproduction approach    7, 16, 17, 75, 94, 100, 201
reproduction of capital    76, 100, 135, 136, 137, 165
reproduction of capitalism    70, 135, 136, 141
reproduction of population    8, 18, 19, 106, 188
reproduction of society    9, 16, 28, 75, 100, 125, 20, 203, 204, 232
reproduction regime    108, 168
reproduction strategy    21, 99, 155, 163, 169
reproductive age    73, 103, 119, 121, 213
reproductive behavior    104n, 113n, 114, 115, 121, 132
reproductive moment    98, 138, 141, 164
reproductive revolution    129
reterritorialization    79
reunification    171
risk society    179
rural-urban migration    47, 50

salary    98, 139, 154, 158, 164, 190, 223, 226, 227n
salary transfers    136
Sassen, Saskia    7n, 8, 43, 66, 82, 84, 179, 176
second demographic transition    8, 73, 98, 106, 108, 113, 114, 115, 119, 130, 131, 148, 163, 186, 188, 192, 204, 205, 207, 213
second generation    92
segmentation    42, 43, 100, 142, 146, 174, 176, 179, 180, 182, 223
segmented markets    40, 42
segregation    31, 142, 154, 159, 165, 179, 180, 182, 188, 223, 230, 231, 232, 233
sending countries    71, 73, 77, 80, 92, 102, 140, 155, 198
settlement    2, 3, 93, 94, 107n, 136n, 156, 161, 169, 170, 171, 200
sex    120n, 130
social capital    16, 17, 29, 42, 43, 44, 60, 61, 155, 161, 163, 164, 166, 169, 173, 200, 201, 203
social change    60, 67, 130
social classes    8, 9, 32, 75, 84n, 98, 100, 163, 168, 172, 179, 180, 182, 183, 185, 189, 193, 224, 231, 234
social exclusion    22, 67, 87, 159, 167
social inclusion    142, 161, 171, 231

## INDEX

social inequality   7, 21, 24, 25, 31, 33, 41, 59, 64, 67, 74, 76, 97, 97n, 99, 100, 132, 142, 166, 167, 167n, 169, 171, 178, 179, 180, 181, 182, 184, 185, 194, 195, 223, 231, 233, 234, 235, 236
social mobility   159, 173, 179, 181, 183, 226
social networks   16, 17, 22, 30, 42, 91, 93, 94, 154, 155, 156, 161, 162, 163, 164, 168, 169, 170, 171, 172, 173, 189, 190, 200, 201, 203
social process of migration   28, 29
social reproduction   17, 21, 22, 28, 29, 32, 33, 39n, 75, 97, 100, 135, 136, 141, 154, 155, 156, 159, 160, 162, 162n, 163, 168, 169, 170, 171, 173, 174, 174n, 175, 177, 179, 180, 181, 182, 183, 185, 187, 188, 189, 189n, 190, 191, 193, 194, 195, 195n, 201, 203, 207, 208, 210, 232, 234
social security   57, 71
social segregation   142, 154, 179, 180
social structure   22, 32, 33, 97n, 100, 104n, 109, 142, 172, 176, 178, 179, 182, 193, 226
social vulnerability   22, 41, 58, 61, 99, 144, 158, 159, 160, 161, 163, 174n, 178
solidarity   29, 91, 155, 161, 163, 169, 173, 200
south   51, 52, 66, 91, 135, 154
sovereignty   83n, 92
Spain   2, 3, 107n, 110, 111, 112n, 115, 116, 120, 120n, 121, 123, 148, 149, 150, 173, 186
Spanish   1n, 14n, 34n, 40n, 54n, 77n, 82n, 87n, 92, 102n, 104n, 135n, 148, 168n, 173, 194n, 196n, 210n
Stefoni, Carolina   2
Stiglitz, Joseph E.   50n, 80, 142
stratification   22, 142, 173, 175, 176, 181, 183, 188, 194, 195, 233, 234
structural adjustment   74, 199
structural changes   13, 106
structural heterogeneities   17, 70
structural imbalance   148, 186, 206
structural transformations   67, 204
structuralism   20, 21, 22, 23, 50n, 136, 137, 138, 139, 147, 166
subordination   162, 165, 172, 236
supernumerary   166
supra-national   4, 82, 84, 194
supremacists   11, 211, 220, 234, 235
supremacy   11, 12n, 129, 133

symbolic goods   3, 59, 86, 156, 169, 200
symbolic relations   21, 169
systems of power   23
systems of succession   21

tasks   171, 174, 182, 186, 186n, 190, 191, 196, 200
technology   60, 82, 137, 138, 146
temporary workers   166
Texas   12n, 129, 182, 216, 220
Third Demographic Transition   9, 127n, 133
Third World   8, 12, 55, 60, 63, 73, 74, 104n, 146, 148, 150, 156, 174n, 190, 206, 207
ties   3, 93, 172
total fertility rate   114, 116, 126, 126n, 213
translocal   81, 84, 85, 91, 160, 165, 166, 188, 200, 203
transmigration   86, 91n, 161
transnational   16, 33, 81, 84, 86, 87, 88, 89, 90, 91, 93, 95, 155, 156, 158, 159, 160, 161, 162, 165, 166, 169, 170, 171, 172, 173, 188, 189, 190, 190n, 191, 192, 193, 194, 200, 203, 232
transnational communities   6, 7, 29, 33, 80, 85, 86, 90, 91, 93, 155, 158, 160, 161, 162, 168, 172, 173, 200, 201, 203
transnational motherhood   189, 190, 193
transnational networks   170, 200
transnational workers   155
transnationalism   6, 7, 80, 80n, 85, 90, 91, 92, 94, 95, 154, 169, 171, 193, 199, 203

underdeveloped countries   73, 107, 154
underdevelopment   24, 25, 31, 32, 55, 66, 71, 74
undocumented migration   56
United Kingdom   3, 112n, 155, 186n
United Nations   9, 54n, 59, 121
United States of America   52
upper classes   32, 60, 100, 168, 170, 173, 187, 189, 191, 192, 195, 196, 232, 234, 235
urban   35, 36, 39n, 47, 49n, 50, 61, 82, 86, 93, 160, 166n

value in use   137
Van De Kaa, Dirk   113, 114, 213
Veblen, Thomas   148, 206

vulnerability   22, 41, 43, 50, 58, 60, 61, 71, 99, 144, 146, 154, 158, 159, 160, 161, 163, 166, 167, 172, 173, 174n, 178, 190, 203, 206, 222, 226, 226n, 231, 235
vulnerable   51, 61, 98, 147, 159, 160, 164, 167, 184, 185, 206, 223, 224, 230

wage   36, 49, 50, 52, 58, 136, 154, 155, 159, 164, 174n, 176, 226, 227, 228, 230
wage discrimination   226, 227, 228, 229
wage inequalities   49, 50, 52
wage transfer   156
Wallerstein, Immanuel   79n, 80n, 83, 84, 88
wealth   59, 138, 139, 190, 194, 227n
welfare state   1, 42, 161, 167, 175, 179
women   103, 113n, 114, 115, 116, 121, 166, 170, 171, 174, 186, 187, 188, 188n, 189, 190, 191, 192, 207, 211, 213, 214, 235
women emancipation   99, 188, 191
women labor   103
work force   41, 136, 138, 181, 191, 227
worker   42, 98, 139n, 154, 162, 165, 174n, 188, 189, 226, 227, 228n
working-age population   102, 125, 126
world system theory   82, 83n

xenophobia   210, 211, 235

young   109, 109n, 110, 115, 119, 122, 129, 148, 150, 166, 171, 205, 213, 218, 219

Zemelman, Hugo   23, 27, 30n, 88, 202

www.ingramcontent.com/pod-product-compliance
Lightning Source LLC
Chambersburg PA
CBHW070915030426
42336CB00014BA/2421